100 GREAT CANADIANS

100 GREAT CANADIANS

GEORGE WOODCOCK

Hurtig Publishers/Edmonton

Hurtig Publishers Ltd.
10560-105 Street
Edmonton, Alberta

Canadian Cataloguing in Publication Data

Woodcock, George, 1912-
    100 great Canadians

    ISBN 0-88830-184-7 pa
    ISBN 0-88830-193-6 bd

    1. Canada — Biography.   I. Title.

FC25.W6   920'.071   C80-091011-7
F1005.W6

Printed and bound in Canada
by T. H. Best Company Limited
Don Mills, Ontario

Contents

Introduction

This is a book of great Canadians. Immediately the questions are likely to come: *Why* do you call them Great? Who are Great Men and Great Women? I don't think there is an absolute criterion of Greatness. Some people have had such an immense influence, even outside their times and places, that the word Great when we apply it to them suggests universality; they are, in some special way, All Things to Many Men! In this universal sense—the sense that applies to Buddha and St. Francis, to Homer and Shakespeare and Tolstoy, to Mozart and Michelangelo—probably very few people who figure in this book could be called Great.

But there is another kind of greatness, and perhaps we should distinguish it with the lower-case initial, since it implies an element of modesty, a willingness to live within a community, to grow with it, and, often at the expense of some degree of individuality, to serve it. Upper-case greatness is usually the product of established civilizations that have passed beyond the needs of nationality and the limitations of language and period. Such civilizations can produce geniuses who express the inner needs and hopes of men in many periods of history and many places. But in societies that are stirring to assert and even to find their identities, and to survive as living cultures (as Canada has been for the past century and a half), greatness is not universal; it is very closely linked to what is going on Now and Here.

In presenting a hundred Canadians who I think showed in their special ways the quality of greatness, I am suggesting that they gave expression with particular emphasis to the experiences and hopes of Canadians as a whole. In a historic sense they were the right people at the right place in the right time. They are not all people I find personally congenial; I have no difficulty in believing that both John Beverley Robinson and William Lyon Mackenzie were hard men to like. But I recognize that they have the appropriateness to their times and places which constitutes the kind of greatness this book seeks to project. Nor does greatness equate with goodness (Napoleon and the Marquis de Sade could both be described as great men but never as good men), and if none of the people who appear in this book can be described as villains, only a few have any great claims to being remembered as saints. Yet each gave something special and unique to the fact of being Canadian, and this is why in our history they stand above the heads of the crowd.

I have chosen people from all ways of life, and I have tried to keep men of power in their place, since greatness and power are not identical, and by no means is every successful politician or general a great man even in the modest sense we are projecting here. I cannot think of any company in which Mackenzie King or Alexander Mackenzie (the prime minister, as distinct from Alexander Mackenzie the explorer) would shine with greatness. But Macdonald and Laurier and Diefenbaker (for all their many faults) had that indefinable quality; they were great men. There are people whose lives were very ordinary except for some single major experience which gave them special meaning, and Catherine Schubert, the Overlander who afterwards settled into a quiet rural life, is here to represent that humble and almost accidental kind of greatness. Writers and painters have been the spokesmen for Canadians in the various stages of our development into a genuine national community. And so they appear in relative abundance, from Thomas Haliburton and John Richardson and Paul Kane in the distant days before Confederation, down to Emily Carr and Margaret Laurence and the Inuit sculptor Tiktak in our own time. All of them are great, in the sense that Margaret Laurence once called Gabriel Dumont "a great man of our people". And Gabriel Dumont himself is, of course, present.

The arrangement of the book is simple. I had first thought of shuffling my people regionally, and then of arranging them in terms of political history—pre-Confederation, post-Confederation, post-Great War, and so forth. But I found that the figures who were unrelated to politics did not fit into such arrangements. So I fell back on the obvious arrangement by date of birth. The results were quite illuminating, since they showed—in every phase of Canada's history—what an extraordinary variety of people were growing up and maturing at the same time. Consider some of the names that appear beside each other. Sir John A. Macdonald, the great Scottish spellbinder, beside Piapot, the great Cree rainmaker; Gabriel Dumont beside Charles Mair; Louis Riel, Brother André, and Alexander Graham Bell, all of whom in their different ways received strange messages, standing—as it were—mouth to ear.

And it is ear to mouth, as well as face to face, that I hope whoever reads this book will stand towards these great Canadians, for in speech and action they show us what we have been, what we are—and perhaps even what we may become.

George Woodcock

The Explorer of the St. Lawrence

When Jacques Cartier sailed into history in 1534 as captain and pilot for the King of France, leading an expedition of two ships to the New World, he was already a man of more than forty. Nothing is known for certain of the first four decades of Cartier's life, except that he was born in the Breton port town of St. Malo in 1491 and that he spent his youth gaining the kind of experience that persuaded King Francis I to authorize and finance his expedition. He appears to have visited Brazil and to have been familiar with the eastern shores of Newfoundland. One historian has suggested that he accompanied Verrazano's French-sponsored expedition of 1524 which reached the shores of Newfoundland and Nova Scotia. However, there is no evidence supporting this conjecture, and it is quite possible that, as a Breton sea captain, Cartier had accompanied the ships which sailed from St. Malo to the cod fisheries of Newfoundland and the adjacent coasts. For business reasons such fishermen did not advertise their discoveries, and it seems likely that these men nosed their ships in the seas around Newfoundland before any of the explorers arrived to claim the credit for themselves and the kings who sent them.

Cartier's voyage in 1534 led him into the Strait of Belle Isle, which he seems to have known already, and down the desolate southern coast of Labrador, which he called "the land God gave to Cain", meaning that it was a country fit only for those who had fled from human society. He entered the Gulf of St. Lawrence, discovered Prince Edward Island—"the best-tempered region one can possibly see"—and on the Gaspé peninsula raised a great cross decorated with a crown and fleur-de-lis to claim the land for France. Donnacona, the Iroquois chief of Stadacona (which we now call Québec), was visiting the local Indians and Cartier persuaded the chief to allow his two sons to accompany the expedition on its return to France. Cartier was the first mariner on-record to sail all round the Gulf of St. Lawrence, though he missed the great river that flows into it.

The next spring, 1535, Cartier set sail for the New World again in a fleet of three ships, led by *La Grande Hermine*. This time he learnt from the Indians of the "river of Hochelaga", and ascended it to Donnacona's village of Stadacona. He proceeded upriver, deep into the new land, until he reached the large fortified Iroquois town of Hochelaga at the foot of the great hill which Cartier named Mount Royal. The expedition returned to winter at Stadacona, where twenty-five of Cartier's men died of scurvy before he discovered the Indian remedy— an infusion of the leaves and bark of the white cedar. When he departed in the spring, Cartier kidnapped Donnacona and eight of his men and took them with him to France where all the Iroquois died—Donnacona in 1539. By this act of bad faith he seems to have aroused a hostility towards the French among the Iroquois that lasted for generations and had a deep effect on the history of New France.

The reports which Cartier brought back with him of fertile lands beside the St. Lawrence, together with his samples of gold, stirred the interest not only of the King of France but also of his courtiers. When a new expedition was organized with the intention of founding a settlement in the new country, Cartier found himself relegated to the position of second-in-command, with general charge of the expedition being given to the Sieur de Roberval.

Cartier set sail in May 1541, with an advance party of five ships, again led by *La Grande Hermine*. He reached Stadacona in August and told the Iroquois of Donnacona's death but he pretended that the other Indians he had taken were living like lords in France. Perhaps his explanations were not believed, for bad feeling developed very quickly between the French and the Indians, and Cartier was forced to sail upriver to Cap-Rouge. There he chose a site for the proposed settlement, calling it Charlesbourg-Royal. He built a fort on the water's edge and one on the hill above, and cultivated some of the ground. He also found what he thought was diamond-bearing rock.

After spending the winter at Charlesbourg, Cartier returned downriver when the ice broke in 1542 and started to sail home. Off Newfoundland he met de Roberval, who had been delayed in setting off from France and who ordered Cartier to return up the St. Lawrence. But the obstinate Breton slipped away in the night and left de Roberval to ascend the river with his group of settlers. After a stark winter this group returned discouraged to France in 1543. Cartier's diamonds turned out to be mica, but at least they enriched the French language with a vivid new phrase—*faux comme les diamants du Canada*—"as false as Canadian diamonds"!

Cartier seems to have gone unreproved for disobeying de Roberval's orders. Indeed, when an inquiry was held into the finances of the expedition, he was exonerated completely. He never explored again, for the wars in Europe between France and Spain distracted royal attention from colonizing New France. Cartier seems to have settled down as a landowner and it is likely that he helped to finance the journeys of other men to distant lands before he died in 1557.

The Founder of Québec

More than half a century passed after Jacques Cartier's third voyage before another French captain journeyed to the St. Lawrence with the intention of establishing a settlement. In the intervening years a few fishermen and fur traders had paid profitable visits to the country. Among these men was the Sieur Gravé du Pont who had traded in the region of Trois Rivières since 1599. When Gravé du Pont sailed to this region in 1603 he was accompanied by Samuel de Champlain, who seems to have travelled with the trading expedition as a kind of geographical observer. The son of a captain in the French navy, Champlain was probably in his early thirties at the time of the voyage. Nothing certain is known, however, about his life before he sailed with Gravé du Pont; he first emerged from obscurity with the account of his 1603 journey which was published on his return to France. His comments on Indian customs were extensive, and his maps were better than any published before, particularly as they included an amazingly accurate representation of the Great Lakes system, reconstructed entirely from the accounts of the Indians that Champlain encountered.

Champlain presented his map of Canada to Henry IV, who authorized him to accompany the Sieurs de Monts

and de Potrincourt when they crossed the Atlantic in 1604 to found the first colony in Acadia. After a poor start at Sainte Croix in Maine, a settlement was established in 1605 at Port Royal. That year Champlain explored southward as far as the Kennebec River and Cape Cod, and prepared the first adequate map of the New England coast. Over the mild winter of 1606–07 he founded at Port Royal the famous *Ordre de Bon Temps*, or "Order of Good Cheer", which whiled away the winter with feasting and entertainment that included a masque, *Le Théâtre de Neptune*, written on the spot by Marc Lescarbot.

In 1607 de Monts decided to abandon Port Royal, and Champlain sailed back to France with him. Champlain did not remain there for long. Next year he was given his first official appointment as lieutenant to the Sieur de Monts, who sent him out to found a fur-trading post on the St. Lawrence. On June 3, 1608, Champlain arrived at Stadacona and, on "the point of Québec", began to build a "habitation". Four buildings were surrounded by a stockade and a fifteen-foot moat, a vineyard was planted, and vegetables, wheat, and rye were sown. The settlement of New France had begun and, though more than half of those who spent the first winter there died of scurvy, Québec became a permanent settlement. It was from there in 1609 that Champlain set out, after receiving reinforcements, on his explorations and followed the Richelieu River to discover Lake Champlain. There, at Ticonderoga, Champlain and the group of Algonkian, Huron, and Montagnais Indians who accompanied him encountered the Iroquois (who had abandoned the settlements on the St. Lawrence that they occupied in Cartier's day). Champlain and his men used their arquebuses to deadly effect, and the enemy fled, only to begin the long frontier war that plagued New France for almost the whole of its existence.

From this time onward, as lieutenant to a number of absentee lieutenants general, Champlain was the virtual governor of New France, making occasional trips back to France (on one of these, in 1610, he married the twelve-year-old Hélène Boullé, who joined him in Québec in 1620). He published his *Voyages* in 1613, which brought him instant renown as a geographer, and in the ensuing years he pushed his explorations up the Ottawa River, and to Lakes Nipissing and Simcoe, Ontario and Huron.

More than once Champlain was wounded in battles with the Iroquois, but he survived the rigours of Indian wars only to be captured by English privateers—the Kirke brothers who laid siege to Québec in 1628. Champlain held out against the siege for almost a year before he surrendered in May 1629, and was taken to England, whence he found his way to France. He returned to Québec in 1633 and set to work rebuilding the settlement

Samuel de Champlain.

and ruling New France on behalf of the Company of a Hundred Associates to which Cardinal Richelieu had entrusted the fur trade. The following year the Hundred Associates began to send out families of settlers, the first real habitants of Québec, and at last, by the time Champlain died in Québec in 1635, the settlement seemed well established.

Cartier opened the St. Lawrence to men's knowledge, but it was Champlain who began the real exploration of the region that later became the provinces of Québec and Ontario. He was the true founder of New France, creating a permanent settlement, laying the foundations for trade, and establishing relations with the Indians which, whether friendly or hostile, continued to shape the history of the colony until the British conquest.

The Laughing Nun

Some of the most vivid accounts of life in Québec during the seventeenth century are contained in the letters written by the woman who founded the Ursuline order of nuns in New France. Her name in religion was Marie de l'Incarnation, but she was born in 1599 as Marie Guyart, the daughter of a baker in Tours. She was well educated and showed two early tendencies that lasted her life. She

Marie de l'Incarnation.

was skilful in practical affairs, and she was mystically inclined. One night she dreamt that God came to her and said: "Do you want to be mine?" She answered, "Yes". Her life seemed to work according to her dream wishes.

As early as fourteen, Marie talked of becoming a nun, but her parents found it hard to reconcile her cheerful disposition with the life of the cloister, and they persuaded her to try marriage. The man she married was a master silk-weaver, Claude Martin. It was an uneasy union, plagued by a difficult mother-in-law and even more difficult financial conditions, and it ended unhappily after two years with Martin's death in 1619. Left with a six-month-old child, Marie returned to her parents' house. Shortly afterwards she had the first of a series of blinding mystical visions that led her by stages towards taking vows of chastity and poverty while still in the lay world. By 1631 she wished to extend her vows. She entrusted her son Claude to her sister, and entered the noviciate of the Ursuline order, to which her inner voice had directed her. In 1633 she took her final vows and became Sister Marie de l'Incarnation.

Marie's practical capabilities showed themselves in religious life as in secular, and soon she was appointed assistant mistress of novices and instructor in Christian doctrine. But she felt her conversion had dedicated her to higher duties than could be performed in a convent at Tours. Her dreams again directed her, for God appeared once more and instructed her to go to Canada and build "a house for Jesus and Mary." Shortly afterwards she met a wealthy and pious laywoman who was willing to give her inheritance to a mission devoted to converting Indian girls. In May 1639, they sailed for Canada and in August they arrived at Québec.

They lived in a cold house in the Lower Town while the convent was being built in the Upper Town. It was completed at last in 1642, but it burnt down on the last day of that year, and the women had to raise money once again and supervise the rebuilding. At the same time they taught Indian girls and some French girls whose habitant parents paid their fees in kind. It was a life which had its perils. The convent's farms were devastated and many of the Indian converts were killed by the Iroquois; once, in 1660, the convent itself was besieged briefly. But Marie de l'Incarnation carried on, keeping an eye on business affairs, teaching her students, and learning Indian languages so well that she could compile Algonkian and Iroquois dictionaries.

Yet all the time that she kept such an admirable control of mundane affairs, and laid a good part of the foundation for an educational system in Québec, her mystical inner life continued, punctuated by dreams and by visions of frightening clarity. In the end the spiritual life

destroyed the physical, for Marie de l'Incarnation practised all the austerities that were customary among religious zealots in her age. She neglected her health badly,
so that only an extraordinarily sturdy constitution kept
her alive until the age of seventy-two, when she said
goodbye to her Indian children and sent a last greeting to
her son, who had entered the Benedictine order. She died
with great serenity, confident that what her visions had
revealed would become reality when she at last saw, face
to face, her God.

Legends say that Marie's face seemed transfigured
when she died, but a surviving copy of a death portrait
made at the time shows only the features of an exhausted
old woman. Nevertheless from the time of her death
Marie de l'Incarnation was treated as a saint, and only the
lack of sufficient miracles connected with her has prevented the Church from agreeing with most pious French
Canadians and officially sanctifying her.

It is in her letters that Marie de l'Incarnation survives
for all people, believing Catholics or not. Here her realistic
attitude towards life and her clarity of mind and spirit
come together. And it is here that a fascinating outward
view of the New France she helped to create is combined
with a moving inward vision of the woman she was. She
is said to have written thirteen thousand letters. Most of
these have vanished but many of the best that have
survived are translated by Joyce Marshall in *Word from
New France: The Selected Letters of Marie de
l'Incarnation.*

Bishop of New France

Samuel de Champlain represented the first phase of
French settlement in North America. He was the explorer
who was ready to engage in Indian warfare but who also
recognized the need to create a balanced colonial society
in which fur traders and farmers would exist together.
During Champlain's lifetime, the early system of giving
trading grants to individual nobles was replaced by the
attempt to organize the fur trade into a chartered company—the Hundred Associates—rather like the later and
more successful Hudson's Bay Company. But after
Champlain's death King Louis XIV decided to organize
New France as an outlying province of the old France.
The colony was given, therefore, a regular government
consisting of a governor, who was the ceremonial head
and responsible for military affairs, and an intendant, who
looked after the civil administration of the colony and
kept an eye on the governor's actions.

François Xavier de Laval, the first bishop of Québec.

In practice there was a third member of the government of New France, the bishop of Québec. From the
beginning the conversion of the Indians to Catholicism
had been regarded as one of the leading objectives of
French colonization. For this reason the Huguenots—
French Protestants—were forbidden to settle in Québec.
Missionary priests shared with the fur traders the task of
establishing contact with the Indians, which meant exploring the country. And inevitably, the person who led
the Church in New France had a large share in deciding
how the colony developed.

The man who in 1659 took up that leadership was
admirably suited to his role. François Xavier de Laval was
born in a French country house in 1623. His father was
squire of Montigny and belonged to a branch of the great
Montmorency family, from which had come twelve
marshals of France and several cardinals. François Xavier
was educated in Jesuit colleges and in 1647 he was
ordained a priest, adding pride in his churchly role to
pride in his ancestry. In 1658 he was appointed vicar
general and representative of the Pope in New France. He
was also given the title of bishop, but his diocese was non-
existent; he was bishop *in partibus* of Petraea, a formerly
Christian city of the Near East now in Moslem hands.

In 1659 Laval arrived in Québec and established his
authority over the clergy there. Then he proceeded to
claim his share of political authority. On his arrival he was

made a member of the governor's council, and in 1663 he joined the much more exclusive Sovereign Council. From this point until his retirement in 1688, New France was really governed by a triumvirate, consisting of the governor, the intendant, and the bishop.

Laval was a difficult man to have on any council, for he was intensely intolerant of opposition and refused to admit that the Church was in any way subordinate to civil authority. He was the first of a long line of French Canadian bishops who believed that their first loyalty was to the Pope in Rome rather than to the King in France. Yet Laval was so much in favour with Louis XIV that no less than three powerful governors with whom he quarreled—the Baron d'Avaugour, the Chevalier de Mézy, and the Comte de Frontenac—were recalled. The main subject of disagreement was the treatment of the Indians. Laval, who had established a seminary in 1663 to train native priests, believed that the Church must look after the welfare of all Indians. The governors, on the other hand, regarded the Indians in New France both as allies in warfare against the British and the Iroquois, and as indispensable partners in the fur trade. In either capacity, the Indians were treated regularly to *regales* of brandy, which the bishop thought highly corrupting, and the dispute over this matter lasted throughout his time in office. Laval was partly motivated by compassion for the Indians, for he saw the harm that alcohol caused, and he was a generous man when his power and pride were not at stake; in times of epidemic he would work in the hospitals of Québec without thought of the danger to himself.

Laval's refusal to compromise gave rise to the dominant role which the Church played in Québec affairs, from Laval's arrival in 1659 until the Quiet Revolution of the 1960s, three hundred years later. It was a role that the Church was to play regardless of whether the reigning government was French or British or Canadian.

In 1674 Québec was made a diocese and Laval naturally became its first bishop. In this role he created the system of parishes which made the priests of New France an integral part of local habitant life and which was one of the reasons for the lasting power of the Church in Québec. At last, in 1688, his health broke down and he resigned his diocese to the Abbé Saint Vallier. He retired to the seminary he had founded, where he lived out the rest of his life, revered by the people as Monseigneur l'Ancien— the Old Prelate. His charitable gifts reduced him to poverty, and when all he had left were the meals the seminary gave him, he shared those with the hungry. In the last years his pride burnt out and he died in 1708 a humble and pious man who had long perceived that human glory is an illusion.

The Indian Saint

Though the Church has never actually canonized her, the Blessed Kateri Tekakwitha, whose relics are preserved in the Saint-François-Xavier mission church at Caughnawaga, is in all but name a Canadian saint.

Tekakwitha was born in 1656 in the Mohawk village of Ossernenon in what later became New York state. Her mother was an Algonkian woman, brought up as a Christian by French settlers near Trois Rivières and captured in an Iroquois raid in 1653; a pagan Mohawk warrior picked her as his wife. In 1660 Tekakwitha's mother and father died in a smallpox epidemic. Tekakwitha also was infected and barely survived; her face was heavily pockmarked and her eyesight was weakened as a result of the disease. She was adopted by her father's brother, who was the leading chief of the village and a determined enemy of Christianity.

Not until she was eleven did Tekakwitha actually learn anything about her mother's religion. In 1666 a French raiding expedition burnt Ossernenon and the other Mohawk settlements, and the Indians were forced to sue for peace. During the parleys they asked for missionaries to be sent to them, and in 1667 three Jesuit priests and two lay brothers arrived at Gandaouagué, the new Mohawk settlement. For the short time they were there Tekakwitha took care of them, and when they left she remembered their piety and their gentle behaviour.

Tekakwitha seems to have learnt of the Ursuline nuns of Québec at this time, and when her relatives tried to force her into marriage she repeatedly refused. She endured the displeasure of her family and other Mohawk members of the settlement for eight years, during which time she tried to live a Christian life without being admitted into the Church. Finally, when Father Jacques de Lamberville arrived in Gandaouagué in 1675, she asked him to baptize her. Her desire was fulfilled on Easter Day, 1676. She took the Christian name of Kateri (Catherine).

After Kateri Tekakwitha's baptism, the displeasure of the Mohawk pagans turned into persecution; more than once she was threatened with death unless she recanted. She spent long periods of time in prayer, and when the situation became unendurable, she fled with other converts in the fall of 1677 to Sault-Saint-Louis near the Lachine falls of the St. Lawrence. There Louis XIV had authorized land to be set aside for a settlement of Christian Indians in 1676. Eventually this land would become the Caughnawaga Reserve.

There, at the Saint-François-Xavier mission, Kateri Tekakwitha began to prepare herself for the Christian life,

Kateri Tekakwitha. An early eighteenth century drawing.

and showed such zeal that she was allowed to take her first communion on Christmas Day, 1677, and in the spring of 1678 she was received into the Confrérie de la Sainte-Famille. Up to that time she had combined the life of a religious devotee with traditional Indian customs, accompanying the winter hunters from Gandaouagué and later from Sault-Saint-Louis. But after 1678 she wished to remain near the mission and even thought of founding a community of Indian nuns. The Jesuits opposed the idea, for reasons which are not at all clear, and instead encouraged her to take in private a vow of perpetual chastity. But though she remained to the end of her life a laywoman, Kateri undertook the kind of physical mortifications usually performed only by members of religious orders. These austerities did not prevent her, however, from displaying the joy in existence which her conversion had brought her.

Whether from the austerities she practised, or because of an undiagnosed disease, her health declined rapidly from 1678, and she died during the Holy Week of 1680, calling—according to the accounts—on Jesus and Mary.

A legend immediately sprang up around her, and the Church was not slow to cultivate it. One priest remarked that after death Kateri's pockmarked features had suddenly become beautiful. Miracles were said to have happened to those who prayed over her relics. A bishop of Québec in 1688 (only eight years after her death) compared her to a popular French saint by calling her the "Geneviève of Canada". She was also called "the Lily of the Mohawks".

Ever since that time there have been reports of miracles connected with Tekakwitha's ghostly presence at Caughnawaga, and the Saint-François-Xavier mission is still the centre of large pilgrimages. Some fifty books have been written about Kateri in many languages.

However much truth may be in the claims for Kateri Tekakwitha's sanctity, and for the remarkable cures and other favours said to accrue to those who have faith in her, there is no doubt that the cult of this early Indian Christian is a remarkable example of the powerful role religious belief has played from the beginning in Canadian history.

Chief of the Whale Hunters

On March 29, 1778, Captain James Cook sailed into Nootka Sound on the west coast of Vancouver Island and was greeted by three canoes. In the bow of each canoe stood a masked dancer who scattered eagles' down on the water as a gesture of welcome and shook a bird-shaped rattle as he made an oration. The leading member of this welcoming group was Maquinna, who enters history at this moment.

We do not know when Maquinna was born or when he died. His people, the Moachat, were a loose confederation of village bands inhabiting Nootka Sound. They belonged to a larger group of peoples who lived in the southwest region of Vancouver Island and on the northern tip of the Olympic Peninsula and who have been identified somewhat erroneously by white historians as the Nootka, a name this group does not accept. Maquinna himself was often described as a "king" by the whites who encountered him at the end of the eighteenth century and who had no idea of the structure of Moachat society. In fact each of the big long houses of Nootka Sound had its own chief, but Maquinna was held in the greatest respect because of the hereditary titles he held; indeed the name we know him by—Maquinna—was really an inherited title. He was the first among equals, for though he held high rank, he did not have great power. He acted as spokesman for the Moachat confederacy in its dealings

Maquinna. A Spanish portrait published in 1802.

with strangers, but John Jewitt's famous *Journal* of his captivity among these people between 1803 and 1805 makes it quite clear that Maquinna could make no decisions affecting the Moachat in general without the consent of the council of chiefs or hereditary noblemen.

Captain Cook visited Maquinna at the village of Yuquot, near the mouth of Nootka Sound. Yuquot was used as a summer fishing base by the Moachat, and Maquinna and the other chiefs would set out from this village to hunt the whale. Winter was spent at sites farther up the inlet, such as Tahsis and Copti, where the potlatches (or giving feasts) and the semi-religious dances of the wolf society were held.

Maquinna received Cook with friendship, and ten years later he was equally obliging to the British captain, John Meares, a maritime fur trader to whom Maquinna granted occupancy of a piece of land. Meares built a small trading post upon this land in 1788 and constructed the *North West American*, the first European-style boat to be launched on the Pacific Coast. In 1789 Estevan Martinez arrived with a Spanish fleet, seized the *North West American* and other ships belonging to Meares, arrested some British sailors, and killed a Moachat chief. Maquinna decided that he was in danger and fled to Clayoquot Sound where he remained for a while as guest of Chief Wickanninish.

Estevan Martinez's actions brought Britain and Spain to the verge of war, but in 1790 the Nootka Convention was signed, limiting Spanish rights in the region. When Captain Vancouver arrived in 1791, Maquinna had returned to Nootka Sound and was lavish in his hospitality. He even made peace with the Spaniards, and in 1792 the Captains Galiano and Valdez attended a potlatch held by Maquinna at the winter village of Copti to celebrate his daughter's attainment of puberty.

In 1803 the name of Maquinna appears again in a dramatic way. By this time American traders on the Pacific Coast were creating resentment among the coastal peoples by acting in a high-handed manner. Trouble broke out when Captain Salter of the *Boston* called Maquinna a liar over an incident with a broken musket. After other insults were added to this, Maquinna and the Moachat warriors seized the ship and killed all but two of the twenty-seven men aboard. John Jewitt, the armourer, and John Thompson, the sailmaker, were the only survivors. Maquinna kept them as personal slaves for two years, and as a result we have in Jewitt's *Journal* an invaluable record of Coast Indian life before white influences radically changed the culture. The two captives were not freed until 1805, when the *Lydia* put into Nootka Sound; the captain of the ship seized Maquinna by a trick and held him hostage until Jewitt and Thompson were released.

But whether this was the same Maquinna that welcomed Captain Cook twenty-five years before is doubtful, for Jewitt's narrative suggests he was too young a man. Since the name Maquinna is a clan title handed down from generation to generation, it is likely that the Maquinna who seized the *Boston* was a successor to the man who greeted Cook and his companions, the first white men to set foot on soil that eventually became British Columbia.

The Mohawk Loyalist

Joseph Brant was a hereditary chief of the Mohawks who eventually became the principal chief of the Iroquois confederacy known as the Six Nations.

Brant, whose Indian name was Thayendanegea, was born in 1742 in a village beside the Ohio River. He was a protégé of Sir William Johnson, the British superintendent general of Indian affairs from 1755 to 1774; Johnson married Brant's sister, Molly, in an Indian ceremony and he seems to have been responsible for giving Brant a private school education.

Joseph Brant. The contemporary portrait by William Berczy.

As a result of this sound education, Brant became a highly literate man, and in his later years he translated parts of the Gospels and the Book of Common Prayer from English into Mohawk. But he was also well educated in Indian ways and he was a brave, resourceful warrior—without these qualities he could never have risen so high in the hierarchy of Iroquois chiefs. In his teens he fought with his people on the British side during the Seven Years' War when New France was conquered. He was among the Indian forces which supported Lord Amherst in the attack on Montreal in 1760, and in 1763 he was among the loyal Indians whom Sir William Johnson led against Pontiac's confederacy of rebel tribes.

In 1774, when he was thirty-two, Joseph Brant became secretary to Sir John Johnson—Sir William's son—and during the American Revolution he led his braves on the British side as auxiliaries of Johnson's Royal Regiment.

When the war ended in 1783, Brant and his Iroquois followers joined the Loyalist trek to Canada, and in 1784 they were granted land along the Grand River in Upper Canada. Joseph Brant had always been a man of two worlds, educated in white ways but equally well versed in Indian customs and warfare, and he realized that the old days when his people could live by hunting and simple maize cultivation were at an end. He encouraged his people to become farmers using European methods, and in 1800 he built himself a large cedar house, which he called Wellington Square, at Burlington Bay near Hamilton. It was more than twenty miles from the land where he had settled his people. He did not find it necessary to dwell among them, and indeed, Joseph Brant regarded himself as no ordinary Indian.

He enjoyed the celebrity that his military exploits and his loyalty to Britain brought him. In 1787 he went to England, where he was feted and where the society painter George Romney portrayed him in the hybrid combination of Indian and European garb he wore on such occasions. Mrs. John Graves Simcoe described this attire when she recorded an occasion on which Brant dined with the governor of Upper Canada:

> He has a countenance expressive of art or cunning. He wore an English overcoat with a handsome crimson blanket, lined with black, and trimmed with gold fringe, and wore a fur cap; round his neck he had a string of plaited sweet hay. It is a kind of grass which never loses its pleasant scent. The Indians are very fond of it.

Brant dressed in a similar way for the splendid portrait which William Berczy executed in the early 1790s and which now hangs in the National Gallery of Canada.

Joseph Brant died in 1807 and was buried at Burlington Bay, but his people wished him to lie among them, and in 1850, his body was transported to the Grand River reservation and reburied there. His house, Wellington Square, was allowed to decay, but a replica of it was built at Burlington Bay and this building now serves as a Brant museum. Brant would have approved.

Lord of the Fur Trade

Two of the Scottish clans stand out above all others in the history of the Canadian fur trade at the end of the eighteenth century. They are the McGillivrays, of whom William was the most important, and the McTavishes.

This pattern began with Simon McTavish, who migrated to America in 1772 and immediately went into the fur trade; by 1775 he had established himself in Montreal and was one of the most energetic of the merchants who took over the trade originated by the French coureurs de bois. In 1779 Simon became one of the original partners of the North West Company, and in 1787 he established the firm of McTavish, Frobisher and Co., which supplied trade goods to the North West Company and virtually controlled it.

William McGillivray.

Simon McTavish's sister, Anne, had married Donald McGillivray, a tenant farmer at Stratherrick in Inverness-shire, and their three sons, William, Duncan, and Simon, all followed their uncle to Canada and joined the fur trade. William was the most prominent of the three; he became the leading figure in the North West Company and in 1821 he arranged its end, which took place by absorption into the Hudson's Bay Company.

There are no records of William McGillivray's birth, but it seems to have taken place round about 1764 at Stratherrick. His uncle Simon paid for his education, and in 1784 he sailed to Montreal and became a clerk in the North West Company's service. For two years he followed the fur trade on the Red River and elsewhere in the Prairies. But, like his uncle Simon, William McGillivray chose against becoming a wintering partner and enduring the hardships of the trade in remote posts and on the brigade trail. He devoted his energies instead to the Montreal end of the business, and in 1787 he conducted the negotiations that brought the rival firm of Gregory, McLeod & Company into the North West Company fold and that re-established unity in the fur trade out of Montreal.

In 1790 William McGillivray became a partner in the North West Company, and in 1793 a partner in his uncle's firm of McTavish, Frobisher and Co. Increasingly Simon McTavish acted through McGillivray, who went each year to the rendezvous at Grand Portage to supervise the exchange between the brigades carrying trade goods from Montreal and the brigades bringing furs from the hinterland.

By 1804, when Simon McTavish died, William McGillivray was unchallenged as the most powerful individual in the North West Company. When the international boundary between British North America and the United States was determined and Grand Portage fell into American territory, the trans-shipment site for the North Westers was shifted in 1805 to a new post at the mouth of the Kamistikiwa River. When construction on this post was finished in 1807, it was named Fort William in honour of McGillivray.

In the War of 1812 McGillivray led a volunteer company of North West Company voyageurs who took part in the capture of Detroit. For this service McGillivray was rewarded in 1814 with an appointment to the Legislative Council of Lower Canada, a position he used without scruple to further the interest of the North Westers during the great struggle with the Hudson's Bay Company for control of the Canadian fur trade.

Between 1812 and 1816 that struggle reached a climax when Lord Selkirk, with the consent of the Hudson's Bay Company, established a farming settlement on the Red River. McGillivray objected strongly to the existence of settlements across the route the North Westers used to reach the rich fur-bearing territory of Athabasca, particularly as the presence of Selkirk's settlers interfered with the buffalo hunt and the supply of pemmican necessary as a food for the wintering voyageurs. It was McGillivray who directed the violence used by the North Westers and their Métis allies against the Selkirk settlers. This violence was to culminate in the tragic massacre of Seven Oaks in 1816, when Governor Robert Semple and twenty settlers were murdered and mutilated. In retaliation, when Selkirk reached Fort William on his way to re-establish the colony, he arrested McGillivray and sent him and other North West partners to Montreal for trial.

Thanks to his influence with the Lower Canadian authorities, McGillivray escaped conviction. But the experience of going through the courts, together with the failure of the North Westers to intimidate the Hudson's Bay men into abandoning Athabasca, convinced McGillivray of the futility of carrying on the struggle between the two companies. He and his brother Simon took leading parts in the negotiations that resulted in the amalgamation of the rival groups in 1821.

After the amalgamation, McGillivray became a member of the board created to regulate the fur trade. He gave up all other company responsibilities and left Canada to retire in England. He bought an estate in the Hebrides, but does not seem to have lived there, and in 1825 he died in St. John's Wood, then a pretty village outside London which must have seemed very distant from the scenes of the fur trade.

William McGillivray, like Simon McTavish, ruled the fur trade with the primitive autocracy of the clan chieftain, treating his traders and his voyageurs as loyal retainers. It was a pattern of authority that did not survive in Canada beyond the early nineteenth century.

By Land to the Pacific

There were Canadian explorers who covered a great deal more territory than Alexander Mackenzie, such as David Thompson, who mapped so much of the Canadian and American West for the North West Company. There were others whose journeys involved more danger or more hardship, such as Samuel Hearne, who made the first journey on foot to the Arctic sea. But the two great journeys that Mackenzie did make were of a kind that changed men's conceptions of the geography of what later

Alexander Mackenzie. An engraving from the portrait by Thomas Lawrence.

became the Dominion of Canada. It was Mackenzie who first opened the routes that united the three great oceans of Canada—the Atlantic, the Arctic, and the Pacific.

Like so many other men who rose to prominence in the Canadian fur trade at the end of the eighteenth century, Alexander Mackenzie was a native of the Hebrides, born at Stornoway on the island of Lewis in 1764. It was a lean time on the islands, and when Mackenzie was ten his family emigrated to New York, where Mackenzie's uncle, "Ready Money John" McIver, was a storekeeper. The Mackenzies and their relatives were Loyalists, and when the American Revolution began, Alexander's father—Kenneth Mackenzie—was given a commission in the "Royal Greens". He died in service in 1780. During the war Alexander had been sent to school in Montreal, and in 1779 he became a clerk in the fur-trading firm of Finlay, Gregory and Co., one of the groups of Scottish and American merchants who were taking over the fur trade established by the French.

After spending several years in Montreal, Mackenzie was sent to Detroit in 1784 to gain fur-trading experience, and in the following year he became a wintering partner and travelled into the west country. When Gregory, McLeod, and Co. (the name by which his firm was then known) joined the other fur-trading groups in 1787 to form the North West Company, Mackenzie became a partner and that year he set off for Athabasca. There he spent the winter with the old trader Peter Pond, who fired Mackenzie's imagination with ideas of an overland route to the Pacific, ideas which Pond had formed after talking with the local Indians.

Mackenzie was put in charge of the Athabasca district in 1788, and after building Fort Chipewyan, he set off in 1789 down the Slave River in an attempt to prove Peter Pond's theories. He found a river running out of Great Slave Lake and called it the River of Disappointment, since the ocean he reached by it on the day the Bastille fell in Paris was the Arctic and not the Pacific; the river was later named the Mackenzie in his honour.

Mackenzie refused to give up his goal of finding a way to the Pacific. In 1791 he travelled to England to buy scientific equipment, and in 1793 he set out westward from the fork of the Peace and the Smoky rivers, crossed the Rockies at Peace River Pass, and made his way down the Bella Coola River to salt water at Dean Channel, where he camped with an uneasy feeling because of the hostile Bella Bella Indians. Before retracing his steps, he wrote on a rock: "Alexander Mackenzie from Canada, by land, the twenty-second of July, one thousand seven hundred and ninety-three."

By his feats of exploration, Mackenzie did more than change men's conceptions of the geography of British North America. He also opened the way for the fur traders to move west of the Rockies, into what is now British Columbia and the American states of Washington and Oregon. But his relationships with the other traders in the North West Company were abrasive, for Mackenzie was proud of his achievements and resented criticism. In 1799 he resigned from the company and went to England. There in 1801 he worked with a ghost writer named Coombes on his travel journals, which were published in the same year, as *Voyages from Montreal, on the River St. Lawrence, through the Continent of North America, to the Frozen and Pacific Oceans*. The book earned him immediate recognition and in 1802 he was knighted.

That year Mackenzie returned to Canada and became leading partner in the new XY Company, trading in opposition to the North Westers. In 1804, after bitter fighting in the Athabasca country, the two companies were united, but Mackenzie returned to the North West Company on the specific condition that he not interfere with its actual workings. His days as an active fur trader were near their end. He lived in Montreal and in 1805 became a member of the Lower Canada Legislative Assembly. In 1808 he returned to Britain, marrying a rich merchant's daughter, buying an estate in northern Scotland, and settling down to the life of a landowner at Avoch in Ross-shire.

It was appropriate that such a great traveller as Alexander Mackenzie should die on a journey, at a wayside inn on the way from Edinburgh to Avoch, in March 1820.

The Indian General

Among a great succession of Indian leaders who tried to unite their peoples against the threat of American domination—which meant the loss of their lands, their freedom, and their ways of life—Tecumseh was perhaps the greatest and certainly the most chivalrous. For over thirty years he fought for the survival of his people and their traditions, and he died in the cause to which his life had been devoted.

Tecumseh was born in 1768 in a Shawnee village beside the Mad River, near the present site of Springfield, Ohio. His father, a chief named Puckeshinwau, was killed by whites in 1774 and Tecumseh was adopted by another chief named Blackfish, who taught him woodcraft and hunting, warfare and the Shawnee code of honour. He had several white foster brothers—boys captured and adopted into the Indian community. One of them, who

Tecumseh.

escaped soon after capture, became famous later as Daniel Boone.

Tecumseh fought at the age of fourteen as a warrior in joint British-Indian operations during the American War of Independence, and he soon showed repugnance for the gratuitous acts of cruelty that occurred frequently in Indian warfare. He once saw a white prisoner burnt alive, and it so horrified him that he set out to persuade his fellow Indians to abandon torture and the slaughter of prisoners. In later campaigns Tecumseh's forces seldom resorted to the kind of atrocities that the Indians had been encouraged in the past to perpetrate by both their English and French allies in the warfare along the borders of New France.

As the tide of white settlement moved westward through Ohio and Indiana after the achievement of American independence, Tecumseh became a guerilla fighter, carrying on small marauding actions against the whites. When the Indians formed an alliance to resist further encroachment, he was one of the leaders; the alliance was defeated, however, at the battle of the Fallen Trees in 1794 by Mad Anthony Wayne and his American troops. When the chiefs negotiated a treaty of surrender at Greenville in 1795, Tecumseh refused to recognize it, since he argued that they had no right to sign away land which, like air and water, belonged to all men.

For a number of years after the Greenville treaty, Tecumseh devoted himself to inducing the Indians to give up fighting amongst themselves so that they could unite against the menace of white intrusion. Round about 1808 he became involved in a movement for cultural regeneration which centred around his brother, Tenskwatawa, who was called the "Prophet" because he claimed to have had a revelation from the "Master of Life". What the two brothers preached was the sharing of property, the abandoning of intertribal conflict, and the discarding of white customs and products, especially alcohol, which was destroying the Indian's ancient way of life. The charisma of the "Prophet" won many converts, and Tecumseh energetically organized them into a new confederacy which united Indians from Ohio south to Florida and from as far west as Iowa—a broad area in which settlement was spreading, game was vanishing, and the economy of native life was breaking down.

The American authorities were fully aware of the danger the new movement represented. In 1811 General William Henry Harrison, governor of the Indiana Territory (and many years later a president of the United States), marched up the Wabash River towards Tecumseh's camp, which was the centre of the confederacy. Tecumseh was absent and the "Prophet" foolishly attacked the American forces. In the battle of Tippecanoe that followed, he and his braves suffered a decisive defeat. His magical powers discredited, the "Prophet" fled over the border to Canada and vanished from history.

Tecumseh also left for Canada, for it seemed the only place in which he could find the support he needed. He foresaw the coming war between Britain and the United States and when the fighting broke out in 1812, he summoned his old followers to join him on the British side. It would be the last Indian struggle for the Old Northwest.

Tecumseh's formidable army of Indians, and the fear it inspired, were important factors in the capture of Detroit. In all some three thousand American prisoners were taken there by General Brock's mixed army of British regulars, Canadian militiamen, and Indian braves. The tide of war seemed to be going in favour of Tecumseh and his allies, and they joined in the British invasion of Ohio, hoping to regain their old homelands. But they were pushed backward, and defeated by Harrison's army in the battle of Moraviantown on the Thames River. There, on October 5, 1813, Tecumseh was killed. His body was carried from the field by his braves and buried secretly; his grave has never been found.

With Tecumseh's death the hopes of the Indians east of the Mississippi vanished. Their lands were lost, their way of life was destroyed, and it was left for other tribes farther west to carry on the struggle, doomed as it was. Tecumseh lived on in the memories of Canadians and in the works of Canadian poets as a heroic figure and as a symbol of the Canadian will not to be submerged by the relentless expansionism of the United States. We see him as one of our own.

Hero of 1812

Canadians have not enjoyed, or rather endured, the kind of violent history that puts a premium on heroism, and it is almost possible to count the universally acknowledged Canadian heroes on the fingers of one hand. Of that sparse company, two at least died in the War of 1812, which involved the only major invasion threat to Canada since the British conquered New France in 1760.

Those two heroes of a long-ago war, whom we still remember with admiration and a good deal of gratitude, are the Indian leader Tecumseh and the British general Isaac Brock. Both of these men died in the process of saving the independent destiny of the British North American colonies that later were to become Canada.

Isaac Brock was born in 1769, the son of a landowner on Guernsey in the Channel Islands. In 1785, when he was sixteen, his family bought for him a commission as ensign in the Eighth Regiment, but it was by merit that young Isaac Brock rose rapidly through the ranks to become, at the early age of twenty-eight, a lieutenant colonel in command of the Forty-ninth Regiment. During the campaigns against France between 1799 and 1801, he served in Holland and at Copenhagen; in 1802 he and his regiment were sent to Canada for what was regarded at the time as peaceful and uneventful garrison duty.

Brock was first stationed in Québec and then transferred to Niagara and finally to York. He was appointed colonel in 1805 and major general in 1811. As major general, he had command of all the British forces in Upper Canada and in October 1811, he was made administrator of Upper Canada, performing the duties of the absent lieutenant governor, Francis Gore.

Aware of the tension rising between Britain and the United States over Britain's insistence on stopping and searching American vessels for deserters from the Royal Navy, Brock began to prepare for the outbreak of war between the two countries. When war did break out on June 18, 1812, he had already strengthened the Canadian militia and had assured himself of the support of Tecumseh and his Indian bands, provided that he could strike quickly in the West. This he proceeded to do by ordering

Captain Charles Roberts who was in command of Fort Saint-Joseph on the Canadian side of the border, to attack the strategically important fur-trading post of Michilimackinac located on the channel that links Lakes Michigan and Huron. This Roberts did successfully on July 17, 1812, and the subsequent retention of Michilimackinac against American attacks gave the British control of the West until the end of the war.

Brock followed up the capture of Michilimackinac by leading a combined force of British regulars, Canadian militiamen, and Tecumseh's Indian warriors against the much more strongly held fort of Detroit. He was outnumbered by the American defenders, but deployed his forces so skilfully that General Hull realized the situation was hopeless and surrendered without a fight on August 15.

Brock was knighted for this exploit, but he did not live to hear the news. On October 13, 1812, less than two months after the capture of Detroit, the Americans, led by General Stephen Van Rensselaer, invaded in force across the Niagara River and ascended Queenston Heights. It was a strategic position from which they had to be dislodged or Brock's whole plan for the defence of Upper Canada would be destroyed. He hastened to the battlefield and himself led the Canadian militia in an assault on the artillery positions that the Americans were preparing on the heights. He was mortally wounded, and legend has it

General Sir Isaac Brock.

that his last words were, "Push on, York Volunteers"; like so many of the good stories that decorate history, it has been proved to be unfounded. But Brock was extremely popular among both the British regulars and the Canadian militia, and the effect of his death was to make them fight more stubbornly. By the end of the day General Robert Sheaffe was able to drive the Americans from Queenston and send those who were not taken prisoner in flight back over the Niagara River.

The war continued for more than two years after Brock's death. But his efficient administration of Upper Canada, his foresight in making sound military preparations for the colony, and his excellent strategy during the early months of the war robbed the American invaders of their initial military advantage. Had the Americans been allowed to capitalize on this advantage, it would have been very difficult to defend the two Canadas against them. Thousands of people—British, Canadian, Indian—contributed to the defence of Canada during those crucial years, and in the process the idea of a separate nation that was worth defending began to take shape. But no single person did more than Brock to ensure that Canada survived to be defended.

Pioneer Reformer

There have been few more remarkable father-and-son teams in Canadian history than the two Baldwins. William Warren Baldwin and his son Robert were among the most dedicated of the Upper Canadian reformers of the early nineteenth century. They disagreed with the more extreme views of William Lyon Mackenzie, their contemporary. Mackenzie was willing to use physical violence to change society, but the Baldwins clung to peaceful methods. Mackenzie favoured American-style republican institutions, while the Baldwins believed that if only the British parliamentary system could be transferred across the Atlantic, it was admirably suited for naturalization in Canada. Mackenzie—and Papineau in Lower Canada—rose in armed rebellion and was defeated. But the Baldwins carried on their policy of constitutional gradualism, and in the end they were successful. During the 1840s Robert Baldwin forged an alliance with the French Canadian reform leader, Hippolyte La Fontaine, and the two led the famous Great Ministry of 1848 which won the battle for responsible government in 1849.

It was Robert Baldwin who reaped the fruits of many years of struggle. But he learnt his principles from his father, who was among the most important of the early reformers in Upper Canada. William Warren Baldwin was born of Protestant stock in the County of Cork, Ireland, in 1775. His family were Anglo-Irish landowners, and he himself studied medicine at the University of Edinburgh, from which he graduated in 1796. In 1798 the whole family emigrated to Upper Canada, and in 1802 William settled in York where he practised medicine and in his spare time studied law. In 1803 he was called to the bar of Upper Canada and until 1822 he practised both the professions of law and medicine. In the tiny community of York (which was later given the name of Toronto), he needed two professions to make a decent living.

In 1822 Baldwin's financial worries were brought to an end when he inherited the estate of an elderly spinster named Elizabeth Russell, who was the sister of Peter Russell, one of the early administrators of Upper Canada. Relieved of the need to labour at two professions, Baldwin turned to politics. He was opposed to the Family Compact, the group of rich Tory merchants and officials who worked in close tandem with a series of British-appointed governors, and he was anxious to gain for the people of Upper Canada a larger share in determining their own system of government. In 1824 he was elected to the Legislative Assembly of Upper Canada, where he was shortly joined by his son Robert, and as a member of that assembly, he was the first colonist actually to give expression—in 1828—to the idea of responsible govern-

William Warren Baldwin.

ment. He wrote a letter to the Duke of Wellington, then prime minister of England, proposing that ministers of government should be removed from their posts if they lost the support of the assembly. In addition, he suggested that all actions of the colonial executive should be authorized by an elected minister.

These very reasonable proposals were ignored, and Baldwin, who had become recognized as one of the leaders of the Reform party, was not returned to the assembly in the elections of 1830. After this defeat he decided to take the route of appealing directly to the people, though he refused to lend his approval to the tactics of direct revolutionary action advocated by Mackenzie. In 1835 Baldwin was one of the founders of the Constitutional Reform Society, which had a considerable influence on the more moderate reformers who believed they would eventually win all they desired by means of peaceful action.

When the two Canadas were united in 1841, Baldwin decided to return to active politics and he was elected to the Legislative Assembly, where he gave his full support to the Reform alliance formed by his son Robert and La Fontaine. During the first ministry of this alliance in 1843, he was appointed to the Legislative Council, but a few months later, in 1844, he died in Toronto.

William Warren Baldwin never held any political office, but his influence on his son Robert, and on the other men who created the first democratic and responsible government in Canada, was very great. He was one of the true pioneers of Canadian independence and, like many pioneers, he followed a rather lonely path of few honours.

John Toronto

The Catholic Church was a power to be contended with in Québec from the early days of New France in the seventeenth century. It was a different church, however, that strove to dominate Upper Canada during the early days of that colony, and for quite a long period of time in the early nineteenth century, the Church of England seemed on the verge of success. Its efforts were bound up with the career of Bishop John Strachan or, to give him his ecclesiastical title, John Toronto. In his own way, Bishop Strachan was as political a prelate as Bishop Laval had been in the palmy days of New France, though Strachan was never quite so powerful.

In 1778 John Strachan, who eventually became Canada's most famous Anglican, was born a Presbyterian

John Strachan, first bishop of Toronto.

in Aberdeen. His father was an overseer in a granite quarry, but his mother had genteel ambitions for her son and she insisted that he be given the best possible education. Circumstances being what they were, he was sent to the Aberdeen Grammar School and to King's College, Aberdeen, where he won a bursary. Strachan's own ambition matched the high hopes his mother cherished for his future; when his father was killed in an accident, and it looked as if his education might be imperilled, he worked as private tutor and village teacher while continuing part-time university studies. He graduated in 1797, but the competition for advancement in the Scottish teaching profession was intense. So he happily accepted an opportunity to become tutor to the children of the Kingston Loyalist, Richard Cartwright, in the hope that he would be appointed principal of a college that Governor Simcoe had planned to establish in Upper Canada. The college did not materialize and, setting his career above his Presbyterian faith, Strachan abruptly changed religious allegiances, joined the Church of England, and was ordained a priest in 1803.

Conversion brought immediate results. Strachan was appointed rector of Cornwall, where he also ran a school

00 218 6799

for the sons of gentlemen. In 1812 he became rector of York (later Toronto), and there his great opportunity came during the War of 1812. In 1813 the Americans occupied York and Strachan was the only person to remain in the town with any kind of authority to negotiate with them; he did so to good effect, protecting the interests of the people of York and preventing the worst excesses of looting.

From this point on, Strachan held political as well as ecclesiastical power in Upper Canada. In 1818 he was appointed to the Executive Council of the province, and in 1820 he was appointed to the Legislative Council. He continued to sit on both councils until 1841, becoming one of the most solid pillars of the so-called Family Compact. This was the group of conservative British and Loyalist families that autocratically ruled Upper Canada and resisted the attempts of the reformers to democratize the system and introduce responsible government.

Strachan's religious and educational careers advanced as his political influence increased. He was made arch-deacon of York in 1825 and when Toronto became a diocese in 1839, he became its first bishop, with the right to sign himself John Toronto. He was the first president of King's College, which was founded in 1827, and when the college was secularized and turned into the University of Toronto in 1850, Strachan founded a new Anglican institution, the University of Trinity College.

In his later years, much of the power that Strachan wielded and enjoyed was a direct result of his talents as a teacher. The men whom he had taught in school and college remembered him when they rose to high posi-tions in Upper Canadian politics and they sustained his influence.

When responsible government came to Canada in the 1840s, Strachan's influence began to wane. He dropped out of politics early in the decade, and in the field of education he watched the principles of his great rival Egerton Ryerson, the Methodist leader who advocated secular schools, gain wide acceptance in English-speaking Canada. Even the power of the Church of England was declining. Although Strachan had tried to assure the dominance of his church by seizing the Clergy Reserves— the land set aside in Upper Canada for the benefit of Protestant clergy—he watched the Church lose its footing in competition with Methodism and Catholicism for the souls of Ontarians. By the end of his life the Bishop of Toronto owed his reputation to his personal strength of character rather than to his role as head of the Anglican community.

The date of Strachan's death was strangely appropri-ate. It was 1867, the year of Confederation,when the old-fashioned Tory ideals of Upper Canada, which John Toronto had so loyally supported, vanished into history.

Founder of Ottawa

Ottawa had gone through many transformations before Queen Victoria selected it in 1857 to become the capital of the Province of Canada, an honour which ensured its selection as the capital of the Dominion of Canada in 1867. In fact the settlement had only enjoyed the name of Ottawa for two years before Queen Victoria put her finger on the map. Previously it had been known as Bytown, a rough logging town celebrated for its riots between Catholic Irish and Orangemen.

The name—Bytown—commemorates Colonel John By, the man who chose the site of the settlement on the south bank of the Ottawa River without any idea that one day it would become the capital of Canada or that the bluffs above the river would make an excellent site for the neo-Gothic towers of Canada's Parliament. For him it was merely the most convenient place to set up a head-quarters for the Royal Engineers while he built the Rideau Canal.

John By was a soldier who won no honours in battle and whose only remembered feat is in fact the building of the Rideau waterway. He was born in England in 1781 of a family of country squires, and he was educated at the

Colonel John By.

Royal Military Academy at Woolwich, which specialized in training artillery and engineer officers. Commissioned in 1799 as a second lieutenant in the Royal Engineers, he was stationed in Canada in 1802 and stayed until he was recalled for service in Europe in 1811, a few months before the outbreak of the War of 1812.

It was the anxiety over further American invasions after the war ended in 1814 that brought John By back. Canada was still at this time a country that depended on waterways for even moderately rapid transport. But the existing routes to the towns of the Great Lakes were along the St. Lawrence and these routes were considered vulnerable, for the southern shore of this river was for a considerable distance American territory. To provide a safer route it was decided to create a waterway, using the Rideau River and Rideau Lake, that would allow troops and military supplies to be taken up the Ottawa River and through the back country to Kingston without passing near American territory.

Because of his knowledge of Canada, John By—a lieutenant colonel by this time—was sent out with a company of Royal Engineers to build the twelve miles of artificial channels and the forty-nine locks that would make the canal a functioning waterway. He arrived in the Ottawa region in 1826 with his sappers and engineers, and found a cedar swamp with a store, a tavern, and a few log cabins like that inhabited by Nicholas Sparks, who owned most of the land in the area, having bought it for $240. By camped in the forest to begin with, but later, when the commencement of the canal brought in merchants and speculative builders, he lived in a house on Major's Hill.

By was a well-fed, genial kind of man, with a strong sense of his military dignity, and it is thus that he appears in W. P. Lett's versified *Recollections of Bytown*, published in 1874:

> As o'er the past my vision runs,
> Gazing o'er Bytown's elder sons,
> The portly Colonel I behold
> Plainly as in days of old,
> Conjured before me at this hour
> By memory's undying power;
> Seated upon his great black steed
> Of stately form and noble breed;
> A man who knew not how to flinch,
> A British soldier, every inch:
> Courteous alike to low and high,
> A gentleman was Colonel By.

The foundation stone for the high tier of locks that led down from the cliff at Bytown to the Ottawa River was laid in 1827 by John Franklin, the Arctic explorer, and the

waterway was completed five years later in May 1832. Colonel By then departed to England, retired from the army, and settled on his estate at Sternfold Park in Sussex. But he was not entirely finished with the Rideau Canal. The construction costs of the canal ran to $5,000,000, a considerable sum in those days, and a British parliamentary committee investigated it, though in the end no blame was laid on John By.

He died in 1856. His canal was never used for military purposes, though for a few years, until the railways came, it provided a more comfortable route for immigrants and a quicker one for merchandise than those via the St. Lawrence. The settlement named Bytown in the colonel's honour continued to grow until it became grand enough to need a new, less awkward name, Ottawa. But Colonel By is not forgotten in Ottawa, for one of the finest features of the capital city is the four-and-a-half-mile stretch of his canal that runs through its heart, a delectable sight in summer and a fine place for skating in winter.

The Gentleman Patriot

Louis-Joseph Papineau is one of the most puzzling men in Canadian history. No label fits him completely; there is always some contradiction that prevents exact definition. In theory he was a conservative; in practice he was a revolutionary. He believed in a republic, but he wanted it to be ruled by country gentlemen like himself. He differed from most Canadian democrats in the early nineteenth century because he did not believe in responsible government—government by ministers chosen from the people's representatives. But he differed also from most Canadian conservatives because he rejected the system of monarchy and the link with Britain. He is usually regarded as the prophet of Québec independence, but there were times when he entertained the idea of Lower Canada, as Québec then was, joining the United States. And though he is often described as leader of the Lower Canada Rebellion of 1837, he fled before the guns began to fire, leaving others to defend the insurrection and—in many cases—to die in battle or on the gallows.

This strange man was born in Montreal in 1786, the son of Joseph Papineau, a notary and landowner who had helped defend Canada against the Americans in 1776; as a volunteer Joseph Papineau had taken despatches from Montreal through the American line to Sir Guy Carleton in Québec. In 1812 Louis-Joseph followed his father's example and served as a militia officer against another invasion of Americans. He was present when a

Louis-Joseph Papineau.

combined force of British regulars, Canadian militiamen, and Indian warriors under General Isaac Brock and the Shawnee chief Tecumseh captured Detroit.

By 1812 Louis-Joseph had already been called to the bar of Lower Canada; he had even been elected, at age twenty-three, to the Legislative Assembly of Lower Canada. He continued to be a legislative representative, with one interval of exile, until 1854. During his early years as a politician he belonged to the moderate Parti Canadien and in 1815 he became speaker of the Lower Canada Legislative Assembly, a position he held almost continuously until the Lower Canada Rebellion of 1837. His brilliance as a parliamentarian was recognized by all parties and in 1820 the governor, Lord Dalhousie, persuaded him to accept an appointment to the Executive Council. But Papineau proved an uneasy councillor. He felt that Dalhousie ignored his advice and used him for his own political purposes, and in 1822 he resigned and became an increasingly extreme opponent of British rule, not only in Québec, but anywhere in North America.

In 1826 the Parti Canadien changed its name to the Parti Patriote; this formalized a change from moderation to radical activism. Papineau had come under the influence of American republicanism, and particularly the teachings of Thomas Jefferson. He never became a true democrat in the sense of believing that everyone should participate in government; he always believed the educated and the genteel should rule like squires over an ignorant peasantry. But if Québec were to be governed by an elite, Papineau wished it to be a French elite, and so, as speaker of the Legislative Assembly, he quarrelled with every governor sent out from Britian. He spent his time gathering grievances against the alien rulers and in 1834 he took responsibility for the Ninety-Two Resolutions, a famous statement of opposition to the existing government.

So extreme were these resolutions that they drove moderate liberals into the arms of conservatives, and left Papineau and his Patriotes so isolated that they turned into a conspiracy rather than a party. In such situations extreme elements predominate, and although Papineau was opposed to violent measures, he found himself unable to resist those who advocated insurrection. But he was like the sorcerer's apprentice; he had set into motion events he could no longer control. As late as October 23, 1837, the date of the Patriotes' assembly at St. Charles, Papineau still opposed insurrection, but the government made such a step inevitable when it began to arrest Patriote activists in November. Papineau avoided arrest and travelled to St. Denis, the rebel headquarters, where he accepted the position of commander of the insurrectionary forces. Then he prudently slipped over the American border while his followers fought it out with British regulars and loyal militia. Their defeat was inevitable.

So was the end of Papineau's effective political career. Exiled in the United States and later in France, he avoided other rebels and took no part in a later rebellion in Lower Canada in 1838. When he received a pardon in 1845 he was living in poverty-stricken loneliness in Paris. He returned to Québec and was immediately elected to the assembly of the united Canadas. But though he influenced a few young liberals who formed the Parti Rouge in the late 1840s, he never again played a leading political role. In 1854 he resigned from the assembly to devote the rest of his life to the cultivation of his estate. He died in 1871.

The Little Emperor

The first Canadian industry was cod fishing, which drew mariners from the ports of Europe to the banks of Newfoundland and into the St. Lawrence estuary. The second was the fur trade. In the early years of Canadian history this industry was conducted from the settlements of Montreal and Québec in New France and from a string of English forts along the shores of Hudson's Bay. It was to Montreal and Québec that the coureurs de bois brought the furs they had gathered from the Indians living in the forests around the Great Lakes. North of the Great Lakes, the trade was in the hands of the Hudson's Bay Company, an English firm which Charles II chartered in 1670. The French traders created elaborate canoe routes that would eventually reach all across Canada; the Hudson's Bay traders had the advantage that in summer their ships came into the heart of the continent. From the beginning there was fierce rivalry between the two groups, and more than once French ships raided and destroyed the English forts on the shores of the bay.

After the conquest of Québec in 1760, Scottish traders took over the Montreal-based fur trade and formed a series of combines; the North West Company was predominant among these firms. As the Hudson's Bay traders and the Montreal traders both moved west into new areas in search of ever-diminishing supplies of furs, clashes became inevitable. One such clash took place on the Red River, where Lord Selkirk established a settlement of Scots in 1812; others occurred when both sides tried to gain control of the Athabasca district, which lay between Lake Athabasca and the Rockies. There were armed encounters, and both groups obtained warrants from Lower Canada to arrest their rivals.

George Simpson.

George Simpson was late in entering this conflict but he played a decisive role. Born in Scotland in 1787, Simpson went to London in 1809 to work as clerk for his uncle, a partner of Andrew Wedderburn. Wedderburn was one of the men who had reorganized the Hudson's Bay Company into a fit competitor for the North Westers, and it was Wedderburn who picked George Simpson to replace the governor of the Hudson's Bay area, William Williams, when he was threatened with arrest. A bookkeeper by training, Simpson had no fur-trading experience, but Wedderburn had observed a strength of character in this small man, and the gamble he took was justified. Although Williams was not arrested, Simpson was given a chance to repay the faith placed in him. When he reached Norway House in June 1820, he was sent with a brigade into the Athabasca country and there he handled a confrontation with the North Westers so audaciously that the North Westers conceded the area to the Hudson's Bay men.

The following year—1821—the two companies united under the name of the Hudson's Bay Company. Simpson became governor of the company's northern department, which conducted the major fur-gathering operations. He ruled with dash and efficiency after first making peace with his old rivals, the wintering partners of the North West Company, most of whom stayed on to become good servants of the new organization. He introduced measures of economy and became celebrated for his cross-continental journeys of inspection, the first of which took place in 1824.

Simpson established records of speedy travel to prove that the fur brigades need not be so long on the road. He carried out such dangerous experiments as descending the Fraser Canyon by canoe, an escapade that not even Simon Fraser had attempted; Simpson concluded that it was not a good route for carrying furs after barely escaping with his life. But he had to find out for himself!

Simpson adopted the style of a Hudson's Bay potentate for he knew how necessary it was to impress the Indians, who played an essential role in the fur trade. Always he would arrive at a trading post sitting top-hatted in his *canot de maître*, with the company's flag flying and his personal piper playing a Highland march. Once, in 1841–42, he went around the world by way of Siberia, a land in which travel was even more difficult than it was in the Canadian West.

In 1839 Simpson was appointed governor-in-chief, which gave him complete control of the Hudson's Bay Company's North American operations. He ruled as a dictator and his underlings found him ruthless, arrogant, cold in personal relations. But he fought like a tiger when the company's existence was threatened. There were many enemies, particularly in the British Parliament, who wished to take away the company's control of the Canadian West, but Simpson staved off the day of reckoning until after his death in 1860. It would be another ten years after that before Rupert's Land, the company's Canadian domain, would be acquired by the new Dominion of Canada.

The Great Ship Master

Nova Scotians have never forgotten that the glory of their province as a separate colony before Confederation was its great fleet of merchant ships. Most of these vessels were built in the colony's own shipyards and many Nova Scotians still blame their province's entry into the Dominion of Canada in 1867 for the loss of that great heritage. In fact, the decline of the province's shipbuilding industry was more likely due to the inability of a small community to compete in the world of sea transport at a time when sail gave way to steam and small wooden vessels were replaced by large iron ones. It is significant that the Nova Scotian shipowner, Samuel Cunard, established one of the world's greatest shipping lines precisely because he understood very early on the advantages of steam and iron, and pioneered a regular system of transatlantic transport that linked the great triangle of Britain, Canada, and the United States.

The Cunard dynasty really began with Abraham Cunard, one of the Pennsylvania Dutch whose ancestors had immigrated to the American colonies in the seventeenth century. In 1783, at the end of the American War of Independence, Abraham accompanied the British forces to Halifax, and there he worked as a master carpenter for the army. Samuel was born in Halifax in 1787.

Abraham Cunard was a thrifty man and every member of his family was expected to work. As a small boy, Samuel sold vegetables from the family garden and largely educated himself, while Abraham invested the family's savings in waterfront property that he intended eventually to use for wharves. As Samuel grew older, he began to follow his father's example, buying goods in the harbour and selling them for a profit in the town, and in his early twenties he became a clerk to the Royal Engineers.

In 1810 Abraham Cunard set himself up as a merchant in the West Indian trade and as a timber exporter to Britain. Samuel entered wholeheartedly into the business, and the Cunards prospered in the War of 1812 and in the Napoleonic wars, which did not end until 1815. It is said that success first came to the Cunards when they bought the cargo of a captured French vessel and sold it at great profit. Whether or not this is true, they did well enough during the wars to survive the recession that came with peace, and soon afterwards they got a contract to carry government mail to New York. Even while his father was alive, Samuel managed to obtain virtual control of the family business, and when Abraham died in 1824 it became S. Cunard and Company.

Samuel Cunard was soon running an extremely complex business. Apart from buying and selling wooden ships, he imported rum and sugar from the East Indies and, in exchange, exported salt, dried fish, and lumber. He traded with Newfoundland and New Brunswick, and imported a great variety of items—from coal to flour; tobacco to books; and nuts to anchors—from London, Boston, New York, and Philadelphia. He obtained the profitable agency for importing tea from the East India Company and in 1825 he was one of the founders of the Halifax Banking Company. Indeed, there was hardly an area of Nova Scotian life in which Cunard did not play a prominent part, for in 1831 he was appointed a member of the Council of Twelve, the senior governing body in Nova Scotia.

But the most profitable and powerful era of Cunard's career began in 1838, when he founded the British and North American Royal Mail Steam Packet Company.

Relying for basic financial support on the mail contract between London, Halifax, and Boston, Cunard pioneered regular transatlantic steamship services, and in the process he transformed ocean travel from an uncomfortable and uncertain form of transport into a comfortable and reliable one. The Cunard Line, as it became known, long outlived Samuel Cunard, though in later years it was amalgamated with competing enterprises. The Cunard liners—growing steadily larger and more palatial with the passage of time—continued to cross the Atlantic until ocean travel finally lost out in competition with the airlines in the 1960s.

Eventually, Samuel Cunard retired to England and in 1858 he was made a baronet—Sir Samuel Cunard—for having loaned his ships during the Crimean War to transport British troops bound for the Black Sea. He died in 1865, rich and envied, one of the first British North Americans to create a business empire. He did not live to become a Canadian at Confederation, nor did he witness the economic decline of the province where he had worked so hard and prospered.

Samuel Cunard.

The Merciless Judge

John Beverley Robinson was perhaps the most distinguished of the talented young men who were educated by Bishop John Strachan and who rose to high political rank in Upper Canada during the early nineteenth century. He was also one of the most capable members of the Family Compact, the group which virtually held power in Upper Canada until responsible government in the 1840s opened the way for reformers such as the two Baldwins and Hippolyte La Fontaine to move peacefully into positions of power.

John Beverley was born in 1791 in Berthier, Québec. His father, Christopher Robinson, was a Loyalist officer from Virginia who had migrated to New Brunswick at the end of the American War of Independence in 1783 and five years later had moved to Québec. When John Beverley was a year old, his family moved once again, this time to Kingston, where his father was appointed surveyor general of the woods and reserves of Upper Canada.

After Christopher Robinson's early death in 1798, John Beverley went to live with his father's friend, the

John Beverley Robinson.

Reverend John Stuart, and in 1799 he was enrolled in the school John Strachan founded in Kingston. When Strachan moved to Cornwall, Robinson went with him and lived in his household until he reached the age of sixteen; his admiration for the older man and his friendship with him lasted until Robinson died in 1863, four years earlier than the long-lived bishop.

On leaving Strachan's care, young Robinson was articled to D'Arcy Boulton, then solicitor general of Upper Canada. But before Robinson could be called to the bar, the War of 1812 began. Since he had already volunteered for the militia, he was immediately given a commission when called for active service, and on the great day when General Isaac Brock captured Detroit, Robinson was in command of the volunteer contingent. Later he served on the Niagara front, and in 1813 he took part in the victory at the battle of Queenston Heights in which Brock was killed.

When Robinson returned from Queenston to York with a contingent of prisoners, he found that—though he had not yet been called to the bar—he had been appointed acting attorney general in place of John Macdonnell, who had been killed at Queenston. Despite Robinson's lack of experience, he had already shown a brilliant grasp of the law, and at the end of the war in 1814, he was appointed solicitor general; he became attorney general in 1818.

Under the colonial system of the time such appointments were made by the governor; they were not, as they are today, held by elected representatives of the people. Only in 1821 was Robinson elected to the Legislative Assembly as member for York. He retained his seat and his position as attorney general until 1830, when he was appointed chief justice of Upper Canada. But in those days there was also no separation—as there is today—between the functions of judges and legislators. So although Robinson resigned from the assembly, he still belonged to the two higher levels of colonial government, being made speaker of the Legislative Council and president of the Executive Council. As systems of government in Canada became more democratic, he shed his two lesser offices, but he remained chief justice of Canada West until 1862. Then, a few months before his death in 1863, he was appointed president of the newly created Court of Error and Appeal.

Robinson was in some ways a man of vision, though his visions were always limited by his essential conservatism of temperament. For example, he was one of the first advocates of the union of all British North American colonies, which did not take place until the Confederation of 1867. But he justified such a solution in 1823 by the unworthy argument that to bring in the Maritime colonies was the only way of ensuring English-speaking control of Canada.

Perhaps Robinson's career is most interesting in showing how narrow the circle of government in Upper Canada was during the colonial rule of the Family Compact. That the same man should be chief justice and should also preside over both the Executive Council and the Legislative Council represented an extreme concentration of power that justified the criticism of moderate reformers, such as the Baldwins, and the anger of rebels, such as William Lyon Mackenzie.

Robinson, who believed in what he called "ancient and venerable institutions" and in "respect for rank and family", was an implacable enemy of rebels. His integrity as a judge and a lawyer, for which he has often been praised, did not seem to him inconsistent with a complete lack of mercy when he was dealing with those who had attempted to destroy the "venerable institutions" he loved. As acting attorney general in 1814 he refused to allow the military authorities to court-martial men suspected of treason in the War of 1812. But once he had established the rights of the civil authorities, he prosecuted the accused so savagely that eight men were hanged in what later became justly known as the "Bloody Assizes". And, as chief justice in 1837, Robinson was responsible for the hanging of the rebel leaders Samuel Lount and Peter Matthews, an act for which Canadians today find it hard to forgive him.

One could well say that John Beverley Robinson, with all his intelligence and personal courage and integrity, and with his racial prejudices and his absence of compassion, personified Canadian conservatism at its best—and also at its worst!

Paper Tiger

William "Tiger" Dunlop was one of the many eccentrics who adorned Upper Canadian society during the years following the Napoleonic wars. Born in Greenock, Scotland, in 1792, Dunlop studied medicine at Edinburgh, and came to Canada for the first time as surgeon to the Eighty-ninth Regiment. He served at Prescott, Gananoque, and Niagara, and took part in the survey of the road from York to Georgian Bay. When the War of 1812 came to an end he returned with his regiment to England. He had developed an interest in writing, and when he was put on half pay in 1817, he set off for India to take up the editing of the *Times* in Calcutta. It was there that he first became involved in land settlement. In 1819 he became

William Dunlop and the tiger.

superintendent of a society for colonizing an island in the estuary of the Hoogly, and he is said to have earned his nickname, "Tiger" Dunlop, for the zeal with which he hunted down the tigers that threatened the settlers and their livestock.

After an alarming bout of malaria, Dunlop decided to leave the unhealthy lowlands of Bengal and return to Britain. Gravitating to Edinburgh, he began to lecture at the university on medical jurisprudence and to write articles on his Indian experiences for the very prestigious *Blackwood's Magazine*. He joined a group of writers connected with that magazine who met for nocturnal gatherings of wit and conviviality, but seeking other challenges, he left Edinburgh for London, where he edited a Sunday newspaper called the *Telescope*.

In 1826 Dunlop returned to Canada; it would be his home for the rest of his life. His Scottish literary connections had brought him to the attention of the novelist John Galt, who was the promoter, and from 1826, the resident superintendent of the Canada Company. The company had been formed to settle large tracts of Upper Canada with British immigrants and Galt gave Dunlop the high-sounding but vaguely defined position of "Warden of the Forests". In 1829 Dunlop became inspector of the company's lands and settlements, and in 1833 he was appointed general superintendent. Dunlop was not entirely pleased with the way the company handled its responsibilities; he often claimed that the interests of the settlers were being neglected for the sake of profit, and after resigning in 1838 he became an open critic of the company.

In some ways Dunlop was the first of the Red Tories of Canada. He had many conservative ideas, and when the Upper Canada Rebellion occurred in 1837, he organized a regiment of loyal volunteers in Huron County. The rebels were defeated before the "Tiger" could lead his men into battle, but Dunlop made up for his disappointment by disbanding his troops with a fiery exhortation urging them to remain patriotic Canadians. Yet he had as much disdain for the ruling group known as the Family Compact as William Lyon Mackenzie had, and when he ran successfully for election to the Legislative Assembly of the united province of Canada in 1841, it was as a Reform candidate. In 1846 Dunlop retired from active politics and was appointed superintendent of the Lachine Canal, a position that he held until his death in 1848.

Dunlop adapted well to the arduous, free-mannered life of the Upper Canadian frontier, for it suited his eccentric personality. He and his brother, Captain Robert Dunlop, settled in Goderich, and their house—Gairbraid—was famous for the amplitude of its bachelor hospitality and for the strange pranks of its hosts.

The "Tiger" continued to write after settling in Canada, choosing for his subject matter immigrant experience, which he portrayed in a much more favourable light than Susanna Moodie did. He wrote with a great deal of humour, and was given to extravagance and exaggeration. When his soberly titled book, *Statistical Sketches of Upper Canada, for the Use of Immigrants*, was published in 1832 under the nom de plume of "A Backwoodsman", it must have been highly misleading to prospective immigrants who took everything he said quite literally.

"Tiger" Dunlop was at the centre of the modest literary world of early Canada. He founded the Toronto Literary Club in 1836 and he was one of the most regular contributors to magazines such as the *Literary Garland* of Montreal and *The Canadian Literary Magazine* of Toronto. Because of his colourful character, Dunlop was the best-known literary personality in Upper Canada, and his reputation was not undeserved. Some of his much neglected writings, such as "Recollections of the American War" which he published serially in the *Literary Garland*, are minor classics, amusing and informative (if taken with cautious pinches of salt). They project a personality of rare geniality.

Upper Canada Rebel

Canadian rebellions have always been small affairs—too small to be described as revolutions or civil wars. A few men take up arms in a cause they believe in, are defeated, and suffer punishment or exile. But in the long run these rebellions provide a stimulus for change in Canadian society. This is why we think of our rebel leaders as great Canadians. They have helped to shape the society in which we live.

William Lyon Mackenzie led the Upper Canada Rebellion of 1837. In December of that year, after months of planning and plotting, a few hundred farmers gathered at the north end of Yonge Street with the intent of marching on Toronto and overthrowing the colonial government. A rival army of a few hundred loyalists, mainly shopkeepers and civil servants who had taken up muskets for the occasion, marched out of the city under the governor, Sir Francis Bond Head. Outnumbered, badly armed, badly led, the rebels dispersed. Except for a few minor skirmishes, the Upper Canada Rebellion was over.

The rebellion was the culmination of a long and frustrated period of political agitation on the part of Mackenzie and his associates, who wished to democratize the system of government in Upper Canada. This government consisted of a governor and an appointed Executive Council, with a Legislative Assembly that had limited powers.

The Executive Council was dominated by a group of prosperous Upper Canadians, popularly known as the Family Compact. The members of the Family Compact were impeccable insiders. Mackenzie by fortune and temper was an outsider. A minute and fiery Scot, whose grandfather had fought at Culloden and whose father was an impoverished weaver, Mackenzie came to Canada in 1820. He started out as a small storekeeper, but his sense of the injustices created by colonial government led him into journalism and then into politics.

In 1824 Mackenzie founded the *Colonial Advocate* in Queenston and the views that he expressed in this paper were those of the pioneer farmers of Upper Canada, who were discontented with the authoritarian form of government and the lack of such elementary public services as good roads. In 1825 Mackenzie moved his paper to York where his attacks on the Family Compact provoked a gang of young Tories to wreck his press in 1826. Mackenzie, who was on the verge of bankrupcy, won enough money in damages to carry on with his paper. In 1828 he was elected to represent York in the Legislative Assembly, but he had made so many enemies by his

William Lyon Mackenzie.

forthright criticism that his fellow members expelled him. Five times the people of York re-elected him; five times he was expelled. In 1835, the year when he was also elected first mayor of Toronto, he was finally allowed to take his seat in the assembly.

By this time Mackenzie was determined to reform the whole political system. As head of the assembly's Select Committee on Grievances, he drew up a five-hundred page report on the injustices Upper Canadians were suffering. He took it to Britain in the hope that the new Reform government would be sympathetic, but in 1837 Lord Russell published a series of Ten Resolutions which supported the existing system.

Other Canadian reformers were willing to continue on the path of peaceful agitation. Mackenzie, who greatly admired the American Revolution, believed that armed rebellion was the only solution and he mobilized his followers. The farmers repaired old muskets and forged pikes out of scythes, and these often served as their only weapons. Their defeat by a better equipped force was inevitable when they decided on a frontal attack on Toronto instead of guerilla tactics. Mackenzie fled to the United States. Many of his followers were imprisoned; some were hanged.

Mackenzie then tried with little success to incite rebellion from across the border, until the Americans imprisoned him for violating neutrality laws. He took out American citizenship, but became disillusioned with United States politics. In 1849, when an amnesty was declared, he returned to Canada and was re-elected to the assembly. But his time had passed. He remained a solitary figure, disagreeing with all parties until he retired in 1858; he died of apoplexy in 1861.

Mackenzie was important because at the right time he gave dramatic expression to intolerable grievances. When the dust of rebellion settled, less violent men were able to carry out the reforms he demanded. Essentially, he was a rebel, not a statesman. It is difficult to decide what Mackenzie stood for, but never difficult to know what he stood against. He hated the abuses which he found in every system of authority.

The Clockmaker's Friend

Thomas Chandler Haliburton was the first Canadian writer to become well known outside Canada. In Sam Slick, the Yankee clockmaker, Haliburton created a comic character who appealed to American and British readers as well as to Canadian. The appeal of this character has not faded; Haliburton published *The Clockmaker; or, the*

Thomas Chandler Haliburton.

Sayings and Doings of Sam Slick of Slickville in 1836, and it is still in print today. It was Haliburton's intention to amuse his readers, but like all satirists he had an ulterior motive. He wanted to show the people of Nova Scotia how other people saw them; he hoped that when they held this mirror up to themselves they might decide to change for the better.

Haliburton was born in 1796 in the little patrician town of Windsor, Nova Scotia. His family belonged to a class of well-to-do bureaucrats in the province and he himself received a blue chip education at King's College in Windsor, graduating in 1815. He went all the way up through the ranks of the colonial establishment. Called to the bar in 1820, he set up a legal practice in Annapolis Royal. He was elected to represent Annapolis in the House of Assembly in 1826 and during his three years there he proved something of a Young Turk, defying the Tory establishment of the province on a number of issues. He supported a motion by the Reform leader, J. B. Uniacke, calling for the removal of regulations discriminating against Roman Catholics. Then he defied the Anglican establishment in an opposite way by supporting a motion for a grant to the Pictou Academy, which had been set up by the Presbyterian minister, Thomas Mc-Culloch. (McCulloch, incidentally, was a satirist who made fun of Nova Scotians even before Haliburton. His best-known work, *Letters of Mephibosheth Stepsure*, began appearing in 1822 in the *Acadian Recorder*.)

During his brief period in the House of Assembly,

Haliburton made his name as a rebel by proposing the establishment of public schools independent of the Church of England, which dominated education in Nova Scotia at that time. The bill was passed by the assembly but it was rejected by the Legislative Council, which was appointed by the governor. Haliburton's angry speech, denouncing the members of the council as "twelve dignified, deep read, pensioned, old ladies" with the prejudices of "antiquated spinsters", resulted in his being called before the bar of the House and solemnly rebuked.

But the establishment had ways of dealing with young and brilliant rebels. In 1829, at the age of thirty-three, Haliburton was appointed as a judge in the Inferior Court of Common Pleas and effectively removed from politics. Later, in 1841, he was made a judge of the Supreme Court, and he retained this position until his retirement in 1856. These appointments had wonderful results, for Haliburton became a seasoned Tory and abandoned his idea of legislating a desirable society. Instead he took to satire, in the hope that sooner or later people would learn to behave more sensibly if their faults were exposed to laughter.

In his younger days, Haliburton had written a serious study of his province, entitled *An Historical and Statistical Account of Nova Scotia*, which appeared in 1829. But there was no market for such solid fare, and he turned instead to satire, for which there was a much wider audience. He began to contribute to a column called "The Club" that Joseph Howe published in his newspaper, the *Novascotian*. It was for this column that Haliburton invented his great character Sam Slick, and his sketches of Sam pungently commenting on Nova Scotian life formed the basis for his first book: *The Clockmaker*.

Sam Slick was in many ways Haliburton's mouth-piece, articulating the observations on life and humanity which the judge had made on the Nova Scotia circuit. But he was also the comic American, full of homespun sayings which concealed an underlying cunning. Ordinary Nova Scotians and English readers could laugh *at* him as a comic Yankee; Americans and more knowledgeable Nova Scotians tended to laugh *with* him at absurdities of colonial pioneer life. But Haliburton was not entirely committed to mockery. He used Sam Slick's sly pontifications to convey his view that the real trouble with Nova Scotia was not the lack of natural wealth—there were abundant resources—but the inclination of the people to avoid hard work and put the blame on bankers and lawyers when they failed to prosper. *The Clockmaker* sold so well that Haliburton wrote a whole series of Sam Slick books, as well as a lively collection of more personal comments on Nova Scotian life, entitled *The Old Judge, or Life in the Colony* (1849).

Haliburton evidently gave up the idea of changing Nova Scotia by satire. When he retired in 1856, he went to live in England and he never returned. Indeed, in 1859 he was elected to the British House of Commons, and he retained his seat there until he died in England in 1865.

English Canadian literature began in the Maritimes, with Thomas Haliburton, Joseph Howe, Thomas McCulloch, and a few others. And Sam Slick was undoubtedly the first memorable character in Canadian fiction.

The Quarrelsome Major

Soldier, adventurer, and romantic novelist, John Richardson was one of the most flamboyant of Canadian writers. His life reads rather like one of his own melodramatic novels, but he holds an important place in Canadian history because he was one of the first writers to create an imaginative world centred on Canada.

Richardson's father was a Scottish surgeon attached to John Simcoe's Loyalist regiment, the Queen's Rangers. His mother was the daughter of the Irish-born merchant, John Askin of Detroit, and John Askin's Métis wife. Born in Queenston in 1796, John Richardson received his early education in Detroit and Amherstburg, but when the War of 1812 began he enlisted at the age of sixteen as a cadet and served more than a year before he was taken prisoner in the defeat of the Canadian forces at Moraviantown in 1813. He spent the rest of the war as a prisoner in Kentucky. After being released in 1814 he was commissioned in the British army and served briefly in the West Indies before he was withdrawn from active service and put on half pay.

For the next twenty years Richardson lived a rather bohemian life in London and Paris. In London he began to commit his experiences to literature. He was always in need of money and his first aim in writing was to earn enough to pay his debts and keep up an expensive lifestyle. The prospect of fame also stirred him but he was not greatly concerned with writing as an art form.

Richardson began his literary career writing verse—a long and very tedious poem entitled *Tecumseh; or The Warrior of the West: A Poem, in Four Cantos, with Notes*, which he published in 1828. In telling the story of the great Indian leader, who died at the battle of Moraviantown on the same day he himself was captured, Richardson drew widely on his own experiences during the War of 1812.

When *Tecumseh* failed to attract attention, Richardson turned to fiction. This time he drew on another kind

Major John Richardson.

of personal experience—his forays into early nineteenth century Paris—to write an anonymous novel about gamblers and gambling entitled *Ecarté, or The Salons of Paris* (1829). It was filled with sensational revelations of Parisian high and low life, and for that reason the book was more saleable than *Tecumseh*. But it was a poorly written book, with a plot as unconvincing as its characters.

Only with his third book did Richardson achieve real success. Published in 1832, *Wacousta; or the Prophecy: A Tale of the Canadas* concerned the Detroit which Richardson had known as a boy, and it dealt with the events of the Indian uprising led by Pontiac in the 1760s, an incident which Richardson had heard a great deal about in his childhood. The plot was intensely melodramatic, but the story was told with a fascinating combination of action and suspense, and the background was vivid and authentic because Richardson was writing of places he knew. *Wacousta* was an immediate success; it ran through many editions, and today it is in print again.

A single literary success like *Wacousta* was enough to turn Richardson back to thoughts of physical action and adventure. In 1834 he joined the volunteer British Legion which fought on the side of Don Carlos during the civil wars in Spain. He remained with the Legion until 1837, rose to the rank of major, and received the Cross of St. Ferdinand, though his belligerent temper involved him in quarrels and court-martials before he finally resigned his commission.

Returning to England, Richardson was sent to Canada by the *London Times* in 1838 to report on the aftermath of the rebellions of 1837 in Upper and Lower Canada. He was dismissed by the paper, however, when he praised Lord Durham, which was contrary to the policy of the *Times*. He stayed in Canada, moved to Brockville, and in 1840 founded his own paper, the *New Era*, which survived until 1842. He also returned to writing books. *The Canadian Brothers*, set in the War of 1812 and largely based on his own experiences as a prisoner, appeared in 1840; his excellent historical work, *The War of 1812*, came out in 1842. From 1843 to 1844 he edited *The Canadian Loyalist*, and in 1845 a Tory friend appointed him superintendent of police for the Welland Canal. He was so abrasive though that he quickly lost his post and returned to writing for a living, producing a very lively volume of autobiography, *Eight Years in Canada* (1847).

But none of Richardson's books sold well in Canada, and after the fiasco at the Welland Canal there were no more offers of employment from his political friends. In 1849 Richardson went south to New York, where he started writing potboilers for the paperback market that existed even then. At first he made friends and seemed on his way to success, but eventually he alienated everyone who might have helped him, and in 1852 he died, alone and destitute.

In many ways it was a sad record of wasted talent. Yet two of the books which Richardson wrote, *Wacousta* and *The Canadian Brothers*, are classics because their author recognized so long ago that Canada and the life of Canadians were interesting in their own terms.

Roughing It in the Bush

Canada is probably unique in its proportion of people who are immigrants, born elsewhere but naturalized here by experience. It is impossible to understand either Canadian history, or the Canadian character, without taking into account the presence of the immigrant among us. Over the years there have been waves of immigration from different points of origin. In the 1830s the immigrant was likely to come from the British Isles; in the 1890s he more probably came from eastern Europe; in the 1960s he was very often a southern European, from Italy, Portugal, or Greece; during the 1970s he was as likely to be an Asian or an African or a West Indian as a European. Immigrants have come to Canada from every country and culture of the world, and their presence has been one of the reasons that the culture we now call Canadian is so rich in content and so diversified in texture. Geography has given us a variety of terrain—of living space—almost unparallelled among the nations of the world; history has given us an equally unique variety of ancestries.

In the Canadian arts immigrants have played particularly important roles. Their influence is most evident in the performing arts, but hardly less so in the creative arts, especially literature. A long series of immigrant writers, including Malcolm Lowry and Frederick Philip Grove, Brian Moore and Roderick Haig-Brown, has contributed to the tradition of Canadian writing. The pioneers among this group of writers were the two daughters of an English businessman turned country squire, Thomas Strickland. One of them is known to Canadians as Catherine Parr Traill. The other, who is the subject of this sketch, wrote some of the most interesting of early immigrant literature under her married name, Susanna Moodie.

Susanna Strickland (born in 1803) and her sisters were brought up, like many pre-Victorian ladies of good family, to cultivate the arts, including writing, in an elegant, amateur way. But when their father died and left the family impoverished, they found that selling their writings was a good way of contributing to the family's finances without offending the accepted standards of ladylike behaviour. Susanna was already a published author in 1831 when she married an unemployed young army officer, Lieutenant John Moodie, formerly of the Royal Fusiliers. Taking up the offer of free land in Upper Canada which was made to former British officers, the Moodies set out from England in 1832 on a sailing ship that was to lie becalmed for weeks off Newfoundland before it could sail up the St. Lawrence to Québec City. When they finally reached Upper Canada they settled on a farm near Cobourg. But Moodie's practical ineptness and his wife's excessive gentility made them ready prey for their pioneer neighbours, who resented Susanna's stand-offish English airs and graces.

By 1834 they were glad to move to the real backwoods in Douro Township, north of Peterborough, where Susanna's sister Catherine and her brother, Samuel Strickland, were already settled. There the Moodies cleared land and at last established a successful farm. But they never really took to the pioneer life, and it was a relief to them both when Moodie was appointed sheriff of Hastings County as a reward for fighting against William Lyon Mackenzie's rebels in 1837. In 1839 the Moodies left the backwoods to live in Belleville and in this quiet little Loyalist town they remained until John Moodie's death in 1869. Susanna moved then to Toronto and stayed there until she died in 1885.

Susanna Moodie's literary activities in Canada began when she moved to Belleville. Small town life relieved her of the endless drudgery of pioneer farming and gave her time to write for the newly founded Montreal magazine, *The Literary Garland and British North American Magazine*, the most important early Canadian literary journal. From 1839 to 1851 Susanna contributed stories and poetry to the *Literary Garland*, as well as some chapters of her best-known book, *Roughing It in the Bush*.

Roughing It in the Bush was a rather harshly written description of the difficulties of pioneer existence, as experienced by an English lady used to a comfortable life. It appeared in 1852. The following year Susanna published another book about her experiences, *Life in the Clearings*, which was much more mellow in temper and which tended to stress the good aspects of pioneer living. These are the two books with which Susanna Moodie made her mark on the Canadian imagination. They gave sharp documentary glimpses into Upper Canadian life in the 1830s, while offering unforgettable sketches of the kind of people who, in the early days of our history, were shaping the Canadian nation. Most importantly, they emphasized more than any other early Canadian books the contribution the immigrant made to our country by his willingness to endure loneliness and hardship in the hope of a better future.

Susanna Moodie.

Susanna Moodie wrote for the short lived *Victoria Magazine*, published in Belleville between 1847 and 1848, and published a few novels that varied between the sentimental and the sensational in tone, before she ceased to write in the early 1860s. None of these later works was as interesting or as important to our understanding of Canadian history as her two books of immigrant experience, *Roughing It in the Bush* and *Life in the Clearings*.

Education for All

Universal education—by which we mean compulsory schooling available without cost to all children—was for many reasons slow to appear in pioneer Canada. For a long time after settlement began in Upper Canada people lived scattered through the forests, and the bad roads made it difficult to gather children into schools. Colonial government funds were scarce and many people thought it was the duty of the churches to provide a religious-oriented education. Until 1807, when Upper Canada began to subsidize grammar schools, all education was privately funded, and though government-sponsored elementary schools appeared in 1815, they provided for a minority of children. Long into the nineteenth century education was a privilege dependent on family income.

The emergence in Canada of a system of education wholly supported by the community and not dominated by any religious sect was mainly the work of Egerton Ryerson. Though he believed education should be secular (not aimed at implanting any particular creed in the student's mind), Ryerson himself was a very religious man. Born in 1803, he was the son of a former colonel who had served in the British army during the American War of Independence. Brought up as an Anglican, he was converted to Methodism, and in 1825 he became a circuit rider—a preacher who wandered through the backwoods from one small community to the next.

From the beginning Ryerson was opposed to the preferential treatment given to the Anglican Church in Upper Canada. Tracts of land known as Clergy Reserves had been set aside for the benefit of Protestant clergymen and Ryerson protested vigorously when Bishop Strachan tried to appropriate them for the exclusive use of Church of England parsons.

Ryerson's opposition to Bishop Strachan and the Anglican establishment led him for a while into political radicalism. He associated with William Lyon Mackenzie for a short time, but he did not like the American-style republicanism that Mackenzie favoured in the 1830s. This led to a break between the two men, and when Mackenzie took up arms in 1837, Ryerson denounced his use of violence.

By this time Ryerson had come to the conclusion that education was the best way to reform society. He took a leading part in founding under Methodist auspices the Upper Canada Academy at Cobourg in 1836; when the academy became Victoria College in 1841, he was its first principal.

But taking charge of a Methodist university did not mean that Ryerson had abandoned his hopes for a system of education open to children of all religions and races. In 1844, when he was made chief superintendent of education for Canada West—a position he held for thirty-two years—he worked ceaselessly towards the creation of such a system. He travelled all over Europe and the United States, examining various methods of education, and came away most impressed with that of the kingdom of Prussia. Although he modified the disciplined approach he found in Prussia for use in Canadian schools, the system he created was much more rigid than any to be found in Canada today.

The 1843 act under which Ryerson had been appointed chief superintendent assured all children of the right to education, but it was a long time before this right was realized. Funds were lacking, and the government had to be persuaded to make grants to supplement the local taxes levied for schools. Teachers were scarce and a normal school had to be created to train them.

Egerton Ryerson.

It was not until after Confederation that Ryerson reached his final goal; in 1871 the new province of Ontario passed the School Act which guaranteed universal education. With this achievement Ryerson changed English Canadian society in a number of important ways. The provision of free education to the underprivileged was a great step forward in democracy. And Ryerson's mass recruitment of female teachers resulted in the admission of women to the profession of education on the basis of merit; it was the first profession to admit women on this basis. By this act, Ryerson launched the long struggle for women's equality with men.

Outpost on the Pacific

If it had not been for the obstinacy and foresight of a fur trader named James Douglas, the region of Canada we now call British Columbia might have been pinched between Alaska and the Oregon territory, and annexed by the United States. More than once, by prompt action, Douglas won the time that was needed for Britain to meet that threat and preserve the colony on the Pacific until it could become part of the new nation of Canada.

In the fur trade James Douglas was called the "Scotch West Indian", for he was born in 1803 in Demerara, British Guiana; his father, John Douglas, was a Glasgow sugar merchant and his mother a Creole woman remembered only as Miss Ritchie. John Douglas took his son to Scotland and enrolled him in a school in Lanark where sound training in French was offered. His knowledge of French was a special asset when James entered the service of the North West Company at the age of sixteen and set sail for Montreal.

For a few months he was stationed at Fort William, the company's base at the head of Lake Superior, to learn the elements of the trade. In 1820 he travelled to Île à la Crosse in the Athabasca region, where the rivalry between the Hudson's Bay Company and the North Westers was reaching its last bitter stage; he actually fought a duel with a Hudson's Bay man, but neither was hurt.

The next year the rivalry came to an end and the two companies united. Douglas stayed on as a clerk in the reconstituted Hudson's Bay Company. In 1825 he was sent west to New Caledonia and served at Fort St. James, where in 1828 he married Amelia, the Métis daughter of Chief Trader William Connolly. Douglas was imperious in his dealings with the local Carrier Indians, and in the end caused so much offense that he was persuaded to move south to Fort Vancouver, the company's Pacific Coast headquarters. He started there as accountant, became

James Douglas.

chief trader in 1834, and reached the highest rank in the company's service, chief factor, in 1839.

As chief factor, Douglas faced a difficult task. The company's position on the Columbia had been made insecure by the arrival of American settlers in the region and the belligerently expansionist mood of the United States government. Under an agreement concluded between the Americans and the British in 1818 the whole area between Alaska and California had been thrown open to trading by subjects of both countries. But the agreement could be terminated at a year's notice, and a movement for annexation arose among the Americans. James Polk fought an American presidential campaign on the slogan "Fifty-four Forty or Fight", 54°40' north being the latitude of the southern border of Alaska. The Hudson's Bay traders had to take into reckoning the chance that at least part of the area between California and Alaska would become American and in 1842 Douglas went north to find a new site for the company's Pacific Coast headquarters. He discovered it on the southern tip of Vancouver Island and there he built Fort Victoria.

The fur traders' forebodings were justified. In 1846, under the Oregon Boundary Treaty, the Americans gained all the territory up to the 49th parallel, with the exception of the southern part of Vancouver Island, which was granted to Britain. By that time Douglas was in charge of Pacific Coast operations and in 1849 he transferred the headquarters to Victoria. In the same year, to prevent further American encroachment, the British government declared Vancouver Island a crown colony and leased it to the company. Richard Blanshard was sent from England to govern the colony, but he received little co-operation from the Hudson's Bay traders and in 1851 the Colonial Office had no choice but to appoint Douglas governor. He remained in his post as Hudson's Bay factor and, over the protests of the few settlers, ran Vancouver Island as a fur-trading outpost rather than a regular colony.

The discovery of gold on the Fraser River in 1857 dramatically changed the situation. When the news of the Fraser River strike reached San Francisco in the spring of 1858, thirty thousand people sailed north to the tiny capital of Victoria (population four hundred) and found their way as best they could to the mainland diggings. The most unruly of the California desperadoes began to clash with local Indians, and the situation became an open invitation to American intervention unless decisive British action were taken.

James Douglas took it. His governor's commission extended only to Vancouver Island and the Queen Charlotte Islands: there was no formal government at all on the mainland. But Douglas did not hesitate to issue technically illegal proclamations regulating the entry of the miners. He used visiting naval ships and their crews to make a show of force. By the time the Colonial Office got round to making the mainland of British Columbia a colony and appointing Douglas its governor, the threat was contained. Douglas settled down to establishing towns such as New Westminster and Derby (Fort Langley) and to building the great road north to the new mines of the Cariboo.

Autocratic Douglas was an excellent man in a crisis, but when the new colonies began to acquire a settled population interested in self-government, he was a liability. He was just too inflexible to adapt to the democratic principles preached by his chief critic, Amor De Cosmos, editor of the *British Colonist*. In 1864 Douglas bowed to change and resigned his governorship. He lived on in Victoria, the town he had created, until he died in 1877, six years after British Columbia entered Confederation. If Douglas had not been present in 1858, the colony might not have survived to become part of Canada.

The Novascotian

The first real breakthrough in democratic government in British North America came in Nova Scotia. Responsible government—a government consisting of the elected representatives of the people—became a reality there in 1848; only later was it achieved in the other colonies of British North America.

If any one man deserves the credit for this achievement, it is Joseph Howe, poet, printer, publicist, and politician. Like so many of the people we now regard as great Canadians, Howe was of Loyalist stock. His father, who had emigrated to Canada rather than accept a republican form of government in the United States, was appointed postmaster and King's printer in the small colonial capital of Halifax, and it was there that Joseph Howe was born in 1804. Although his formal education was scanty, he showed great discipline in learning and became a self-taught man with remarkable reserves of knowledge. He also had natural writing ability and he combined this talent with his skills as a printer when he began to publish a series of local journals that were partly news and partly opinion.

His first effort, the *Acadian*, appeared in 1827 and it was followed by the *Novascotian* in 1828. Writing a great deal of the material for the *Novascotian* and printing it all, Howe quickly made it the liveliest paper in the Maritimes. It played a great part in the upsurge of literary and intellectual life that Nova Scotia enjoyed in the 1830s. But the paper also had a political focus. Howe tried to seek out controversial subjects for the *Novascotian* and he found plenty to write about in the backward, authoritarian, and rather corrupt colonial system of the time.

In his own column, which he called "Legislative Reviews", Howe freely criticized men in public life and fearlessly exposed the political abuses that came to his attention. He made himself unpopular with the authorities and when he went beyond the accepted limits of the freedom of the press in 1835, they decided to suppress him.

Howe had delivered a spirited attack on the Halifax magistrates and police for the way in which they exacted money from accused persons, and he was prosecuted for criminal libel. According to the law of the period, which was loaded against honest criticism, Howe was in all probability technically guilty. But he decided to conduct his own defence and he did so with such spirit and eloquence, that the jury acquitted him; Howe was carried home in triumph on the shoulders of his supporters, followed by an applauding crowd. He had won a great victory for the freedom of the press, but it was only the first of his triumphs.

The sensation caused by his trial led to Howe's election in 1836 to the Nova Scotia assembly, and in 1840 he was appointed to the Executive Council. He accepted the appointment on the understanding that the governor, Lord Falkland, intended to make the council into a genuine coalition of Conservatives and Reformers, but Howe soon began to suspect that the governor was intriguing with the Conservatives and in 1843 he re-

Joseph Howe.

signed. He returned to opposition journalism, publishing a series of bitter attacks on Lord Falkland in the *Novascotian* and writing articles demanding responsible government. He presented the case most eloquently in 1846 when he published his well-known pamphlet, *Letters to the Right Honourable Lord John Russell, on the Government of British North America.*

We do not know what Lord John Russell, then prime minister of Great Britain, thought of Howe's pamphlet, but its publication was certainly followed by rapid and radical changes in the attitude of the imperial authorities. In 1848 the Nova Scotia government, appointed by Lord Falkland according to the old colonial system, was defeated in the assembly. The new governor, Sir John Harvey, called on the Reform majority leader, James Boyle Uniacke, to form a government that would rule at the assembly's pleasure. In this new government Joseph Howe became provincial secretary; he was in fact the "grey eminence" behind Premier Uniacke, shaping the government's policy until in 1854 he left politics to become chief commissioner of the Railway Board. In this role he foresaw the day when trains would run from the Maritimes to the Pacific Coast.

When Howe returned to politics as premier of Nova Scotia in 1860, he proved that a brilliant opposition member does not always make a good government leader. His performance as premier was uninspired, and in 1863 he left politics to become fishery commissioner.

Howe took up politics once again to lead the local opposition to Confederation. He believed entry into the Dominion of Canada would destroy the shipping economy of the Maritimes; many people today think he was right. Under his leadership, the Nova Scotian government that had accepted Confederation was defeated in an 1867 provincial election. But the British government refused to modify the British North America Act and Howe had to be content with obtaining slightly better terms for Nova Scotia in Confederation and a federal cabinet post for himself.

He was by now a spent man. The great period in his life had been that of the struggle for responsible government. He was a brilliant political critic and a fine prose writer but he never developed into a statesman. In 1873 Joseph Howe was put out to grass as the lieutenant governor of Nova Scotia, but he had no time to enjoy the paddock; within three weeks of being inaugurated he was dead.

Remembering Past Glories

If the people of Québec have kept, for more than two centuries since the British conquest of 1760, a strong sense of being a separate people with their own culture and traditions, it is largely due to the historians who revived a pride in the past of New France and a determination that the French language and culture must survive. Perhaps the most important of these historians was François-Xavier Garneau, whose *Histoire du Canada depuis sa découverte jusqu'à nos jours*, published in three volumes between 1845 and 1848, is a French Canadian classic that has inspired successive movements of Québec nationalism.

François-Xavier Garneau was born in Québec in 1809 of old French Canadian stock; his ancestors came to New France in 1659. He studied at the local seminary but instead of entering the priesthood he became a notary public in 1831. In the same year he left for London to act as secretary to D. B. Viger, who represented the interests of the Lower Canada assembly there. In Europe Garneau associated with Polish revolutionary exiles and observed the British parliamentary system in practice. He returned to Canada in 1833 and resumed his occupation as notary; he also edited a literary review, *L'Abeille Canadienne*, and played an active part in the agitation for constitutional reform. Though Garneau was not associated with Papineau in the events that led to the Lower Canada Rebellion of 1837, his views during this period became increasingly nationalistic and this sense of nationality helped him to become a historian.

François-Xavier Garneau.

The two events that actually turned Garneau from a very minor poet into a major historian were the publication of Lord Durham's *Report on the Affairs of British North America* in the spring of 1839, and the Act of Union of 1840, which joined Upper and Lower Canada into a single province. Like many Englishmen in the 1830s, Durham had little but contempt for the traditions of French Canada, and he expressed his opinions in a famous passage that aroused Garneau's anger:

> There can hardly be conceived a nationality more destitute of all that can invigorate and elevate a people, than that which is exhibited by the descendants of the French in Lower Canada, owing to their retaining their peculiar language and manners. They are a people with no history and no literature.

It was Durham who recommended the union of the two Canadas, and if Garneau was angered by the noble earl's belittlement of Québecois traditions in the *Report*, he was alarmed by the prospect of Québec's cultural and linguistic submergence in a united province.

Garneau believed that the French Canadian heritage was a great one, as reflected in the deeds of the people who had created La Nouvelle France, and he felt that if the Québecois could be reminded of this heritage their culture would survive. He therefore started on his history, a sixteen-hundred page work that covered the period from Cartier's voyages in the sixteenth century to 1792. Perhaps inevitably, Garneau went to the opposite extreme from Lord Durham. He set out to prove that his people had not only a history but a great one and gave the past of La Nouvelle France an epic glory which removed his work from the realm of the literal. The facts in the *Histoire* are generally correct, but the interpretation is often overly heroic.

Yet this was what the French Canadians needed at the time. The *Histoire* united past and present in a dramatic way. It presented a powerful vision of the lost past and it gave a shape to the new consciousness of identity that was emerging in Québec at the midpoint of the nineteenth century. Garneau believed that by remembering what they had been, the French Canadians could recover a sense of collective dignity and prepare the way for their own liberation.

The *Histoire* was Garneau's only important work. During the later years of his life he worked as the town clerk of Québec and devoted his free time to preparing new editions of the *Histoire* and to dealing with the controversies he created by criticizing the role of the Church in Québec. He enjoyed poor health in those final years, and died in 1866, a year before the separate Province of Québec came into existence at the time of Confederation. The motto which the province took—*Je me souviens*, meaning "I remember"—was entirely in the spirit of Garneau's great book which, whatever its flaws, gave back to his people a pride in their past and their culture.

Portraits of Chiefs

Sometimes painters and writers are more important for what they record in terms of fact than for the appealing forms they create in paint and words, which we are often told is the purpose of art. Paul Kane was one of the artists whose work we value for what it tells us about our past rather than for its patterns or colours and shapes. He travelled through the wilds of the Canadian West during the 1840s, before the Indian cultures there had succumbed entirely to their fatal contact with the civilization of the white men. The observations he made on his travels give us an invaluable picture of how the native peoples lived before Canada, as we know it, existed.

Paul Kane was born in Ireland in 1810, but his father was English, a former artilleryman born in Lancashire. In 1819 the Kane family migrated to Upper Canada and the elder Kane set up business in York as a wine and spirit merchant. We know very little about Paul's education, except that Thomas Drury, the art teacher at Upper Canada College, recognized that he had artistic talents and gave him painting lessons. But Kane did not immediately become a professional artist. He painted signs for shops in his early twenties and later he moved to Cobourg where he worked in a factory painting decorations on furniture.

In Cobourg Kane began to paint portraits in a rather primitive manner, and in 1836 he crossed the border into the United States, where he wandered about for five years, making his living from portrait commissions that he picked up along the way. It was at this time that Kane began to mix with professional painters; he may have taken lessons from some of them. Certainly it was on their advice that he sailed to Europe in 1841. He divided his time between Italy, where he studied the works of the great masters, and London, where he met the American painter, George Catlin. Catlin told Kane that he believed it was a North American artist's duty to record the cultures of the native peoples before they vanished entirely, and Kane was so impressed by this conversation that he made Catlin's remarks his creed for the rest of his life.

He sailed back to the United States in 1843 and spent a year painting portraits in Mobile, Alabama. In the spring of 1845 he returned to Toronto, intent on recording in

Paul Kane.

paint the Indians of British North America, and in June 1845, he set off with a gun and his artist's materials, bound for the Pacific Coast. Neither British Columbia nor Canada, as we know them, yet existed; the whole territory west of the Lakehead was held under charter and licence by the Hudson's Bay Company.

During the summer of 1845 Kane worked among the Ojibwa and other Indians around the Great Lakes. He intended to continue westward, but a Hudson's Bay trader in Sault Ste. Marie persuaded him that he would get nowhere without the approval of the company's governor, the "little emperor", Sir George Simpson. So Kane went back east to Lachine. Simpson was interested in his project, and not only gave him permission to travel west in the spring with the company's fur brigades, but also—which was even more important—arranged for him to receive hospitality in the Hudson's Bay posts.

Kane made his own way to Fort William, where he joined one of the brigades. He reached Fort Garry in time to take part in the annual buffalo hunt of the Red River Métis and he then travelled west over the Prairies to Fort Pitt and Fort Edmonton on the North Saskatchewan. After crossing the Rockies with the fur traders, Kane followed the Columbia River down to Fort Vancouver at its mouth. Not long before he arrived there, late in 1846, the Oregon Boundary Treaty had established the international border at the 49th parallel, so the region was now in American territory. Kane spent some time making vivid little oil sketches of the Indians around the mouth of the Columbia

and then went north to Fort Victoria on Vancouver Island. There he saw people from the northern tribes, such as the Haida, who had come south to trade, and he painted Indian life around Puget Sound and the Juan de Fuca Strait before returning at the end of June to Fort Vancouver. He set off east then through the region of Walla Walla and the country of the Nez Percé Indians and spent the winter in Fort Edmonton attending and sketching the Cree festivals. In May 1848, he left Edmonton and reached Toronto in October. Although he returned to the Red River in 1849 for a brief visit, he never again journeyed to the far West.

Kane's great travels were ended and he settled in Toronto to work his seven hundred oil sketches into enormous canvases. The result was an example of how artistic conventions can destroy authentic perceptions. Kane's sketches, which have fortunately been preserved, are so vivid that even now they retain their freshness of impact. But his great canvases are deliberate compositions which portray the Indians in artificially heroic attitudes and perpetuate the European myth of the Noble Savage. Fortunately Kane kept not only his sketches, but also the diary he had written during his long journey, and in 1859 he published it as a book, *Wanderings of an Artist among the Indians of North America*. It is a classic among the travel narratives of early Canada.

Kane was neglected as an artist once the novelty of his paintings of Indian life had worn off. He retreated into embittered loneliness and then went blind before he died, suddenly, in Toronto in 1871.

The Gallant Engineer

In Poland history tends to repeat itself. Today the Poles are nominally independent, but in fact they live under the dominating shadow of Russia. During the nineteenth century Poland also came under Russian domination but its position was even worse. After the Napoleonic wars had ended in 1815 the ancient and independent kingdom of Poland was dismembered. Part of it was annexed by Prussia and part by Austria, but most was swallowed by the empire of the Russian tsars. Several times during the nineteenth century the Poles rose in rebellion; each time they were defeated and each time Polish refugees fled to the free world.

One of these refugees was Casimir Stanislaus Gzowski, who became a well-known engineer in his adopted country of Canada and whose great-grandson is the Canadian journalist, Peter Gzowski.

The Polish rebellion that led Casimir Gzowski into

exile took place in 1830. The tyrannical Tsar Nicholas I was the ruler of Russia and his brother, the Grand Duke Constantine, was the equally tyrannical governor of Russian-occupied Poland. In 1830 there was a revolution in France and King Charles X was overthrown: Tsar Nicholas thought of invading France to restore the king to power, and it was rumoured that the Polish regiments would be sent. But there was a traditional friendship between Polish nationalists and French revolutionaries, and the junior officers in Warsaw started an insurrection which first spread throughout the Polish regiments and then to the civilian population. The Sejm—traditional national assembly of the Polish people—met to reassert independence and to formally sever the links between Poland and Russia. Casimir Gzowski, born in 1813 and in training as a military engineer at the time of the insurrection, was one of the young rebel officers.

There were a few heady months of freedom in Poland and then Tsar Nicholas sent a Russian army to crush the rebellion, which came to an end in November 1831. Casimir was wounded and taken prisoner. He was luckier than many of the rebels, who were sent to exile in Siberia, for he spent a short time in prison and then was released and allowed to leave for western Europe.

He first went to Paris, which was full of refugee Poles who dreamt of their country and split into rival political factions. Most lived in poverty, since it was hard to find work befitting their sense of aristocratic dignity. But Gzowski was not a political theorist. He had rebelled from an instinctive hatred of tyranny. The life of the Paris exiles struck him as futile and he set out for New York, where he arrived in 1833. He earned a living by teaching French and fencing, while he studied law to teach himself English. In 1837 he passed his bar examinations and began to practise in Pennsylvania. But engineering was still his real calling and eventually he found work as an engineer on a New England canal project.

In 1841 Gzowski moved north to Canada and made

Casimir Gzowski en famille, *Toronto, 1855.*

the acquaintance of the Governor General, Sir Charles Bagot, who was so impressed with Gzowski's aristocratic manners that he immediately appointed him to the position of engineer in the department of public works. Gzowski took up this position at the beginning of the first railroad boom in Canada, at a time when Allan MacNab said: "All my politics are railroads." And after setting up a private consulting practice in 1848, Casimir became chief engineer of the St. Lawrence & Sarnia Railroad in 1849.

But it was the contractor rather than the engineer who made the greatest profits out of the early Canadian railroads, so in 1853 Casimir established the construction firm of Gzowski and Company, which won the contract for building the Grand Trunk line between Toronto and Sarnia. The cycle of profit did not end there, however; money was also to be made out of the materials contractors used to build the railway, so in 1859 Gzowski and his partners founded the Toronto Rolling Mills to make their own rails. Gzowski combined his knowledge as contractor and his talents as engineer to build between 1871 and 1873 his masterpiece, the international bridge at Niagara.

Before he came to Canada, Gzowski had married Maria Beebe, an American doctor's daughter, and he posed with her and their children in the 1850s for the family portrait we present. His military youth he never forgot: he always loved parades and ranks and uniforms. Never again, after those distant days in Poland, did he see any military action. But he became lieutenant colonel of the Toronto Volunteers in 1872, honorary ADC to Queen Victoria in 1879, and Knight Commander of the Order of St. Michael and St. George in 1890. All these honours he added to his hereditary Polish title of Count Gzowski, which he never abandoned.

Living off the Barren Land

Perhaps the greatest tragedy of the Arctic was the loss of Sir John Franklin and the men who accompanied him when he sailed in 1845 from England, in the hope of finally solving the mystery of the North-West Passage. Franklin's ships, the *Erebus* and the *Terror*, were last seen by a whaler on July 28, 1845. After that there was no news and in 1848 the British Admiralty instituted a search in which many explorers took part. It lasted more than a decade until Captain F. L. McClintock's expedition finally discovered in 1859 the cairn containing Lieutenant Gore's record of the expedition's failure and the death of its members.

But the first clues to Franklin's fate were discovered in 1854 by Dr. John Rae. There was an ironic appropriate-

John Rae.

ness to this fact, since Rae was the man who perfected the skills of survival in the Arctic which Franklin had so tragically ignored. Franklin travelled by ship; Rae by small boat. Franklin depended on the supplies he himself transported to the Arctic; Rae learnt from the northern Indians and the Eskimo how to live off the land. Franklin was an alien in the Arctic environment and it destroyed him; Rae adapted to it and survived. His style of exploration became after the 1850s the model for Arctic travel.

Rae was born at Stromness in the Orkney Islands in 1813. As a child he learnt the island skills of fishing and managing small boats, but decided to study medicine in Edinburgh. Upon qualifying as a surgeon, he was given employment by the Hudson's Bay Company and in 1833 he became physician and clerk at Moose Factory, where he lived for the next ten years. Rae felt as much at home in the Arctic as a fish does in water. He spent his spare time wandering the northern woodland and tundra on long trapping and shooting journeys, adapting so well to the terrain that he was said to be able to travel fifty miles a day on foot. The novelist R. M. Ballantyne, who knew him during this period, described him as "full of animal spirits" with a "fine intellectual countenance".

Sir George Simpson, governor of the Hudson's Bay Company, kept a shrewd eye on his employees and he chose well in 1846 when he picked Rae to lead a survey of the unexplored coast of the Arctic sea from Boothia Isthmus to Fury and Hecla Strait. Rae gathered for the trip a mixed company of Orkneymen, Métis, Indians, and

Eskimo, every one of them possessing some skill that would be useful in the barren lands; he took only four months' supplies, intending to travel light and live mainly by hunting and fishing. He was entirely successful. The land fed instead of starving him; he charted six hundred miles of coastline, proved that Boothia was a peninsula and not an island, as had been thought, and came back with a full team of healthy men.

By the time he returned south in 1848, the search for Franklin was already under way and he joined Sir John Richardson as second-in-command of an overland quest. They followed the coast from the Mackenzie River to the Coppermine, but the ice prevented them from reaching Victoria Island and they returned having found no clue bearing on Franklin's fate.

Rae was put in charge of the Hudson's Bay Company's Mackenzie district upon his return, but he had lost his taste for fur trading, and in 1850, when the Admiralty asked him to undertake another search, he set off immediately. From Fort Confidence he travelled down the Coppermine River with a minimal party of two men and two dog sleighs. He and his companions stayed out the whole winter, travelled five thousand miles, charted another seven hundred miles of unexplored coastline, including Cambridge Bay, and got within forty miles of the place where Franklin's ships had been abandoned. The only clues they found though were two bits of wood that might have come from Franklin's boats.

It was on his fourth journey, which he began in 1853 with some Eskimo companions, that Rae was finally successful. Having proved that King William Land was an island, he wintered at Repulse Bay, and in the spring he encountered Eskimo who told him of a group of white men who had starved to death. He acquired relics of the Franklin expedition that left little doubt of their fate and heard further Eskimo accounts which suggested that before the end some of Franklin's men had turned cannibal. Rae returned with his news in 1854 and was given the award of £10,000 offered for the discovery of Franklin's fate. He was attacked for his suggestion that cannibalism had taken place and he became involved in a particularly vigorous debate with Charles Dickens in the novelist's magazine, *Household Words*.

That was Rae's last Arctic journey. He retired from the Hudson's Bay Company in 1856. For some years he worked as a surveyor on the Prairies, before moving to Hamilton and later to England, where he died in 1893. In the brief period of his Arctic exploration—eight years in all—he had not only charted thousands of miles of Arctic coastline. He had also developed a highly mobile form of Arctic exploration which was rarely to result in the loss of human lives.

The Politics of Railways

The argument between federalists and separatists that dominated the 1970s in Canada was nothing new to the people of Québec. From the early days of Confederation, some Québecois have been devoted to the idea of remaining within a federated Canada, while others have desired independence for Québec, fearing that their language and culture would be submerged by Canada's English-speaking majority.

Perhaps the most dedicated of the original Québecois advocates of Confederation was George-Étienne Cartier, who for many years was John A. Macdonald's closest political ally. Cartier came of an old family of Québec seigneurs or landowners. Family legend had it that they were linked with the sixteenth century voyager, Jacques Cartier, but this has never been proved. George-Étienne was born in 1814; the War of 1812 was still in progress and he was given the name of George after King George III of England, whom the Americans hated.

The loyalty to the British crown which his name suggested did not prevent George-Étienne, as a young law student in 1831, from supporting Louis-Joseph Papineau, the defender of French democratic rights. Nor did it prevent him from joining the radical organization known as Les Fils de la Liberté, for which he composed a song still remembered in Québec, "O Canada, mon pays, mes amours". Even after being called to the bar in 1835, Cartier did not loosen his links with Papineau and the Patriotes, as French Canadian nationalists were then called. When the Patriotes took up arms in the Lower Canada Rebellion of 1837, Cartier fought among them with great courage at the battle of Saint-Denis. He escaped to the United States; when he returned to Québec in 1838 his radicalism had cooled and he supported the non-violent moderates led by Louis-Hippolyte La Fontaine, who advocated collaboration with the English-speaking Reformers of Upper Canada to attain democratic goals.

Cartier did not take up politics actively again until 1848, when he was elected to the Legislative Assembly. It was during this period that Canada experienced its first railway boom and Cartier soon became involved in the political aspects of this development. In 1852 he introduced into the assembly a bill creating the Grand Trunk Railway and, when he became the line's legal adviser in 1853, people suspected that he was not above profiting from his political influence. Cartier's involvement in railway politics continued to the end of his life, and he did not die a poor man.

After brief terms as provincial secretary in 1855 and attorney general in 1857, Cartier joined Macdonald as

George-Étienne Cartier.

50

head of a coalition government of Conservatives and moderate Reformers. The alliance stayed in power until it was defeated in 1862 on a militia bill. After two years in the opposition, Cartier brought down John Sandfield Macdonald's government in 1864 with a famous thirteen-hour-long speech and awakened Canadians to the instability of their governmental system. When the Great Coalition of 1864 was created to explore ideas for a new system, Cartier became attorney general once again. As a strong supporter of Canadian union, Cartier posed Confederation to the people of Québec as the practical alternative to absorption by the United States. It was a stance that was to convince the majority of Québecois of the benefits of Confederation, though even then many French Canadians feared a federal Canada would merely substitute English for American domination.

Cartier was active in all the conferences leading up to Confederation, including the Westminster conference that framed the British North America Act as Canada's substitute for a constitution. In the first Dominion government of 1867, Cartier was minister of militia, but in practice he was almost John A. Macdonald's equal, and when the prime minister—for various reasons—was incapacitated, Cartier took his place. He carried out the negotiations for the surrender of the Hudson's Bay Company's charter rights over the Canadian West. He also negotiated British Columbia's entry into the Dominion of Canada in 1871 by promising a railway that would unite the Pacific Province with the rest of Canada.

His interest in railways proved Cartier's political downfall. It was he who introduced into the House of Commons the bill providing for the construction of the Canadian Pacific Railway; when it was passed in 1872 he shouted exultantly: "All aboard for the West!" But during the election campaign of that year Cartier had accepted campaign funds from the syndicate headed by Hugh Allan that expected to build the railway. The Liberal opposition discovered that Cartier alone had received $85,000 and that through his intervention Sir John A. Macdonald's campaign had been lavishly funded. The Pacific Scandal broke Macdonald's government. But though Sir John returned to power, Cartier did not; he was ill with Bright's disease, and in 1873 he died in England, where he had gone in search of a cure. Cartier was a complex man and though at times his political morality was lax, the standards of the times were different from ours, and Cartier was at heart a true patriot.

Canada's Wayward Father

When we compare statesmen with politicians, we are really talking about two different ways of handling public affairs. The politician is concerned with the interests of his party and with policies for the present. The statesman takes the long view and sees his actions in historical perspective, realizing that their effects are not confined to the present; he also has a greater understanding of the gap between the desires of a people and their capabilities. And when he has also that elusive quality called charisma, the power to attract and inspire people quite apart from the logic of what he tells them, then he is the most effective kind of statesman.

Canada has had many politicians and few statesmen. But Sir John A. Macdonald combined the qualities of historical foresight and charisma. And that is why, though the Confederation of Canada in 1867 was the work of many men, we still tend to regard Sir John as the founder of our nation.

In his early years, not a great deal distinguished John Macdonald from the small-time lawyers who were so numerous among the politicians of Canada West, as Ontario was then called. He was a Scot by birth—born in Glasgow in 1815 and brought to Canada by his immigrant parents in 1820. The family settled near Kingston and his father set up a rather unsuccessful business as a merchant. Young John went into law and soon became well known for his skill in defending criminals. While still in his twenties, he became involved in politics, first at the municipal level as a Kingston councillor and then as a Tory member of the Legislative Assembly of Canada. In 1847 he was briefly receiver general.

Early in his career Macdonald showed himself to be a master of political manoeuvre. Once in jest he declared his profession as "cabinet-maker", but he was a maker of parties as well. When he put together the coalition that formed a cabinet under Allan MacNab in 1854, he also laid the foundations for the Liberal-Conservative Party, the direct ancestor of the present Progressive Conservative Party.

Macdonald was the attorney general in the MacNab government, but in 1857 he became titular prime minister in the Macdonald-Cartier government; Macdonald, as the leader of the English-speaking Conservatives of Canada West, worked in alliance with George-Étienne Cartier, leader of the French-speaking Blues, as the Tories of Canada East (Québec) were then called.

The alliance illustrated the difficulties that plagued the government in Canada at that period. The separate colonies of Upper Canada and Lower Canada had been

Sir John Alexander Macdonald after the scare of the Pacific Scandal.

united in 1840 into one, and in the Legislative Assembly the two regions, now called Canada West and Canada East, had equal representation. The government of the united colony was usually formed from an alliance between groups in the two Canadas, with joint English-French leadership. And it soon became accepted that any piece of legislation needed a double majority to be passed—that is a majority among the representatives from Canada West and a majority among representatives from Canada East. By the 1850s language differences and other disputes made this system unworkable. No government held office for very long, so unstable were the shifting alliances. The weakness of the colony became all the more alarming with the threat of American expansionism—a threat created by the aggressive nationalism which arose in the United States as the Civil War drew to an end.

By 1864 most Canadian leaders had become convinced that the government of the united colony had failed and that only a federal system, allowing each region to manage its local affairs, would work. A coalition government was established to explore this possibility. Once Macdonald had accepted the idea of federalism, he managed the series of conferences at Charlottetown and Québec so skilfully that the provinces of Ontario and Québec were joined by Nova Scotia and New Brunswick when the Dominion of Canada was established in 1867.

Macdonald became Canada's first prime minister and he remained prime minister for twenty out of the first twenty-four years of the Dominion's history. He was not always successful in the position. The completion of the Canadian Pacific Railway was delayed until 1885 because of the Pacific Scandal, which arose when the Liberal opposition discovered that Macdonald and others had received immense campaign subsidies from the railway promoters. The rebellion of Métis and Indians on the Saskatchewan River, led in 1885 by Louis Riel and Gabriel Dumont, was caused largely by Macdonald's failure to understand the plight of the native peoples. But the National Policy that Macdonald formulated in 1878 gave Canada a sense of unity. He died in 1891, not long after his last successful election, which he had fought under the slogan: "A British subject I was born—a British subject I will die." In fact, by the time of his death, he had transformed Canada from a scattering of settlements beside the St. Lawrence River and the Great Lakes to a transcontinental dominion moving rapidly towards independent nationhood.

The Raindancer

Travelling the Trans-Canada Highway westward from Swift Current, with the distant outlines of the Cypress Hills looming to the southwest, you reach a prairie hamlet where the grain elevators carry in bold lettering the word, *Piapot*. The hamlet was given that name as an ironic gesture by the engineer responsible for this section of the CPR. He wished to commemorate the trouble he had had with the Cree chief Piapot, who was one of the most active Indian opponents to the construction of a railway across the Prairies. To Piapot, the Prairies were his people's homeland, the heritage of nomadic hunters.

Unlike Poundmaker and Big Bear, Piapot never actually went on the war path against the Canadian government. Unlike Crowfoot and the other chiefs who regarded assimilation as the inevitable fate of the Indians, he believed that the heart of Indian life lay in retaining the old beliefs and ceremonies, and he remained faithful to them until his death as a very old man in 1908.

Piapot was born about 1816. The name he was given at the time of his birth was Kisikawawasen, which means

Flash in the Sky. Very early in his life he felt the effect of the intrusion of white men into the West, for when he was a child the smallpox imported by white strangers devastated the camp to which he belonged. Only he and his grandmother survived the epidemic. Eventually the two were captured by a group of Sioux, who adopted the boy and trained him in the arts of prairie survival and Indian war. When he was fourteen the Sioux camp was raided by the Cree and Kisikawawasen was reunited with his own people. But he still retained his link with the Sioux and often acted as mediator between the two tribes which were traditional enemies. In war against the Blackfoot he became a noted brave and when he was finally made a chief, he was given the name of Piapot. Piapot's growing fame on the Prairies was in fact due less to his warlike prowess than to his reputed feats as a medicine man. He was believed to have prophetic visions, and his powers as a rainmaker were known throughout the southern Prairies.

So long as the white men merely traded for furs and did not try to change the Indian way of life, Piapot was friendly with them. His relationship with the Hudson's Bay men, who in 1855 established a post in his hunting territory in the Qu'Appelle Valley, was so good that in 1869—when the local Métis were fired up by the example of Louis Riel's insurrection on the Red River and threatened to attack the post—Piapot and his braves protected the traders.

White settlement was another matter. That, Piapot foresaw, would bring an end to the traditional nomadic life of the Plains Indians. When in 1874 the Indian peoples of the southern Prairies handed over their land rights to the Dominion of Canada under Treaty No. 4, Piapot chose to go off hunting in the Cypress Hills to avoid being present for the ceremony of signing. Later he refused to settle down on a reservation. But he was on friendly terms with James Morrow Walsh and other Mounted Police. He recognized that the American whisky traders were the most dangerous of all white men to the Indian way of life and he was grateful that Walsh and his men had frightened them away.

During the 1880s Piapot and his band based themselves in the Cypress Hills area. The Canadian authorities tried to remove them from this region for the government feared that with Sitting Bull and his thousands of restive Sioux also camped in the hills, the concentration of Indians might result in warfare. Piapot not only resisted all attempts to send his band back to the Qu'Appelle Valley; he and his braves also harassed CPR surveyors and in 1882–83 they tried to halt construction of the line, which Piapot rightly believed would mean the final destruction of the old Indian way of life.

At last, in the fall of 1883, the Mounted Police persuaded Piapot to settle on a reservation near Indian Head, but after enduring a winter of sickness and starvation, he moved back in 1884 to the Qu'Appelle Valley, and during the North-West Rebellion of 1885 he and his braves remained neutral.

This did not mean that Piapot accepted the idea that the Indians should forget their past and imitate white men. He refused conversion to Christianity, sustained the pagan beliefs and ceremonies of his people, and when the Dominion government forbade the rain dances, he defiantly continued to stage them. In retaliation, the government deposed him as chief in 1899, but his band refused to elect a successor. Piapot remained the chief in fact, if not in law, and until his death in 1908 he was a revered figure among the Indians of the Canadian Prairies.

Piapot's resistance to white culture on behalf of his people's traditions was not in vain. Today the old beliefs are being reasserted and the rain dance is openly performed once again.

Piapot.

Founder of the Globe

D'Arcy McGee was not the only Father of Confederation to suffer assassination. In 1880, twelve years after McGee's death in 1868, the same fate overtook the Liberal leader, George Brown. But while McGee's murder was almost certainly political in motivation, Brown's seems to have been mainly due to the autocratic way in which he ran his famous newspaper, the *Globe*.

Brown was one of the many Scots who played key roles in the creation of Canada. His father, Peter Brown, was an Edinburgh merchant, and George was born in 1818 at Alloa on the Firth of Forth. Running into debt, Peter Brown decamped for New York with his family in 1837 and set up a dry goods store there. But his heart was not in trading. He was a good Liberal; even more, he was a devout Presbyterian. He was interested in promoting both causes and in 1842 he founded the *British Chronicle* in New York. George Brown helped his father with the newspaper and eventually became its publisher.

When it came to the test, Peter's religious convictions were stronger than his political interests. When the Free Kirk split off from the Church of Scotland in 1843, he moved to Toronto to establish a paper—the *Banner*—in support of the cause. But George Brown was more interested in politics than in the infighting of the religious sects and in 1844 he founded his own paper, the *Globe*, dedicated to the cause of political reform. In 1853 he made the *Globe* a daily and soon it became the most influential paper in British North America. Even after entering politics, Brown never abandoned control of the *Globe*. At heart he was a journalist rather than a politician.

This preference showed up clearly in George Brown's political career. He was an intelligent political analyst and a brilliant and abrasive public speaker, but he was at his best in lonely opposition. He detested the necessary compromises of political life that men such as Sir John A. Macdonald were so adept at making.

Nevertheless, Brown felt his duty called him to play a part in the politics of his country, if only to control abuses. In fact it was through the investigation of abuses that he became politically active. In 1848 he served as secretary of a commission to investigate the Kingston penitentiary. The findings of the commission revealed many abuses and the resulting scandal turned Brown into a political figure.

He was elected to the Legislative Assembly in 1858 and he immediately started a long campaign to end the arrangement by which Canada West and Canada East sent equal numbers of representatives to the assembly. Owing to heavy immigration, the population of Canada West had become considerably larger than that of Canada East, and in the assembly and in the *Globe*, Brown began to push his slogan of "Rep. by Pop." (representation by population). It was an idea that alarmed the French Canadians of Canada East though, for they feared the possibility of being swamped by the English-speaking majority. Logically, however, it was hard to deny the justice of the demand, and to find a way of resolving the problem of adequate representation, George Brown turned to the ideal of a federal union, in which each province would control its local affairs.

Brown was the prime minister of Canada for a few days in 1858, and the president of the council in the Great Coalition cabinet from 1864 to 1866, but he was much more effective as a committee man than as a minister. He chaired brilliantly the Select Committee of the Legislative Assembly that examined Canada's political future and recommended "a federative system". And it was he who devised, and presented to the Charlottetown and Québec conferences, the dual system of central and provincial governments that eventually became the basis of the Canadian political system. He also went to Westminster at the end of 1864 to conduct the early negotiations with the imperial government which assured the Canadian and Maritime ministers that their proposals would get a friendly hearing.

George Brown.

Yet it was typical of Brown that in 1866, the year before the Dominion of Canada actually came into existence, he resigned from the cabinet, picking a minor disagreement as his excuse, but wiring to his wife on the same night, "I am a free man once again."

And he remained a free man, in the sense of avoiding any political office, to the end of his life, though he used the power he wielded as proprietor of the *Globe* to influence political events. His editorials helped to bring down Macdonald's government in 1873 over the Pacific Scandal. But the dictatorial way in which Brown ran the *Globe* proved his undoing in the end. He was almost fanatically anti-union, and in 1872 he had picketers arrested in an attempt to break a printing strike. At last, in March 1880, a worker he had dismissed for drunkenness shot him, and after six weeks of agony, he died from the effects of the wound.

George Brown's great flaw was that he loved political influence but did not want to soil his hands with the intrigue that was inevitable in political life. This basic contradiction was the reason why his intellectual brilliance and his powerful personality seemed in the end so wasted.

The Riding Judge

Some men are badly served by the legends that grow up around them. Sir Matthew Baillie Begbie was one of these men. A great figure in the early days of British Columbia, he has gone down in folklore as the "hanging judge", and there is even a tale that once, when a hangman could not be found, Sir Matthew tied the rope himself.

The truth about Begbie is not so grim. But in its own way it is just as extraordinary. Until 1858, when there was a sudden need for a judge to deal with the turbulent miners stampeding north from California in the Fraser Valley gold rush, Begbie had been regarded by his London friends as a man of great talent whose expectations had not materialized; in other words, a bit of a failure.

He was born in 1819, but it is not certain whether his birth took place aboard a ship sailing into the Indian Ocean or on land in Mauritius where his father, Colonel Begbie of the Forty-fourth Foot, had been posted. Certainly, he grew up in England, attending St. John's College, Cambridge; in 1844 he became an M.A. and was called to the bar at Lincoln's Inn in London. He spent a few months making the Grand Tour of Europe and learning French and Italian. Then he settled down to a career as a lawyer.

Matthew Baillie Begbie.

Begbie had an appearance and manner that should have guaranteed quick success. He was very tall for his period: six feet four inches. He was handsome, with bold eyes and dark beard, and he dressed with dash, in a great black cloak and a wide-brimmed soft black hat. Yet success never came to him in England, either in law or—it is said—in love, and when he was offered a judgeship in remote British Columbia, he accepted with alacrity.

As it turned out, the task was perfectly suited to Begbie's flamboyant personality, which would have been wasted in the English law courts. His task was to impose British law, with the help of a few untrained constables, on some tens of thousands of miners used to nothing better than the lynch law of the California goldfields. Many of them hated Britain and the British, and they would gladly have created a lawless situation that might have justified American intervention. Begbie realized that half measures would be of no use: it was necessary to carry the law in all its dignity into the mining country. And this he did, tirelessly riding over the mountains from one camp to the next. He set up his court in any store or saloon that was convenient, and sometimes passed judgement sitting on horseback, but he always observed strict protocol and inspired awe by the sheer contrast between his long wig and scarlet judge's robes and the rough clothing of the miners who filled the courtroom.

Begbie was fearless and tough: he could outride

almost any man of the far West. And he conducted his trials with a grim humour that has become part of the folklore of British Columbia. Sometimes the juries were obstinate, insisting on freeing men whom Begbie regarded as guilty and once, when a mugger was acquitted, Begbie dismissed him with the remark: "The jurymen say you are not guilty. I do not agree, but it is now my duty to set you free. I warn you not to pursue your evil ways—but if you are ever again so inclined, I hope you will select your victim from among the men who have acquitted you."

What made Begbie so effective as a judge was his knack of appearing quickly at any trouble spot and administering the law strictly as soon as he arrived. On one famous occasion Begbie rode into Wild Horse Creek just as a riot seemed to be developing and guns were being brandished. "Boys," shouted Begbie to the mob of armed and excited miners, "if there is shooting in Kootenay, there will be hanging in Kootenay." There was no shooting. Begbie ensured that throughout the gold rushes in British Columbia a completely different atmosphere existed than in the violent California settlements.

In 1866, when Vancouver Island and British Columbia were united to form the enlarged colony of British Columbia, Begbie became chief justice. He retained the position when the colony became a province of Canada in 1871, and continued to hold it until his death at the age of seventy-five. As a judge Begbie was always autocratic, but this meant that he did not allow the state, any more than the individual, to infringe on his interpretation of the law. When a new law was brought in forbidding the Indians to hold potlatches (or giving feasts), Begbie threw it out of court because it was ill-defined and, in any case, he thought the potlatch a good custom that did no harm unless it turned into a riot. Outside the courtroom, Begbie was a man of compassion rather than strict justice and there are many stories of his quiet kindness. He was a man of elaborate courtesy, celebrated for the great parties he gave at his Victoria house, where the Chinese servants would hang bunches of cherries on the ornamental trees for his guests to pick as they wandered in the garden. He was pious without ostentation, and when he died he had the simple epitaph carved on his gravestone: "God be merciful to me, a sinner."

The First Cardinal

In 1886 the first Canadian was elevated to the College of Cardinals of the Roman Catholic Church. He was Elzéar Alexandre Taschereau, archbishop of Québec. In recent generations the princes of the Church have often been men who came from humble origins, but Cardinal Taschereau was as near to an aristocrat in descent and upbringing as one could find in the Canada of his time.

His ancestors had been seigneurs, members of the gentry of old Québec. His great-grandfather, Thomas Jacques Taschereau, was a member of the Superior Council of New France. His grandfather was a judge and member of the Legislative Council of Lower Canada; his father and brothers were also judges. On the maternal side his great-grandfather, Jean Claude Panet, was the first French Canadian judge appointed under British rule and his grandfather, Jean Antoine Panet, was for more than twenty years speaker of the Legislative Assembly of Lower Canada. It would be hard to find more solid antecedents in a community, such as that of nineteenth century Québec, which depended heavily on tradition.

Yet Elzéar Alexandre Taschereau was a strong and independent personality in his own right, and undoubtedly he was elevated in the Church more for the qualities he possessed than for the social position of his ancestors.

He was born at Ste. Marie de la Beauce in Lower Canada in 1820. At the age of eight he began to attend the Québec Seminary, but it was characteristic of Taschereau and his freedom of spirit that even as a boy he did not accept as a foregone conclusion that he would enter the priesthood. Only after a visit to Rome at the age of seventeen did he decide that the Church was his vocation. He was ordained in 1842, but he never served as a parish priest. His talents lay in the direction of teaching and in his early twenties he was appointed professor of philosophy at the Québec Seminary. Eventually he became director of the seminary and then its superior and in 1860, when Laval University was founded in Québec as a daughter institution of the seminary, he became the university's first rector.

Taschereau was not only a man of great learning, but also of great humanitarian feeling. While many French Canadians resented the flood of impoverished Irish who arrived in Canada during the 1840s, Taschereau showed his compassion for them in many practical ways. In fact, in 1847 he almost died of typhus fever contracted while caring for the epidemic-stricken immigrants on Goose Island. As a result of his kind acts, he became very popular among the Irish Catholics.

Elzéar Alexandre Taschereau, the first Canadian cardinal.

Thomas D'Arcy McGee.

In other ways Taschereau showed himself a man of open mind, in so far as the doctrines of the Church allowed it, and at a time when the hierarchy was sharply divided on the political role of the Church, he eventually came down on the side of tolerance. He was appointed vicar general of Québec in 1862 and archbishop in 1871. At this time the two other leaders of French Canadian Catholicism, Bishop Laflèche of Trois Rivières and Bishop Bourget of Montreal, were ecclesiastical conservatives who believed it was the duty of Catholic priests to influence politics to the extent of telling their parishioners how to vote. At first Taschereau found it difficult to resist the pressure that Laflèche and Bourget placed upon him and in 1875 he signed a pastoral letter they had composed, declaring that nobody could become a Liberal and remain a Catholic. But after consulting such prominent Catholic laymen as Wilfrid Laurier, Taschereau withdrew support from his fellow bishops, and in 1876 he issued a statement declaring that the Church's position must be one of neutrality between conservatism and liberalism.

Given the political situation in Canada at the time—a Liberal government was in power—it was obvious that Taschereau had acted with more churchly statesmanship than Bourget and Laflèche. He helped to heal the deep wounds that had been caused in Québec society by the feuding between the liberal elements and the clergy, and in this way he kept alive the great influence of the Church in Québec's cultural life, and particularly in education. This was perhaps why, when the time came to appoint a Canadian cardinal, Taschereau was chosen to receive the symbolic red hat.

Taschereau himself contributed in many practical ways to the Church's role in Canadian life. He founded new colleges, reformed old ones, established a hospital in Québec City, and reconstructed the old pilgrimage shrine of St. Anne de Beaupré into a great basilica. He resigned his archbishopric in 1894 and died in 1898, widely respected throughout Canada by Catholics and non-Catholics alike.

Poet and Politician

D'Arcy McGee began his career as an Irish nationalist who demanded the annexation of Canada by the United States; when he died from the bullet of a fellow Irishman in 1868 he had become a Canadian patriot and one of the most dedicated of the Fathers of Confederation. In the course of his life he never ceased to be devoted to the cause of Irish freedom, but he did reach the conclusion that peaceful constitutional change was a better way of attaining it than violent revolution.

McGee was born in 1825 at Carlingford in Ireland; his father was a coast guard. When he was seventeen, D'Arcy, like so many Irish people of his time, sailed across the Atlantic and settled in Boston, where he began to work collecting subscriptions for a Catholic Irish newspaper, the *Boston Pilot*. In 1844 the editor of the *Pilot* resigned, and at the age of nineteen D'Arcy took his place and began a career in journalism that was to continue, despite his involvement in politics, for the rest of his life.

Like most young educated Irishmen of his time, McGee had become fervently anti-British and had adopted the idea of the Fenians—the militant Irish organization in the United States—that a good way of causing harm to Britain would be to assist the United States to seize Canada. When he returned to Ireland in 1845 he became editor of the *Freeman's Journal*, but his politics were too extreme for that paper. So he joined the staff of the *Nation* and helped to found the Irish Confederation, which was dedicated to severing the union between Ireland and Great Britain.

During this formative period in his life, McGee's political beliefs oscillated from one extreme to the other, for when he returned to New York in 1848 and founded a *Nation* there, he fell out with the Fenians because they advocated violent insurrection. He became so unpopular among New York Irish that he moved to Boston and founded yet another paper, the *Irish Celt*.

While in the midst of all these journalistic ventures, McGee was writing novels and patriotic poetry and delving into the Celtic past. The best of his historical works was the *Popular History of Ireland* (1863) in which he not only celebrated his country's traditions but declared a faith in its destiny of independence which he never abandoned.

What he did abandon was his faith in American republicanism. As early as 1855 he began telling Irish immigrants to pick Canada rather than the United States and in 1857 he followed his own advice and moved to Montreal. There he founded the *New Era* and immediately became involved in Canadian politics, demanding better representation for Irish immigrants. He was attracted to the reformers and when he was elected to the Legislative Assembly, he at first supported George Brown, the leading Grit from Canada West and the editor of the *Globe*. But when Brown opposed separate schools for Catholics, McGee parted company with him and drifted towards the Conservatives, allying himself with George-Étienne Cartier and becoming minister of agriculture and immigration in 1864.

Even before John A. Macdonald became converted to

federalism, McGee was advocating it. He sensed the desire to shake off colonialism that was stirring in Canada and he talked of a "kingdom of the St. Lawrence", ruled by one of Queen Victoria's sons. He hoped that this kingdom would emerge from a "federal compact" between the British North American colonies; he even advocated the annexation of Rupert's Land, the Canadian West that was still in the possession of the Hudson's Bay Company.

McGee played a great role in the achievement of Confederation, taking part in the conferences at Charlottetown and Québec that paved the way for a union of the colonies. There is no doubt that his eloquence as a public speaker and journalist helped greatly in bringing about acceptance of the idea of a Dominion of Canada. But the achievement of his political goal meant, ironically, the end of his political career. He denounced the Fenians for their plans to attack Canada and in 1865 he made a speech in Ireland renouncing the extreme nationalism he had espoused in the past. This lost him the support of the Montreal Irish, and when Macdonald and Cartier realized that McGee had become a political liability, they decided against inviting him to join the first Dominion cabinet in 1867.

McGee was disappointed and disillusioned with the men who had welcomed him when he could deliver the Irish vote and he decided to abandon politics and return to full-time writing. He did not have the time to do it. Less than a year after the Dominion of Canada came into existence, on April 7, 1868, he was shot on the steps of his Ottawa lodging. An Irishman, Patrick James Whelan, was hanged for the murder, but his motives were never established, and though the Fenians were suspected of inspiring the assassination, their involvement was never proved.

Lover of the Universe

In the portraits of Amor De Cosmos the real man seems to be hiding behind the luxuriant dark beard. In a rather similar way, a man with a real name hid behind the invented appellation of Amor De Cosmos. His real name was very ordinary: William Alexander Smith. Smith was born at Windsor, Nova Scotia, in August 1825, and transformed on February 17, 1854, by an act of the California legislature, into Amor De Cosmos.

When he assumed his new name, which he claimed projected the things he loved most in existence—"order, beauty, the world, the universe"—De Cosmos was a photographer and property speculator in a California mining village which also had recently changed its name—from Mud Springs to El Dorado. Three years before that he had been clerk to a wholesale grocer in Halifax, where he had imbibed the democratic principles of the great Nova Scotian reformer, Joseph Howe. In 1851, however, he left the eastern seaboard and crossed the United States in a wagon train; he wintered in Salt Lake City and in 1852 reached the California goldfields. Cannily scanning the situation, he realized that there was more money to be made from providing a service, such as taking accurate photographs of mining claims, which could be used as evidence in law courts, than by panning gold.

But Amor De Cosmos was not entirely happy among the Americans and when the news of gold on the Fraser River reached San Francisco in 1858, he was one of the first to take ship northward into British territory. Once again, he had no intention of performing hard manual toil, and he settled in Victoria, which was the commercial capital of the gold rush. He bought and sold properties, and used the profits to finance his ambition to become a radical journalist and eventually a politician.

"I am one of those"—Amor De Cosmos once said—"who believe that political hatreds attest the vitality of a State." Certainly, when he founded his newspaper, the British Colonist, in Victoria late in 1858, he did not hesitate to denounce very bitterly the autocratic rule of Governor James Douglas. He advocated the kind of responsible government which he had seen established in Nova Scotia in 1848. By 1860 he was also advocating the amalgamation of all the British colonies of North America into a single nation. Responsible government and Canadian Confederation remained the main policies to which De Cosmos dedicated his political life.

His task was not an easy one in the crown colony of Vancouver Island, where Hudson's Bay interests were strong even after the gold rush. In 1859 Governor Douglas actually tried to suppress the British Colonist under an old English law that required a large cash deposit before a newspaper could be published. But De Cosmos had already so many supporters that the necessary surety was collected in a single public meeting and very soon the Colonist became a daily rather than a weekly thorn in the side of Douglas and the Fort Clique, as Douglas's followers were called.

By manipulating the voting, the Fort Clique kept De Cosmos out of the island's Legislative Assembly until 1863. But when he was finally elected, he immediately became the leader of the opposition. He was a flamboyant parliamentarian. Like Sir John A. Macdonald, he was often drunk when he spoke, and occasionally he used his walking stick on the heads of his opponents. Once, when De Cosmos and another member of the assembly were in

Amor De Cosmos.

a minority over a motion, they spoke in turn for twenty-six hours until they wearied the majority into surrender.

By such means De Cosmos attracted and held public attention, and accomplished a great deal. He was largely responsible for the union of British Columbia and Vancouver Island. When he could not persuade the Legislative Council of the united colony to agree to Confederation with Canada, he turned directly to the people and organized the famous Yale Convention of 1868, to which delegates came from all over the colony to express their desire for Confederation. And he continued his agitation until British Columbia finally entered the Dominion of Canada.

By 1871 De Cosmos had attained everything for which he had fought; union of the colonies, union with Canada, responsible government. From this point on his life seemed to lose direction. He had been an admirable opposition leader, but as premier of British Columbia in 1872 he was unimaginative and unpopular, resigning after a mob attacked the legislature. As a federal Member of Parliament for eleven years he showed little initiative. And on one of the rare occasions when he did, he brought his political career to an end.

De Cosmos was one of those who foresaw Canadian independence, and one day in the House of Commons he declared: "I was born a British subject. . .I do not wish to die without all the rights, privileges and immunities of the citizen of a nation." His Victoria constituents, devoted to the British Empire, were infuriated and voted him out of office in the 1882 general election.

Amor De Cosmos retired to private life. He became steadily more eccentric as he roved the streets of Victoria, fixing people with a compelling eye like the Ancient Mariner and engaging them in increasingly incoherent conversation. Shortly before his death in 1897 he was declared insane. By this time he was almost forgotten. Yet more than any other man he had ensured that the motto which Canada adopted in 1867, *A mari usque ad mare*, really meant "from sea to sea", from the Atlantic to the Pacific.

Indian Rebel

As discontent boiled up in the Prairies during the years that led to the North-West Rebellion of 1885, the great Indian chiefs were divided between those who chose the path of peace and those who chose the path of war. Crowfoot chose the path of peace and kept the powerful Blackfoot confederacy out of the war that followed the Métis uprising. Poundmaker, like Big Bear, chose the path

of war and led a good part of the Cree nation into the rebellion, in alliance with Gabriel Dumont and his tiny Métis army.

Pito-kanow-apiwin (which means Poundmaker in the Cree language) was born in 1826 beside the North Saskatchewan River, near the site where Battleford now stands. He got his name from the old way of hunting in the days when the buffalo herds were driven into great enclosures or pounds and slaughtered in vast numbers. It was a wasteful method that had become almost obsolete by the time Poundmaker was a young man. If he ever indeed made a pound, it must have been one of the last constructed.

In fact, during his early life Poundmaker seems to have done little that aroused great attention. He was not a celebrated warrior like Crowfoot and he did not really become influential among his people until the old way of life began to disintegrate as the buffalo herds diminished in size and white settlers began to demand a share of the prairie lands that the Indians had always regarded as their own. Then he became a focus for Indian discontent.

Early in the 1870s he had played a part in a movement to end the old warfare between the Indian peoples now that they were faced with a more dangerous enemy, the white man. And in 1872 when the Blackfoot and the Cree settled their ancient differences, one of the guarantees of the treaty between the two peoples was Crowfoot's adoption of Poundmaker—already a man of forty-six—as his son.

Later, in 1876, Poundmaker was a signatory to the treaty concluded at Fort Carlton between the Cree and the Canadian government, but he signed his mark with misgivings. There were many provisions in the treaty he did not like, since they seemed to restrict freedom of movement and hunting, and he refused to settle down on a reservation. For three years he wandered over the prairie as a moving focus of discontent, gathering resentful Indians around him. Then, in 1879, he was forced to recognize that there was no future for nomadic hunters in a country where their basic food—the buffalo—had vanished, and he and his followers settled on a reservation at Battle River.

At first Poundmaker was unexpectedly docile. He became a farmer and his behaviour so pleased the authorities that in 1881 they picked him as guide for the Governor General, Lord Lorne. It was a role for which his rather aristocratic good looks made him especially suited.

But in the early 1880s the Dominion government began to cut back on maintenance grants to the Indians and, with the loss of the buffalo hunt, this meant growing distress and near starvation. Recognizing that his misgivings about the treaties were justified, Poundmaker

Poundmaker.

joined other chiefs in demanding better treatment. But, like Gabriel Dumont and his Métis, Poundmaker and his Indians were ignored by Sir John Macdonald, who was trying to administer Indian affairs as well as carry on his many duties as prime minister.

At first Poundmaker was reluctant to resort to force. When Dumont sent a message inviting him to join the proposed uprising, he refused. But by the time that the Métis actually rose in rebellion and defeated the Mounted Police at Duck Lake in March 1885, Poundmaker's supplies of food had run out and he was unable to restrain his angry braves. They invaded Battleford, demanding food, and pillaged the town while the settlers and the Mounted Police took refuge in Fort Battleford.

Poundmaker was aware that he and his men would be no match in the long run for the Canadian army that General Middleton was leading into the Prairies. What he seems to have hoped was that the desperate raid on Battleford would at last make the government aware of the Indians' plight. When Colonel Otter's troops reached Battleford at the end of April, Poundmaker withdrew his men from the town and only engaged in battle when Otter

staged an early morning surprise attack on the Indian camp at Cut Knife Hill. Poundmaker deployed his men so well that the Canadians were put to flight, but he did not follow up his victory or join forces with Dumont at Batoche. On May 26 he surrendered voluntarily to General Middleton.

At his trial Poundmaker behaved with dignity. "You did not catch me, I gave myself up," he told the judge. "You have me because I wanted peace. I cannot help myself, but I am still a man." He was sentenced to three years in prison, but it soon became clear he was dying of tuberculosis. Crowfoot pleaded for his release and after six months Poundmaker was freed. A few weeks later, in July 1886, he died in Crowfoot's home at Blackfoot Crossing. Like Crowfoot, he represented the best traditions of the prairie Indians. And if he distrusted the white men's promises, his own fate seemed to prove him right.

Peacemaker of the West

During the nineteenth century many priests left Québec for the Prairies to serve the Métis who had inherited the Catholic religion and to act as missionaries among the Plains Indians. Perhaps the most famous of all these priests was Albert Lacombe. Certainly he was the most loved by the Indians and especially by the Blackfoot, whose name for him can be translated into English as "Good Heart".

Albert Lacombe was himself part Indian. His great-grandmother, the daughter of a habitant of New France, was kidnapped by the Ojibwa and married a man of the tribe according to the customs of the forests. Their child was Albert Lacombe's grandfather. Albert's father, a farmer at Saint Sulpice in Québec, was wealthy enough to dedicate one of his sons to the Church; in those days the dedication of a son to the priesthood was a custom among prosperous French Canadian peasants, just as it was among the Irish until recent years.

Albert was born in 1827. He attended L'Assomption College, and after being ordained as a priest in 1849, he set out immediately for the Red River, which was then the centre of the Hudson's Bay Company's domain. It was a region inhabited by a mixture of Métis hunters and Scottish farmers, the descendants of the settlers Lord Selkirk had brought there in 1812.

Father Lacombe first settled at Pembina, which is now in North Dakota, and there he encountered the Métis, then at the height of their pride as the horse lords of the Prairies. He went out as chaplain in 1850 on the greatest of all the buffalo hunts and was present at the hunt of 1851

Father Albert Lacombe with the great chiefs, Crowfoot and Three Bulls.

also played a great part in inducing the Blackfoot chief, Crowfoot, to sign the 1877 treaty with the Canadian government.

By this time though, Lacombe was back in Winnipeg, helping French-speaking settlers from Québec and New England to set up farming colonies on the Prairies. But in 1880 he returned to the plains as Catholic chaplain to the CPR construction camps. Again he prevented warfare by working out compromises between the railway builders and the Blackfoot, who were angered by the iron road which encroached on what they regarded as their lands. And a few years later, when he was running a mission at Fort Macleod, in what is now southern Alberta, Lacombe again influenced the course of Canadian history by persuading Crowfoot to deter the Blackfoot chiefs from joining Gabriel Dumont's forces in the North-West Rebellion of 1885. He certainly prevented the violence of an Indian war from spreading over the Prairies, yet it is possible that with the Blackfoot as their allies the Métis might have gained some of their demands from the rebellion.

As the West became settled and the old Indian way of life drew to an end, Father Lacombe took up new activities. He founded residential schools intended to help Indian children understand the world of the white men. He wrote his memoirs of life among the Métis. And in 1909, when he was already eighty-two, he founded the Lacombe Home for the Poor near Calgary. He died there in 1916, and was buried at St. Albert among the Métis. They were the people to whom, through his own mixture of ancestries, he had always felt closest.

when a party of the Métis, including the young Gabriel Dumont, fought and won the famous battle of Grand Coteau against the Sioux.

The following year—1852—Lacombe went west to Fort Edmonton, where he spent the winter learning Cree, and in 1853 he took over the mission at Lac St. Anne from its founder, the Oblate Father Thibault. Lacombe stayed at Lac St. Anne until 1861. By this time he had become concerned with the fate of the Métis. He realized that time was running out on the old nomadic way of life associated with the annual buffalo hunt; very soon the Métis would have to take up a sedentary farming life. Accordingly, he founded a settlement for them at St. Albert, where they could begin to live an agrarian life; he persuaded Gabriel Dumont, the uncle of the famous Gabriel, to become its leader.

St. Albert made a good centre for Lacombe's missionary work among both the Cree and the Blackfoot. There was a traditional hostility between the two tribes sanctified by centuries of warfare and Lacombe set out to reconcile the two peoples. He was not always able to stop the bloodshed—there were times when he even got caught up in the fighting—but he did help to bring an end in the 1870s to the endemic warfare that had persisted in the Prairies and the Rocky Mountain foothills. His influence

Prophet of the CPR

Sandford Fleming was one of the first men to dream of a railway that would go from the Atlantic Ocean to the Pacific and unite the whole of North America. He was fortunate enough, many years later, to play a leading part in turning this vision into reality through the building of the Canadian Pacific Railway.

Fleming was born in Kirkcaldy, Scotland, in 1827. He had some kind of training in surveying and engineering before he arrived in Canada at the age of eighteen and found employment in the engineering department of the Simcoe and Huron Railway. He first attracted public attention in 1849, when a Tory mob in Montreal burnt down the Canadian Parliament building in its rage over the Rebellion Losses Act, which gave compensation to people who had actually been rebels in 1837. Fleming ran into the burning building and saved the portrait of Queen

Victoria which hung there. In doing so he revealed two traits that became all the more evident in later years—his audacity of temperament and the value he placed on Canada's imperial links.

Fleming rose rapidly in his profession and by 1857 he was chief engineer at the Northern Railway. But his vision was already leaping far beyond the small lines that were being built in Upper Canada during the 1850s; in 1858 he published his pamphlet entitled *A Railway to the Pacific through British Territory*, one of the first of the proposals that eventually led to the building of the CPR.

It would be a long time before Fleming could turn his attention to the problems of railway building in the West. In the meantime his attention turned eastward. The colonial governments of Canada, New Brunswick, and Nova Scotia simultaneously commissioned him to carry out the survey for the Intercolonial Railway, which would link Halifax with Montreal. The Intercolonial was planned for strategic as well as commercial purposes; it would provide quick winter transport of troops to the colony of Canada from an ice-free port, in the event of an American invasion. Once the survey was complete, Fleming became chief engineer for the construction of the Intercolonial; the assignment lasted until 1874. During this period he was also supervising railway construction in Newfoundland, which had not joined Confederation in 1867. But already, when the last spike was driven for the Intercolonial, Fleming was busy with the task he rightly considered his great life work. In 1871 the Dominion government appointed him as its chief engineer, with the assignment of planning the railway to the Pacific Ocean. The following year Fleming made a journey by horse and foot across the Prairies and through the succession of mountain ranges that lie between the Rockies and the Pacific Coast. He suggested that the railway should cross the Rockies through the Yellowhead Pass, the route now used by the Canadian National Railway.

But there were many political hurdles to be cleared before work began seriously on the CPR in the early 1880s. Fleming had retired from the government service in 1880, but when the way was finally open for the construction of the railway, he could not resist the challenge. It was he and his surveyors—particularly Major A. R. Rogers—who showed the feasibility of the more southerly route the railway actually took; this route crossed the Rockies by the Kicking Horse Pass and the Selkirks by the Rogers Pass.

Fleming showed his belief in the West by investing his money there; he became a director of both the Canadian Pacific Railway and the Hudson's Bay Company. But his interests went far beyond balance sheets and rail beds for he was a man of political and scientific vision and was always deeply involved in the cultural and academic life of Canada. As early as 1849 he took part in founding the Royal Canadian Institute. He was president of the Royal Society of Canada in 1888 and was chancellor of Queen's University from 1880 to his death in 1915. It was he who designed the first Canadian postage stamp, the Three-penny Beaver of 1851. And it was Fleming who devised the present system of standard time, by which the world is divided into twenty-four equal time zones. He proposed the idea in 1879; it was adopted by an international conference in Washington in 1884. Undoubtedly Fleming's travels across Canada had impressed on him the difficulties of running an efficient transport system without an efficient time system. He was also an enthusiastic supporter of imperial federation, for he believed that Britain and its colonies should form themselves into a great confederation of equal states, for which Canada already provided a model. And to further this aim he was a keen advocate of the development of imperial cable communication.

Luck made Fleming a rich man; intelligence made him a practical visionary.

The Overlander

When the news of rich finds of gold in the Cariboo Mountains reached the outside world, thousands of people set off in the spring of 1862 in the hope of joining in the bonanza. Some were seasoned miners from the

Sandford Fleming.

Fraser Canyon or the worked-out diggings of California; others were Chinese immigrants willing to pan the sand bars that were not deemed rich enough by white men; but there were many thousands who came from eastern Canada, the American midwest, and even as far away as Britain and the European continent. Most reached the British Columbia mainland by boat and then made their way up the newly constructed Cariboo road to the gold mecca of Barkerville. But a few particularly adventurous or foolhardy spirits from Eastern Canada decided to make the arduous overland journey to British Columbia that has earned them in history the gallant title of the Overlanders.

The best-known group of Overlanders was comprised of a number of small parties from Canada West and Canada East that had made their way by rail to St. Paul in the United States. After joining forces there these Overlanders took a steamer up the Red River to Fort Garry.

By the time they reached Fort Garry a few had already decided that the enterprise was too arduous. But there were still 136 people prepared to start the great trek over the prairie and through the mountain passes, and having elected Captain Thomas McMicking as their leader, they set out on June 5, 1862. They were soon joined by a family who caught up with them outside Fort Garry. The family was that of the German, Augustus Schubert, and his Belfast-born wife, Catherine; they had three children with them and Catherine was pregnant. Although the Over-

Catherine Schubert.

landers had originally decided against including women in their group, it was impossible to refuse the Schuberts' request to travel with them.

The Schuberts, as one of the Overlanders recollected, had "a milch cow or two and some riding or pack horses" and "a light spring and covered carriage", which were added to the ninety-seven Red River carts that creaked their slow way westward over the trackless prairie. Every day except Sunday the group travelled at ox pace from two in the morning until six in the evening, taking only three brief breaks for meals; Sunday was a day devoted to rest and worship in camp. The wagon train was half a mile long and each night the Overlanders imitated the Métis and drew their carts into a triangle within which they slept for fear of attacks by Indians.

No Indians appeared, but muskeg often delayed the Overlanders and it was July 21 by the time they reached Fort Edmonton. Here they gave up their wheeled vehicles in favour of pack animals—horses and oxen. A few more of the party dropped out, fearing the mountains ahead, but among those who continued were the Schuberts.

Métis guides from Fort Edmonton took the Overlanders over the Yellowhead Pass, but these guides did not know the country beyond the Rockies, and the information the Overlanders obtained from the Shuswap Indians was confusing. Finally the party decided to divide into two. The larger group built rafts to sail down the Fraser River while the smaller group set off overland on foot in the hope of reaching Fort Kamloops by following the North Thompson River. There were more than thirty of them in the smaller group, driving over a hundred horses and cattle that the large group had left them. The Schuberts were among this overland party.

After experiencing great difficulties they finally reached the North Thompson River. It then became obvious to the group that they too would have to make rafts to descend the river. At a place they afterwards called Slaughter Camp they killed all the cattle and made jerked beef, and on September 22, they took to their rafts. But it was no easy run downriver. At Murchison Rapids the rafts and most of the food had to be abandoned by the group; they spent three days traversing a long portage before building new rafts and setting out again. Their food supply ran short and they ransacked potato fields in an Indian village that had been ravaged by smallpox. They had difficulties with some of the Indians. Finally, on October 11, the first raft reached Fort Kamloops, and on October 13 the raft with the Schuberts arrived. Mrs. Schubert was already in labour, and next morning, assisted by an Indian woman, she gave birth to the first white girl born in the interior of British Columbia. The baby was named Rose.

The Schuberts eventually settled at Spallumcheen in the Northern Okanagan, where they farmed for many years. Catherine Schubert not only survived her great experience; she lived on for more than fifty years after it and died in 1918. A British Columbian folk ballad celebrated the memory of her courage, and she deserved such acclaim.

Canada's First Woman Doctor

It is impossible to talk of Emily Howard Stowe without mentioning her daughter, Augusta Stowe-Gullen. Their names are remembered together, for Augusta's career brought to completion the struggle her mother began for the right of women to practise medicine in Canada.

Emily Stowe was born in 1831 as Emily Jennings in the little Upper Canadian community of South Norwich. Educated at Toronto Normal School, she joined the legion of young women that Egerton Ryerson had recruited to staff the new schools he was creating; she started teaching at the age of fifteen and continued in this profession for ten years, until in 1856 she married John Stowe from the neighbouring community of Norwich.

During her time as a teacher, Emily Stowe had become convinced that the male monopoly of the medical profession was not only unjust, but also impractical, since there were certain functions a woman doctor could almost certainly fulfil more effectively. Besides, Emily found it demeaning that women should have no alternative but to consult a man in sickness and in childbirth. She resolved that she herself would help to change this situation by becoming a doctor. But when she sought training at a Canadian institution, she faced an unbroken wall of refusal. No medical school in the country would enroll a woman among its students.

Undeterred, Emily Stowe tried the United States. She eventually gained admission to the New York College of Medicine for Women, studied for several years in the United States, and in 1867 became—in a foreign country—the first Canadian woman to receive a medical degree.

But possessing a degree did not mean that she could practise medicine on home ground. After returning to Canada, Emily Stowe had to fight a battle thirteen years long against the medical establishment before she was finally admitted to the Ontario College of Physicians and Surgeons and was allowed to practise in her native province.

Emily Stowe became a successful Toronto physician, but her profession did not usurp her interest in women's

Emily Howard Stowe.

rights. Her personal struggle for professional status had made her highly conscious of the problems women faced in nineteenth century Canadian society. She recognized that women needed greater access to higher education, but that even education would not be completely effective without political influence. Such influence, she believed, could be assured by the right to vote in elections. Accordingly she helped to establish the Toronto School of Medicine for training women doctors and in 1893 she was a founder of the Dominion Women's Enfranchisement Association, of which she became the first president.

Emily Stowe, who died in 1903, did not live to see women participating freely in Canadian political life, but her daughter Augusta did. Born at Norwich before her mother began to study medicine, Augusta was one of the first students of the Toronto School of Medicine and in 1883 she was the first woman to receive a Canadian medical degree. The same year she married another doctor, John Gullen. Augusta Stowe-Gullen inherited her mother's concern for the liberation of woman from all constraints as well as her mother's belief that education was one of the means to that end. She succeeded Emily Stowe as president of the Dominion Women's Enfranchisement Association and was one of the founders of the National Council of Women. But she also found time, in a busy medical career, to act as a school trustee, as a member of the Toronto Board of Education, and as an active senator of the University of Toronto. In Augusta's lifetime the goals that Emily Stowe had spent so many years struggling for were finally fulfilled, as professions and politics alike were opened to women.

*Gabriel Dumont arriving over the American border after his
flight from Batoche, May 1885.*

Captain of the Buffalo Hunt

In Canadian history Gabriel Dumont has always been remembered as the lieutenant of Louis Riel in the North-West Rebellion of 1885. Yet Dumont was a man of power on the Prairies long before he fought Louis Riel's battles for him, and he was far more representative of the Métis people than the Québec-educated Riel.

Long before either Gabriel or Riel was born, the Dumont family were leaders of the Métis in the western Prairies. Sometime in the 1790s a French Canadian voyageur, Jean-Baptiste Dumont, arrived to work at Fort Edmonton, a Hudson's Bay Company post. He married a Sarcee Indian woman; the sons they had became famous hunters. One of these sons was Isidore Dumont, who hunted from Fort Pitt on the North Saskatchewan until the 1830s. Isidore then migrated to the Red River; his son Gabriel was born there in 1837.

On the Red River even the Métis were beginning to settle on long strip farms and life seemed so tame to Isidore, accustomed to the wandering life of the West, that in 1840 he returned to Fort Pitt. There Gabriel grew up without schooling but with a kind of education that was well suited to his time and place. He never learnt to read or write, but he could speak six Indian languages as well as French. And he knew the vital skills of prairie life better than any man. He was a superb rider and an accurate marksman, as good with a bow as a gun. He was an excellent tracker, and he could call the buffalo, an art even the Indians had begun to forget.

Gabriel also had a way of dealing with men that made him a natural diplomat and leader. Though as a boy of fourteen he took part in the battle of Grand Coteau between the Métis and the Sioux in 1851, he recognized that the Indians and the Métis had a common interest against the strangers who would soon be flooding into the Prairies. Thus he and his father Isidore were responsible for treaties between the Métis and the Sioux, and later between the Métis and the Blackfoot.

By the 1860s the Métis had already formed themselves into two groups—those who remained in settlements along the Red River, and those who followed a mainly nomadic life near the Saskatchewan rivers. By 1862 Gabriel Dumont had been elected chief of the Métis along the Saskatchewan and captain of their annual hunt.

When the Red River rising took place in 1869, the western Métis were not directly involved, but they were concerned about the fate of their brethren. Gabriel offered to bring five hundred horsemen for guerilla warfare against the Canadian forces that marched to the Red River under Colonel Wolseley in 1870. Riel refused his offer and

Dumont returned west, where he consolidated his alliances with the Indians and told the Métis that it was time to establish settled communities, since the buffalo herds were diminishing and would not survive for ever.

In 1873 the Métis gathered at St. Laurent on the South Saskatchewan in a great meeting outside the town church. They established a virtually autonomous little republic there, voting in laws and electing a council, with Dumont as president. For two years Gabriel and his council ruled their people with fairness and foresight, introducing sensible regulations to cover land and timber rights and to conserve the buffalo. Then, in 1875, the Mounted Police arrived and the little republic of St. Laurent was dissolved.

Gabriel Dumont withdrew into his private affairs, building a store and operating a ferry across the Saskatchewan River at a place still called Gabriel's Crossing. But the Métis continued to regard him as their leader, and they turned to him in the early 1880s when settlers began to flow into the country of the two Saskatchewan rivers. The Métis, who held no titles to their land, feared that their farms were threatened. In vain they petitioned the successive governments of Alexander Mackenzie and Sir John Macdonald to guarantee their holdings. When it was obvious that their appeals had fallen on deaf ears, Gabriel rode off in 1884 to fetch Louis Riel from Montana in the hope he could help them. But the petition that Riel and Dumont framed was also ignored, and in March 1885 the Métis declared a provisional government, with Riel as head and Dumont as "adjutant general".

Dumont and his men defeated a force of Mounted Police at Duck Lake, and this was the start of hostilities. It took the Dominion government some weeks to organize an army, and in the meantime the South Saskatchewan region was in Dumont's control. He organized a tiny army of three hundred men and planned a guerilla war which he hoped would last long enough to force the government to compromise. But Riel refused to give consent to such tactics until it was too late. The Canadian forces were already near the Métis stronghold of Batoche when Dumont ambushed and defeated them at Fish Creek. It was only a temporary triumph. The defeated Canadians reorganized and advanced on Batoche, which they finally took after four days of bitter resistance.

When Riel surrendered, Dumont fled south to Montana. He tried to rescue Riel, and when that was impossible he joined Buffalo Bill's Wild West Show. The rest of his life was uneventful. He returned to Batoche in 1893 and in 1906 he died of a heart attack after a hunting trip.

Dumont was one of the great Canadian rebels and one of the few true Canadian heroes, a brave and chivalrous man whom even his enemies remembered with respect.

Canada First!

Charles Mair was a poet and a patriot. He was one of the founders of the Canada First movement and he played an important part in the events leading up to the Red River rising of 1869–70.

Mair was an Upper Canadian, born in 1838 in the small Ottawa Valley town of Lanark. His family ran a small lumber business and encouraged Charles in his ambition to become a doctor. But though he went for two spells to Queen's University, he had to interrupt his studies to help the family business out of difficulties, and he never took his degree. But he did acquire at Queen's an enthusiasm for poetry and in 1868 he published his first book, *Dreamland and Other Poems*, which attracted a good deal of attention because of the vividness with which Mair perceived and portrayed natural scenes.

The year 1868 was in other ways a critical one in Mair's life. Abandoning his thoughts of a medical career, he went to Ottawa to take up journalism and there he met Captain George Denison and the other young men who had come together to form the early nationalist movement known as Canada First. Mair immediately joined the group. The Canada Firsters were enthusiastic advocates of an immediate extension of the Dominion of Canada—

Charles Mair.

founded the year before—across the North American continent. They were especially anxious for Canadians—which in practice meant Ontarians—to take over the Red River colony, with its rich farmlands, as a prelude to annexing the whole West.

When Mair was given the chance to work as paymaster for the company building the road from Lake of the Woods to the Red River, he immediately took the opportunity to visit the West. It was also a chance to begin work as a journalist; he arranged for his brother to send his letters from the Red River to the Toronto *Globe*.

Mair's behaviour at Red River was, to say the least, injudicious. He associated with the extreme Canadian faction led by Dr. John Schultz, who advocated forcible seizure of the Red River, which still belonged to the Hudson's Bay Company, and he married Schultz's niece. Just as offensive to the Métis and other inhabitants of the colony were the scurrilous descriptions of Red River society that appeared in the extracts from his letters printed in the *Globe*. These descriptions so angered Mrs. Bannatyne, wife of a leading merchant, that she pulled Mair's nose and horsewhipped him publicly in the Fort Garry post office.

When it became obvious that the inhabitants of the Red River colony were to have no say in the negotiations for the transfer of the territory from the company to the Dominion, the Métis under Louis Riel created a provisional government in 1869 to arrange for better terms. John Schultz led an armed rebellion of the Canadian minority, in which Mair took part. He was captured by the Métis militia and Riel threatened him with execution, but Mair escaped and fled through the United States to Ontario, where he and Schultz embarked on a campaign designed to inflame Ontario opinion against Louis Riel and the Métis. But Mair and his associates failed to prevent the main achievement of the uprising, which was the creation of the Province of Manitoba.

Mair could not keep away from the West. He returned to set up a store in Portage la Prairie and in 1878 he moved on to Prince Albert, the newly founded settlement on the Saskatchewan River. There he dabbled unsuccessfully in real estate. As the threat of a second Métis rebellion grew in the 1880s, Mair was much more understanding of the people's grievances and he warned Sir John Macdonald of the dangers of the situation. When Macdonald did nothing, Mair left Prince Albert in 1884, though he served in General Middleton's expedition to suppress the rebellion. In 1886 Mair published his famous verse play, *Tecumseh. A Drama*, a sprawling work celebrating the Indian leader in the War of 1812 and containing some fine passages describing the virgin prairie before the settlers arrived. What is most interesting about *Tecumseh* is the way its obvious patriotism is fused with a growing sympathy for the native peoples of Canada.

For many years Mair lived a wandering and financially unsuccessful life, trading as far west as Kamloops in British Columbia. Only when he was sixty did he finally get a government post; in 1898 Clifford Sifton took him into the immigration service. He remained a civil servant for the next twenty-three years, retiring at the age of eighty-three. Although it was a largely uneventful period in his life he did attend the signing of the treaty in 1899 between the Canadian government and the Indians of the Peace and Mackenzie rivers. Mair lived another six years after his retirement and died in 1927. He was not one of the best of Canadian poets, yet he was something of a literary pioneer; he believed in the reality of Canada as a nation and expressed it in his verse, particularly in *Tecumseh*, and he saw the Canadian landscape more sharply and authentically than any poet before him.

Grandpapa Chocolat!

Sometime towards the turn of the last century a rather plump and benign-looking old man could be seen walking the streets of Québec and hailed by schoolchildren as "le grandpapa chocolat", from his habit of distributing candies from his well-filled pockets. Louis-Honoré Fréchette, "le grandpapa chocolat", was also Clerk to the Legislative Council of Québec. But this respectable occupation, which gave him a comfortable salary for very little work, was really another disguise for the best-known French Canadian poet of the nineteenth century and the first poet in either of our languages to become famous abroad.

Fréchette, whose best poems recalled the glories of the Québec past, of New France and its eventful history, was himself a member of one of the oldest Québec families. He was a seventh-generation Canadian; his ancestor, François Frichet, came to New France in 1677 and in the century and a half that preceded Louis-Honoré's birth in 1839, the family name had changed gradually to Fréchette.

Louis-Honoré was born into a very different world from that of seventeenth century New France, with its strange mixture of chivalry, piety, and barbarism. Two years before Fréchette's birth at Lévis, the Lower Canada Rebellion had taken place. The rebellion had been followed by the arrival of Lord Durham, whose famous *Report* on the state of the Canadas resulted in Québec losing what little independence it possessed when it was

Louis-Honoré Fréchette.

united with Upper Canada into a single colony. All through his childhood Fréchette was made aware of the danger of extinction that threatened his culture and even his language. But the rebelliousness which he showed in his youth was more a personal revolt against authority in general than a political rebellion against English domination. It led to his expulsion from two different classical colleges before he finally settled down to study law at the newly founded Laval University in Québec. After periods of study at McGill and Queen's universities, he was admitted to the bar of Canada East in 1862.

But the law as a career soon lost its attractions for a young man of Fréchette's romantic inclinations. Radical politics and poetry were much more interesting. He joined the Parti Rouge—the Reds or left-wing liberals—and edited two short-lived political papers, *Le Journal de Québec* and *Le Journal de Lévis*, while writing his first rather fragile and sentimental poems which appeared in 1863 under the title *Mes Loisirs*. In his newspapers Fréchette freely attacked the Roman Catholic priests who wielded such influence in Québec affairs and the priests took their revenge by discouraging clients from giving their business to the law office Fréchette had set up in Lévis.

Realizing that there was no living to be earned by practising law in Canada, the young poet set off in 1865 for the United States, where he settled in Chicago. After editing two unsuccessful papers for French Canadians living abroad, he took up the best employment he could find, as a clerk in the land department of the Illinois Central Railway.

Fréchette returned in 1871 to the very different Canada of Confederation. The Liberals in Québec had survived the censure of the Catholic Church and Fréchette, who had decided to try a career in politics, was elected to the House of Commons in 1874, the year that Alexander Mackenzie's Liberal government took power. But in 1878, the year of Sir John A. Macdonald's comeback, he was defeated by a Conservative and he dropped out of active politics.

By this time he had decided to devote himself to poetry and other kinds of writing, and though he found this difficult in the early years, everything changed when his fourth book of poems, *Les Fleurs Boréales*, was awarded in 1881 the famous Prix Montoyon by the Académie Française. This established Fréchette's repute both in Canada and abroad, and gave him the impetus to write his masterpiece, *La Légende d'un Peuple*, published in 1887.

La Légende was a kind of epic poem celebrating the heroes and heroic deeds of the Canadian past before the conquest of 1760, and it evoked with great eloquence the landscapes in which these historic events took place. It was the first major Canadian poem in either French or English.

La Légende was regarded by the French Canadians as a great patriotic work and it was for this reason that Fréchette was given his sinecure at the Legislative Council. It was a position that enabled him to live without anxiety and with plenty of time for the books of poems, the plays, the tales, the essays, the histories that flowed from his pen until his death in 1908. For Fréchette was more than a fine poet; he was also a man of letters who took pride in being able to express himself in prose as well as poetry, in fiction as well as non-fiction. More than any of his predecessors or contemporaries, he gave a dignity to the profession of writing which it had not enjoyed in the Canada of earlier days, for the arts do not flourish in pioneer societies.

The Mountain Man

John George Brown started his career as an Anglo-Irish gentleman and an officer in the British army in India. He ended it as Kootenay Brown—one of the most celebrated mountain men of the Rockies—who knew the western Prairies and the great mountain ranges like the palm of his hand and who could live off the land as well as any Indian.

Brown was born in 1839, and after he had finished his public school education he set off for India, where he served as a subaltern in the Eighth Regiment of Infantry. A year of soldiering was enough for Brown. Far off in the Indian hills he had heard of the fortunes that were being made in the gold fields of British Columbia and he decided that there might be more adventure in the mountains of North America than in the cantonments of the Deccan. So he resigned his commission in time to join in the rush northward to the Cariboo in 1862.

Brown was unlucky as a prospector, but he was tough and adaptable, and for two years he survived by wandering as a trapper over the mountains and plateaus of central British Columbia. It was then, still in his twenties, that he built up his knowledge of the ways of the land. In 1864 Brown returned to civilization at Boston Bar in the Fraser Canyon and while he was buying stores there, he heard of the discovery of gold at Wild Horse Creek in the Kootenay district near the American border.

Once again, Brown arrived too late to stake a good claim, so to earn a living he enrolled as a constable in the police force organized by the chief gold commissioner, Chartres Brew. He was responsible for rounding up a gang of counterfeiters, but instead of being promoted for this act he found that his pay was cut in a government economy drive. So he resigned and wandered off again as a prospector, finding his way through the Rockies and eventually reaching Medicine Hat, where he and his companion were ambushed by the Blackfoot. They escaped with difficulty, Brown with an arrow in his back. After pulling it out Brown rode all the way to Fort Edmonton, where he recuperated. Then he went to Duck Lake and lived for a time with Gabriel Dumont and his wandering band of Métis hunters.

After leaving Dumont, Brown went east to Fort Garry, bought trade goods, and wandered for a couple of years buying furs from the Indians of the Canadian plains. He then travelled south and became a pony express rider, carrying United States mail in Dakota. On one of his mail runs the Sioux ambushed him and robbed him of everything, including his clothes. Brown saved his life by jumping into a lake and hiding in the reeds until the Indians had gone. He then walked naked to the nearest military post, where he accepted an offer to work as a scout for the American army. But scouting turned out to be as perilous as carrying mail. Once Brown was lost in a blizzard for three days and almost died. But he continued to work for the army for several years, not only acting as scout but also becoming an interpreter; he had a good ear for Indian languages and could speak several of them.

Kootenay Brown.

As the years went by, Brown became increasingly disturbed by the policy of extermination that the American army had adopted towards the Indians, and in 1874 he moved back into Canadian territory and built a cabin on a remote lake in the western foothills of the Rockies. It was then called Kootenay Lake, and hence Brown became known as Kootenay Brown. Later the lake was renamed Waterton.

Using Kootenay Lake as a base, Brown lived the typical mountain man's life. He wandered as a commercial buffalo hunter, and when his efforts and those of his kind had thinned down the great herds, he took to hunting wolves. He worked often with Métis bands, hunting on both sides of the international boundary until 1877, when in a fit of anger he killed a man named Louis Ell in Montana. The jury was sympathetic and acquitted him, but Brown decided to leave American territory in case Ell's friends tried to avenge the death and he stayed north of the border for the rest of his life.

In partnership with a former whisky trader named Fred Kanouse, Brown set up a store near Lower Waterton Lake and traded with the Indians. During the North-West Rebellion of 1885 he became a scout again, for a hastily raised volunteer group called the Rocky Mountain Rangers, but he took no part in the actual fighting against the Métis. Later, when the newly built Canadian Pacific Railway brought travellers and hunters to the Rockies, Kootenay Brown acted often as their guide. He became a popular companion of the ranchers who settled in the Fort Macleod area, for they enjoyed listening to his tales of gold prospecting and buffalo hunts and encounters with Indians in the legendary days of the old West. In 1910, when Waterton National Park was established, his role as a pioneer was recognized by an appointment as the first park superintendent; he kept the post until he died in 1918 among the mountains he had loved.

Spokesman for the Provinces

When Canada was created in 1867, its constitution was enshrined in the British North America Act. This act provided for a federal system, with two levels of government: a central government based in Ottawa and a local government in each of the provinces. Matters that were obviously of general interest, such as foreign affairs, military matters, and currency, would be controlled by the central government. Matters that were obviously of local interest, such as education, administration of laws, and control of natural resources, would be in the hands of the provinces. But the act left room for disagreement on the exact limits of the two jurisdictions, and differing interpretations of federalism began to emerge. Sir John A. Macdonald and his followers believed that federalism was consistent with strong central government, but others conceived of a more basic federalism. For these men regions and localities were the true foundations of society; as many powers as possible should be vested in provincial governments and as few as possible in the federal government situated in Ottawa.

By the 1870s a number of provincial premiers were demanding more power for the regions. One of these was Oliver Mowat, premier of Ontario from 1872 to 1896. But the most forceful among the dissidents was Honoré Mercier, premier of Québec from 1887 to 1891. Mercier was the first important post-Confederation Québec nationalist; he differed from modern nationalists of the Parti Québécois though, for he never advocated the separation of Québec from the rest of Canada.

Born at St. Athanase, Québec, in 1840, Mercier was a farmer's son. He was educated at the Jesuit college in Montreal, and ever after he remained under the influence of that religious order. Like so many men of the nineteenth century—an era when lives were usually shorter than they are today—he became politically active at an early age. At twenty-two he was already editing a local newspaper, *Le Courrier de St. Hyacinthe*. *Le Courrier* supported the conservative Parti Bleu, and in the sense that he was deeply attached to the traditions of Québec, Mercier remained a conservative for the rest of his life.

Mercier abandoned journalism when he was called to the bar in 1866, but he remained deeply interested in politics. Even before the Dominion of Canada came into being, he was disillusioned with Confederation, for he thought it did not really guarantee French Canadian rights. He broke away from the Parti Bleu, which supported Sir John Macdonald's federal government, and with a group of equally disillusioned Conservatives and disgruntled right-wing Liberals, he founded the Parti National in 1871. It was a party devoted to expanding the rights of the Province of Québec.

Mercier had to wait a long time though for a chance to gain his objective. He sat in the federal House of Commons from 1872 to 1874; then he concentrated on his law practice until 1879, when he was elected to the provincial assembly of Québec. The Parti National had dwindled away by this time, but Mercier had joined the provincial Liberal Party, on to which he succeeded in grafting nationalist ideas. For a brief period he served as solicitor general and then, in 1883, he became leader of the opposition. In this role he made great political capital out of the execution in 1885 of Louis Riel, leader of the rebel Métis of Saskatchewan. Sir John Macdonald's refusal to

Honoré Mercier.

commute Riel's sentence aroused such anger in Québec that Mercier was able to defeat the Conservative provincial government in 1886 and take over the administration in 1887.

He ruled only four years, but during that time he gave vigour and direction to the struggle for provincial rights. In 1887, working closely with Oliver Mowat in Ontario, he called a gathering of provincial premiers. In this meeting the premiers passed strong resolutions on provincial rights that helped to frustrate Macdonald's attempts to create a highly centralized government in Ottawa.

Within Québec Mercier pursued a course of favouring the Church in exchange for its support. He recruited a priest, Antoine Labelle, as deputy minister of colonization. In 1888 he compensated the Jesuits out of public funds for property they had lost when the order was banned in the eighteenth century.

Such acts angered the Orange Order and other Protestant groups, but Mercier had so much support in Québec that he would certainly have weathered the political storm if he had not in 1891 been implicated by a Senate committee in a scandal over railway contracts in Québec. The lieutenant governor immediately dismissed Mercier's government, and in the elections that followed he lost heavily. Unlike Sir John A. Macdonald, who had been involved in a railway scandal in 1873 and made a comeback five years later, Mercier did not outlive the great scandal of his career. He died after three years of retirement in 1894.

The Silver Voice

Wilfrid Laurier was the first Canadian prime minister whose mother tongue was French, though he was more fluently bilingual and bicultural than any of his predecessors or successors. He was also a liberal in the broadest sense of the word. In 1877 he proclaimed his disagreement with certain Catholic bishops who tried to equate the Liberals of Québec, popularly called Rouges, with European revolutionaries, often called Reds. "I am a Liberal," Laurier said in a famous speech, and defined his position by adding: "I am one of those who think that everywhere there are abuses to be reformed, new horizons to be opened up, and new forces to be developed." The idea of *reform* was essential to Laurier's liberalism; never did he imagine that society could be improved by violent revolution.

Laurier's family—originally called Champlaurier—traced their ancestry to settlers who came to Montreal with Maissonneuve in 1642. In the early nineteenth century they were farmers at St. Lin in Québec; Laurier's father was also a surveyor. Wilfrid was born in 1841 and owed his name to his father's enthusiasm for the works of Sir Walter Scott. In Scott's novel *Ivanhoe* the Saxon Wilfrid is one of the more heroic characters. Laurier's parents were anxious that he should enjoy the best of both Canadian cultures and they sent him to an English school in New Glasgow before he went on to the French language classical college at L'Assomption. He finally studied law at McGill and made history in that English-speaking institution by delivering the first valedictory ever spoken there in French.

By this time—1864—Laurier was already interested in Liberal politics and had joined the Institut Canadien, a society devoted to the free discussion of intellectual and social questions which Ignace Bourget, the extremely conservative bishop of Québec, denounced as heretical and subversive. Laurier, who believed that the Institut was not heretical and knew that it was not subversive, defied the bishop's ban although he was a pious Catholic.

However, he did not immediately engage in politics. His lungs were weak and he retired to the country at L'Avenir in the Eastern Townships, where he edited a small Liberal newspaper, *Le Défricheur* (The Settler). When his health recovered he set up a law practice in Arthabaskaville and only in 1871 did he become a member of the Québec Legislative Assembly, after conducting a campaign stressing his opposition to the clergy interfering in politics.

Three years later, in 1874, Laurier was elected to the House of Commons. In 1877 he became minister of inland revenue in Alexander Mackenzie's Liberal government. The next year, 1878, Mackenzie was defeated; Sir John A. Macdonald returned to power and the Liberals went into opposition for many years. Laurier came into prominence in 1885, after the North-West Rebellion, when he led the French Canadian protest against Sir John Macdonald's decision to allow the execution of the Métis leader, Louis Riel. "Had I been born on the banks of the Saskatchewan," he said, "I would myself have shouldered a musket to fight against the neglect of governments and the shameless greed of speculators."

When Edward Blake resigned the Liberal leadership in 1887, Laurier—who led the Québec wing of the party—was the natural man to take his place, and in 1896, when the disintegration of the Conservative government after Macdonald's death had become evident, he led the Liberals to victory. He remained as prime minister until 1911.

It was a time of great progress and many problems. The new provinces of Saskatchewan and Alberta were carved out of the North-West Territories; new railways

Wilfrid Laurier campaigning in 1910.

opened up the northern Prairies; a vast immigration program filled the empty lands with people from all parts of Europe and North America. Yet there were difficult problems, particularly over schooling in the West; Laurier never quite reconciled the desire of new provincial governments to secularize education with that of the Catholics to operate their own schools.

Laurier was undecided over other difficult issues. He was in favour of Canada's connection with Britain, yet at the same time he wanted his country to follow its own foreign and military policies. He supported Canada's participation in the South African war (which most French Canadians opposed). But at the same time he freed the Canadian army from the last vestiges of British control, established a separate Canadian navy in 1910, and secured Canada's right to sign commercial treaties without referring them to Whitehall.

His great mistake was that in freeing Canada from British political rule, he failed to see the threat of American economic domination. He was finally defeated because the Canadian people did not share this blind spot. When he proposed a Reciprocity Treaty that would have meant large scale commercial co-operation with the United States, his government lost the 1911 election and he never returned to power. During World War I he opposed conscription on principle and many English-speaking Liberals deserted him. In 1917 his remnant of the Liberal Party was beaten everywhere but in Québec. He died, a man defeated by the strength of his own convictions, in 1919.

James Morrow Walsh.

Sitting Bull's Friend

The American frontier was the advancing edge of a democracy founded on revolution, a place where men worked out the shape of their new society through violence and disorder. The Canadian frontier was the advancing edge of a country whose people had rejected revolution. It moved west according to the principle of order, and in western Canada the manifestation of that order was the North-West Mounted Police, founded in 1873, three years after Canada took over the domain of the Hudson's Bay Company. The task of the Mounted Police was to ensure that the violence of the American frontier would not be repeated in Canada. The contrast between the attitudes of the two countries was emphasized by the fact that the North-West Mounted Police was founded after a particularly appalling example of American frontier behaviour: in May 1873, a group of Montana wolf-hunters had massacred on Canadian territory in the Cypress Hills a party of Assiniboine Indians they accused of being horse thieves.

When the call went out in 1873 for recruits to the newly founded Mounted Police, it was answered by a strange variety of romantics and adventurers. Many were remittance men, sons of wealthy English families sent out to redeem their youthful errors in the colonies. Others were former soldiers who could not settle into civilian life. Flamboyant as they were, many of them were men of courage and enterprise who played an invaluable part in ensuring that order in the Canadian West would not disintegrate and tempt the watchful Americans to intervene. James Morrow Walsh was a good example of these Mounties in his mixture of flamboyance and capability.

Walsh was born in Prescott, Canada West, in 1843. He was attracted by stories of military life, but the ambitions for glory that he fostered as a boy were hard to fulfil in nineteenth century Canada. He joined the militia and saw action only briefly during the Fenian raids of 1866. When the establishment of the Mounted Police was announced, he was one of the first recruits. On the strength of his militia background, he was immediately appointed inspector, with the courtesy rank of major.

Walsh rode in the great march of 1874 when the Mounted Police carried the flag across the Prairies as far as the Rockies; the next year he led his troop into the Cypress Hills, a favourite wintering place of Métis and Indian hunters, but also a centre of the whisky trade. The very news of Walsh's approach sent the American traders running south. To maintain this atmosphere of order, he built a stockaded post which, with characteristic vanity, he named Fort Walsh.

Almost immediately after its establishment, Fort Walsh became a focal point of international attention. South of the border in 1876 the Sioux massacred the cavalry of General Custer at the battle of Little Big Horn and soon after they began fleeing north from the vengeance of the American army. Their leading chief, Sitting Bull, arrived in 1877.

The Canadian policy was to contain the Sioux and pacify them without letting them take up permanent residence, lest they provoke unrest among the Blackfoot and other powerful tribes. Walsh had to deal with Sitting Bull and his thousands of braves. He took advantage of the good impression made by the Mounties' red coats, which reminded the Indians of the British soldiers who had treated native peoples more fairly than the blue-coated American cavalry. Walsh acted with deliberate bravado. He would often ride into the Sioux camps with small escorts and calmly tell the braves about the "Queen's Law" which they had to obey. Walsh's fearlessness appealed to Sitting Bull, who was the same kind of man, and a genuine friendship sprang up between these two leaders of such different backgrounds.

Walsh's friendship with Sitting Bull was fatal to his career as a Mounted Policeman. By 1880 the buffalo were almost exterminated, but the Ottawa government refused to feed the starving Sioux, in the hope that such a policy would force them back over the border. Since Walsh was planning to take a trip east, Sitting Bull asked him to plead with the American president on behalf of his people. Walsh agreed, only to find that his superiors disapproved; it seemed to them that a mere policeman was dabbling in international affairs. Walsh's willingness to help the Sioux was regarded as insubordination and he resigned, disillusioned, in 1883.

It took a major crisis before he was called back to the Mounted Police from the coal and transport business he operated after leaving the force. In 1897 strong and decisive men were needed to deal with the Klondike gold rush and Walsh was persuaded to return and take the dual post of police superintendent and district commissioner at Dawson City. But again there were suggestions of wrongdoing; Walsh was accused of corruption in connection with recording gold claims and he resigned in 1898. It was later proved that his errors were due to bad bookkeeping, not to graft, but the taint of wrongdoing clung until he died in 1905. Few people remembered Walsh's feat of keeping the peace on the border in the 1870s when he and his handful of men, by firmness and bluff, prevented violent Indian warfare from sweeping into the Canadian Prairies.

Prophet and Martyr

During recent years Louis Riel has become in Canadian eyes a strange combination of hero and martyr. Biographies, plays, and operas have been written about him; he has been the hero of novels and television spectaculars. His portrait has even appeared on a Canadian postage stamp. Yet not long ago many English-speaking Canadians regarded Riel as a traitor. Only in Québec was he seen as a martyr for French Canadian traditions.

Why have we changed? Partly it is because we have become more tolerant of each other's traditions; English-speaking people in Canada are much more inclined to respect the aspirations of French-speaking Canadians, whether they live in Québec or, as Riel did, in other parts of Canada. And partly it is because as time passes we get a better sense of the perspectives of history. Now that Riel has been dead almost a hundred years, we look back and realize that the two rebellions he led were part of the process by which the Canada we know came into being. Every society grows by change, and rebellion is one way by which change occurs.

But if Louis Riel now looms very large in our history, the two insurrections his name recalls—the Red River rising of 1869–70 and the North-West Rebellion of 1885— were small affairs in which only a few thousand people played an active part. Both were rebellions in which most of the participants were Métis—the people of part-Indian and part-French descent who for decades ruled the Prairies as buffalo hunters and who were feared even by the fierce Sioux. When the buffalo herds were destroyed and settlement began to move in, the nomadic hunting life of the Métis was doomed, and the two rebellions were part of the painful process of adjustment.

Louis Riel, the son of a Métis miller, was born at St. Boniface in 1844. His intelligence soon attracted the attention of Bishop Taché, who sent him to the College of Montreal. It was thought he would become a priest, and indeed Riel had a deeply religious mind, but it was not one that could be disciplined within a priesthood. By the time he was twenty-one he had left the college to become articled as a lawyer. He soon realized, however, that he was as little fitted for the law as for the Church. He drifted south of the border and worked for a couple of years as a store clerk in various American cities. By 1868 he was back on the Red River.

It was a critical time. The new Dominion of Canada was trying to buy out the Hudson's Bay Company's rights over the West, and the Canadians had started to build a road from the head of Lake Superior to the Red River. They were even surveying the prairie where the Métis had their long strip farms facing on to the Red River. The Métis were naturally alarmed, and when Louis Riel stopped the surveyors by standing on their chains, he became the leader of the Red River people. It was a role he

Louis Riel speaks from the dock during his trial in Regina in 1885.

took seriously, for in 1869 he helped to found the Comité National des Métis to protect his people's rights.

When Canadian representatives finally tried to enter the Red River country to set up a territorial government, the Métis stopped them and shortly afterwards they seized Fort Garry. There Riel set up a provisional administration which enjoyed the support of most of the people in the region. He was able to deal with the small groups of Canadians who tried to overthrow the provisional government by force, and if it had not been for the execution of a single Orangeman, Thomas Scott, for rebellious behaviour, it would have been a bloodless revolution. The Canadians were forced to negotiate; the insurrection ended when Manitoba was declared a province with its own government. Riel, however, had made a serious mistake in executing Thomas Scott and had to flee. Twice the people of Red River elected him to the House of Commons, but he was not allowed to take his seat and was eventually banished from Canada for five years.

The years of his exile were trying ones for Riel. He suffered periods of mental imbalance and became convinced, while being tended secretly in Québec institutions, that he had a special role as a prophet. After travelling through the United States he settled at last in Montana as a teacher and became an American citizen. But in the early 1880s the Métis of the South Saskatchewan River began having trouble over land surveys similar to those carried out in the Red River country years before. When they could not settle their claims, they thought of Louis Riel, and in 1884 Gabriel Dumont rode south to summon him to their help.

Riel went back with Dumont to Batoche on the South Saskatchewan. For a whole winter he and the Métis tried by peaceful means to settle their land claims, but Sir John A. Macdonald was deaf to their pleas and to the warnings of people who knew the West. In March 1885, the impatient Métis rose in rebellion. They held out until May, when the Canadian columns captured Batoche and the rebellion was put to an end. They might have held out longer and gained better terms if Riel had not been so concerned with his idea of founding a holy empire on the Prairies and had listened to Dumont's plea for effective guerilla warfare.

When it was all over, Riel surrendered. He was tried in Regina and found guilty of treason. Sir John Macdonald ignored the jury's recommendation of mercy and Riel was executed on November 16. His death aroused great bitterness in Québec where the execution was regarded as an attack on the French community in Canada. For many years the Conservatives have had no political influence in Québec; Riel's death at the orders of a Conservative prime minister has never been forgotten by French Canadians.

The Humble Healer

Every country and every religion has its tradition of spiritual healers, men and women who are able to cure ailments without the use of ordinary medical means. Often they are called "faith healers", and indeed the faith, or at least the fervent hope, of the person cured seems to play an important part in the healing. It is often suggested that only psychosomatic sicknesses—those caused by the action of the mind on the body—can be cured in this way, but whether that is the case or not, the evidence in favour of spiritual healing is too extensive to be ignored. Many thousands of people who have gained no benefit from ordinary medical treatment claim to have been cured by such healers. Where their power comes from is not certain, for almost every healer has a different explanation for his feats of curing. What cannot be denied is that the cures take place.

Perhaps the most famous of all Canadian healers was a small, frail man generally known as Brother André. Brother André was born as Alfred Bessette in 1845. His father was the wheelwright in the village of Saint-Grégoire d'Iberville, Canada East. Alfred Bessette was a sickly child; throughout his life he remained frail and every year people expected he would not survive until the next: every year, that is, until he finally died at the age of ninety-one!

Misfortune hovered over Alfred Bessette's early life. When he was ten his father was killed by a falling tree: when he was twelve his mother died of tuberculosis. After his mother's death he was handed over to a vigorous but insensitive uncle who did not realize his nephew was not as strong as he. Alfred received virtually no education and his poor health made it impossible for him to carry on with the trades he attempted to learn—baking, tinsmithing, blacksmithing. Despairing of ever mastering a trade in Québec, he went south to work in the textile mills of New England, where he at last learnt English, but found that his weak lungs made factory work impossible.

The one thing that remained constant in Alfred Bessette's life was his religious devotion. He decided that he would like to become a member of a community in which he could devote his whole life to religious service, but his ill-health and his virtual illiteracy were both against him. Eventually, in 1870, he was accepted as novice by a teaching order, the Holy Cross Brothers, and he entered the Notre Dame College at Côte-des-Neiges in Montreal. He accepted the name of Brother André and did whatever menial work was required. After a year the brotherhood decided that his health was too poor for acceptance into the order, but he was allowed to continue as a novice for another six months. During that time he

Brother André, an old man sitting in the sun in 1925.

encountered Bishop Bourget, who was so impressed by Brother André's evident dedication that he persuaded the Holy Cross Brothers to accept him. Brother André took his vows in 1872, and from that time on he served as the porter or doorkeeper for Notre Dame College.

It was not long after he took his vows that Brother André's first cures became manifest. He was a devotee of St. Joseph, the carpenter-saint who had become the patron of those who worked with their hands. Seeing people who were suffering without prospect of cure, André began touching them with oil from a vigil lamp that burnt before St. Joseph's statue in the college chapel. Remarkable cures took place, not on every occasion, but often enough for rumours of miracles to circulate, and people began to come to Brother André for relief from their illnesses.

As in all such instances, there was a long period when the church authorities refused to acknowledge the special powers of this mystic who lived among them. They feared that the flocks of sick people who came to Brother André might create a fear of infection among the parents of their students. So Brother André began to meet his "patients" in a street-car shelter outside the college gates. But the street-car passengers objected, and finally, in 1904, he got permission to build an open-air shrine to St. Joseph on the slopes of Mount Royal. There he met sick people and talked to them and laid on hands that were usually smeared with a little of the oil from St. Joseph's lamp.

But the shrine was only suited to fair weather. In winter the people continued to collect at Notre Dame College for Brother André's ministrations, and finally, in 1908, he built an all-weather chapel. It quickly became popular and the vestibule was filled with the crutches and sticks of cured people.

Like most such healers, Brother André was highly conscious that whatever power he exercised came from outside himself. He attributed it to the intercessions of St. Joseph and his ambition was to build a great basilica on Mount Royal in honour of the saint. He collected money tirelessly for the construction fund, while he healed people in his chapel and walked the streets of Montreal visiting the sick who could not come to him. The cornerstone for the basilica was laid in 1916. In 1937, before it was finished, Brother André died, and it would be another thirty years before work on the building could be brought to completion. But before he died, Brother André's chapel was visited by three million people. Many claimed they were cured; the cures, it was said, continued to be performed after his death. In 1978 Brother André was beatified by the Pope. Long before that millions of people had come to regard the little doorkeeper as a saint.

Voices from Afar

Canadians make more use of the telephone than any other people in the world, and it is appropriate that the inventor, Alexander Graham Bell, should have been himself a Canadian and that the telephone should have been first used in Canada. There have been many Canadian inventors, but few of them became as famous as Bell, whose name is an everyday word in most of Canada because of the Bell Telephone Company which he founded.

He was born as Alexander Bell in 1847; the middle name of Graham was added eleven years later. His father, Alexander Melville Bell, was a Scottish expert in the correction of speech defects; he invented a system called Visible Speech, by which people who had been born deaf could learn to speak, and he wrote a book—*The Standard Elocutionist*—which became a nineteenth century best-seller and ran into two hundred editions.

Since he was an educational expert, Alexander Melville Bell preferred to teach his son at home, according to his own methods. Later on, however, young Alexander spent periods of time at both Edinburgh and London universities without completing his courses. He too had developed an interest in teaching, and after taking employment briefly as a teacher, he began to assist his father in speech training.

When two of Alexander's brothers died of tuberculosis, the Bell family decided to leave Scotland for a healthier climate. They chose Brantford, Ontario, and settled there in 1870. By 1873 Alexander had become such an expert in voice training that, at the age of twenty-six, he was appointed professor of vocal physiology at Boston University.

Vocal physiology is the study of the ways that the human body produces speech and other sounds. Alexander Bell's studies in this field had led him to consider various mechanical means by which human speech might be recorded, projected, and transmitted. During the summer vacation he took in 1874 at Brantford the idea of transmission by wire—the basic idea of the telephone—occurred to him and he worked on it at Boston University with a repair mechanic named Thomas Watson, until in 1876 they were able to put the invention into practice. The first long-distance telephone conversation in history took place between Brantford and Paris, Ontario, a distance of eight miles.

In his application to patent his invention, Bell described it as: "The method of, and apparatus for, transmitting vocal or other sounds telegraphically... by causing electrical undulations, similar in form to the vibrations of the air accompanying the said vocal or other

Alexander Graham Bell in 1913 during his final, most imaginative phase.

sounds." Other inventors who had been trying to use the electric telegraph to transmit speech challenged Bell's claims, but the courts found that he was the first to devise a practical telephone and history agrees with them.

Bell was one of the great inventive geniuses of history. In 1885 he bought a property on Cape Breton Island called Beinn Bhreagh, where he spent all his summers experimenting and where eventually he died in 1922. One of his inventions was the photophone, by which he transmitted sound on a beam of light. Another was the graphophone, a system of sonic recording that rivalled Edison's phonograph. He worked on problems of sonar detection and solar distillation that still concern scientists today, and with young Canadian researchers he founded the Aerial Experiment Association and worked on various heavier-than-air craft. He designed a man-carrying tetrahedral kite as well as inventing the hydrofoil. In 1918, four years before his death, Bell and his assistants constructed an experimental hydrofoil that weighed five tons and reached a speed of seventy miles an hour. Yet for every one of the ideas Alexander Graham Bell had time to carry through to the point of achievement, there are hundreds which he conceived and simply jotted down in notebooks; many inventions that have been carried to fruition in our time were first sketched out there.

But Bell had been led to this great career of invention by a simple concern for people deaf from birth; he wanted to know how they could be taught to speak when they had heard no speech. And he devoted a considerable amount of time to helping such people. Much of the royalties he earned from his inventions were used to finance the Volta Bureau, an international information centre for the oral education of deaf people, and the American Association to Promote the Teaching of Speech to the Deaf. One of the things he remembered most proudly was the part he played in teaching the famous Helen Keller, who was born not only deaf but also blind and dumb, to speak and eventually to write.

The Great Surveyor

Everywhere in the records of western Canada during the last decades of the nineteenth century you come across the name of a minute and restless man, George Mercer Dawson. In the photographs of geographical or survey expeditions he stands there, hunchbacked and a head shorter than his companions, but emanating the strange decisiveness that made him such a natural leader on audacious expeditions. He is the Dawson after whom Dawson City on the Yukon is named. He is the Dawson whose photographs of the groves of Haida totem poles in the 1880s have become historical classics. He was a Jack-of-all-sciences, and besides being a brilliant geologist and geographer, he was a better observer of our native peoples than most professional anthropologists.

Dawson was a Nova Scotian, born in Pictou in 1849. His father, Sir William Dawson—who six years later became principal of McGill University—was a noted naturalist of the pre-Darwinian school and a friend and collaborator of the great geologist, Sir Charles Lyell. He was also a writer of prodigious energy, publishing a long series of books concerning popular science, and was a familiar figure at international scientific gatherings.

George Mercer, his son, was a sickly boy; a childhood illness halted his growth and left him with a hump on his back. But an extraordinary will power inspired that stunted frame, and as Dawson grew up he resolved not to be daunted by his father's example, but to create a life of his own as productive and as interesting.

He studied at McGill and then at the Royal School of Mines in London, England. In 1873 he was appointed geologist and botanist to the North American Boundary Commission, whose surveyors were establishing the international frontier along the 49th parallel. His work took him to the Prairies and offered him an excellent

George Mercer Dawson.

opportunity to study the natural life of that region in the days before the buffalo died off and the ploughs of the settlers irrevocably changed the ecology of the great plains. The report of these observations which Dawson published in 1875 immediately drew attention to him as a promising young scientist.

Working with the Boundary Commission whetted Dawson's appetite for adventurous travel, and when he joined the Geological Survey of Canada in 1875, he availed himself of all the opportunities it offered to extend his scientific knowledge by observation in the field. He rose up the ranks to assistant director of the Survey in 1883 and director in 1895, but these responsibilities never made him into an office-bound bureaucrat. He spent as much of his short life as he could wandering and gathering facts in the pristine wilderness of the far Canadian West. No kind of travel seemed too tiring or too perilous for Dawson. By the very frailty of his appearance he seemed to challenge his crews, so that they would work harder under him than under any of the other government surveyors who at this time charted the untravelled mountains west of the Rockies. "He climbed, walked, and rode on horseback over more of Canada than any other member of the Survey at that time," one of his colleagues remembered, "yet to look at him, one would not think him capable of a day's physical labour."

Dawson did the first intensive surveys of such vital development areas in Canada as the Peace River and the Yukon, and he was the first to draw attention to the rich coal fields on each side of the Crow's Nest Pass. He investigated the great geological formation known as the Missouri Coteau, which runs up from the United States into Saskatchewan, and he demonstrated that it originated in glacial action. He explored the interior plateaus of British Columbia and recorded much about the lives of the Indians on the Pacific Coast; his survey of the Queen Charlotte Islands was particularly valuable in this respect, since it provided the first thorough account of the great culture of the Haida Indians. In 1892 Dawson spent a year investigating the sealing industry in the Bering Sea and preparing a joint report with Sir George Baden-Powell.

Dawson was extraordinarily modest about his great achievements. While his father published a veritable flood of books aimed at a popular audience, Dawson allowed his most valuable observations to be recorded in documents that never reached a wide public. Yet he had earned the worldwide respect of geologists and geographers and anthropologists by the time the flame burnt out in his frail body and he died in 1901 in his early fifties. He was one of the most important of the men who described and defined our vast land and, in that sense, gave Canada to us.

Poet of the Canadian Land

It was in the Maritimes, at the settlement of Port Royal which later became Annapolis Royal, that the first Canadian poetry was written. It was written by a Frenchman, Marc Lescarbot, who lived in Acadia between 1606 and 1607 and who later published in Paris a book called *Les Muses de la Nouvelle France.* Thus it seems appropriate that the first really original Canadian poetry written in the English language should also have come from the Maritime region. For the earliest great Canadian poet was undoubtedly Charles G. D. Roberts, who was born in 1860 in Fredericton, New Brunswick, a member of a large Loyalist family that had links with both New England and Oxford.

Roberts was the son of Canon George Goodridge Roberts and the brother of Theodore Goodridge Roberts, who was a poet of minor reputation. His cousin was Bliss Carman, who was perhaps even more celebrated as a poet than Roberts during their common lifetime.

Charles G. D. Roberts (left) with his cousin and fellow poet, Bliss Carman. The third member of the group, whom the two poets seem to be considering throwing off the raft, is not identified.

In 1880, when he was only twenty, Roberts published his first book of verse, *Orion, and Other Poems*, which brought him immediate and unexpected acclaim. The other young poets of the time, such as Archibald Lampman, Duncan Campbell Scott, and Bliss Carman, recognized that Roberts had at last shown that a Canadian poet could write as well in traditional forms and tones as any writer in England, and they acknowledged him as their leader.

But Roberts did more than compete with the English poets on their own terms. Having mastered nineteenth century poetic techniques, he used them to present a fresh vision of Canadian country life. He was determined to portray the Canadian countryside as it actually was and not—as earlier Canadian poets had done—as if it were a modified English setting. With books such as *In Divers Tones* (1886), which included his most famous poem, "The Tantramar Revisited", and *Songs of the Common Day* (1893), Roberts began to move Canadian poetry away from the colonial attitude that always compares the immediate environment with "the Old Country" and never sees it freshly, as it is.

As with many Canadian poets since his time, the need to make a living forced Roberts to combine writing poetry with teaching. He taught in a small school in Chatham, and in his early twenties he became principal of the York Street School in Fredericton. Then after spending a short period in Toronto editing a paper called the *Week*, owned by Goldwin Smith, he became at the age of twenty-five a professor of English at King's College in Windsor, Nova Scotia. He remained there until 1895 when, at the age of thirty-five, he abandoned teaching for good and became a professional writer.

Roberts wrote all his best poems while he was working as a teacher. When he took up writing fiction, history, and journalistic articles, the need to produce large quantities of prose in order to survive seems to have sapped his poetic energy. In 1897 he moved to New York and worked there for a decade. Then he wandered abroad for four years until he settled in England in 1911. He was already fifty-four when World War I broke out in 1914, and too old for active service, but he was accepted for training duties. Having transferred from the British to the Canadian army, in which he attained the rank of major, he was relieved of ordinary military duties to work on the official Canadian history of the war. After peace came, he remained in England until 1925; then he returned to live in Toronto until his death in 1943.

During these years Roberts turned out many books, including historical novels and romantic tales. In works such as *The Heart of the Ancient Wood* (1900) and *In the Morning of Time* (1919) he portrayed one of his favourite themes: man's attempts to become reconciled with the world of nature. These books were not very successful, but Roberts's best fictional works—the stories he wrote about wild animals—were even better known during his life than his poetry. The best of these stories, included in books such as *The Kindred of the Wild* (1902) and *The Watchers of the Trails* (1904), succeed because they help us imagine how animals feel and even think: they do not portray animals as human beings in skins. Roberts gave us in his poetry the Canada we know and experience, and in his stories he populated the countryside with its real natural inhabitants.

Populator of the Prairies

More than a quarter of the people of Canada are neither British nor French by descent, and there are large areas of western Canada where the grandchildren of immigrants from continental Europe considerably outnumber the descendants of both "founding peoples". Such groups—our own Third World of Ukrainians, Poles, Germans, Scandinavians, Czechs, and peoples of many other origins—retain many of their special traditions and make Canada one of the most intricately multicultural countries in the world.

More than any other individual, the publicist and politician, Clifford Sifton, was responsible for bringing into Canada the great migrations of central and eastern Europeans which between the 1890s and World War I created the regional way of life of the Canadian Prairies.

Sifton himself was the son of an immigrant within Canada, for his father moved to Manitoba from London, Ontario, in 1875, when Clifford was fourteen. The elder Sifton became a contractor for railway and telegraph lines and he started a family trend towards politics by successfully seeking election to the Manitoba Legislative Assembly, of which he became speaker in 1878.

Like many other Canadian political leaders, Clifford Sifton started out by studying law, but in 1888 he followed his father into politics. He was elected to represent North Brandon in the assembly, and at the age of thirty, in 1891, he had already reached cabinet rank as attorney general and minister of education in Thomas Greenway's Liberal government.

These appointments meant that Clifford was involved in the Manitoba schools controversy. The terms under which Manitoba had been established in 1870 gave French-speaking Catholics the right to operate schools with provincial grants. But Greenway's government, which believed schools should be free of sectarian reli-

Clifford Sifton.

gion, revoked the Catholics' right. Sifton represented the provincial government in the long negotiations with the federal government; the matter was finally settled with Laurier's compromise, giving the Catholics limited rights that fell considerably short of what they had demanded.

The negotiations brought Sifton to Laurier's attention, and by the time the compromise was reached in 1897, Clifford had been elected to the House of Commons and at the age of thirty-six was federal minister of the interior. It was a key post at that period, since it involved administering the vast North-West Territories, which included the lands that were to become the provinces of Saskatchewan and Alberta.

Sifton was aware that the economic progress of Canada depended on the Prairies being settled quickly; the same was true of Canada's political security, since if the Prairies remained sparsely inhabited they would be a temptation to American expansionists. He immediately launched an intensive campaign to bring in Europeans with farming experience. When he found that British farmers were not responding in sufficient numbers, he turned to Scandinavia and after that to the Slavic peoples of Russia and the old Austro-Hungarian Empire.

Sifton brought into Canada the first Ukrainians, then called Galicians. He also brought in religious groups persecuted in Tsarist Russia, such as the Mennonites and the Doukhobors. These actions aroused a good deal of criticism among people who wanted to keep western Canada Anglo-Saxon. The Ukrainians and Doukhobors arrived wearing sheepskin coats, with the fleece on the inside, and Sifton's critics declared that "the men in sheepskin coats" were "the scum of the earth". Sifton defended the Slavic immigrants by arguing that they came from the Russian steppes, which were similar to the Canadian Prairies, and that this made them worth double as much as ordinary settlers. He refused to be deterred by criticism and it was his policy that made the Prairie Provinces of Canada the cultural mosaic they became and have remained.

Sifton not only defended himself in Parliament. He made sure that he also had the support of a newspaper by purchasing in 1898 the *Manitoba Free Press*, which under the editorship of John W. Dafoe became one of the great Canadian papers.

Sifton was not an unquestioning Liberal who always followed the party line. When Prime Minister Laurier made concessions to church-dominated schools in the newly founded provinces of Saskatchewan and Alberta, Sifton resigned as minister of the interior. And when Laurier in 1911 proposed a Reciprocity Treaty with the United States that Sifton thought would damage Canadian interests, he led a revolt of Liberal M.P.'s and ensured the Liberal defeat in that year's elections.

Sifton never returned to active politics, but earlier than most Canadians he understood the power of the press, and through the *Manitoba Free Press* he wielded an influence on the Liberal Party until his death in 1929. More than most people who become involved in politics, Sifton remained his own man; he was always ready to put his convictions before his career.

The Great Forecaster

Cora Hind was one of those irrepressible Victorian women who refused to accept the professional limitations that a man's world tried to force upon them. She was born—Ella Cora Hind—in Toronto in 1862, and even as a girl she rejected the stuffy conventionality of the nineteenth-century capital of Canada West. She had no desire to settle down to a humdrum married life and she refused to enter the one respectable profession that was then regarded as appropriate to women—teaching. When her relatives tried to persuade her to attend Normal School, she simply removed herself from their presence and travelled west to Winnipeg in 1882.

Cora was attracted to the profession of journalism, but none of the Winnipeg papers at that time would take a woman into their offices. Then she heard that a local distributor was intending to introduce typewriters into the city. She saw immediately that the expanding trade of the West would create a demand for good typists, so she persuaded the distributor to lend her a typewriter and taught herself to use it and to write shorthand. Then she advertised her services as the first stenographer in Winnipeg.

As she had anticipated, there was so much demand for her work that by 1893 she was able to open a typing and shorthand bureau and employ other stenographers, which left her free to make another attack on the world of journalism. This time she was known to the local editors and she expressed a willingness to accept any journalistic task to establish herself. For years the only items she published were accounts of local meetings and conventions, the humblest kind of reporting.

But Cora Hind was energetic and enterprising. She saw the need for good agricultural reporting in an area that depended on farming for its existence, and she set out to make herself an expert in the field. She began learning about agriculture in a very practical way, by establishing a marketing service for cheese and butter factories. The task took her travelling over the prairie farmlands, and after mixing with the grain growers and watching the crops

Cora Hind forecasting the harvest.

tireless weeks of looking at farmers' fields, she announced that the American experts were entirely wrong; the harvest would be between 50 and 55 million bushels. It turned out to be 54.5 million bushels. In 1905 nobody consulted the Americans; they waited to see what Cora Hind would say, and this time she was even more uncannily exact. Her estimate was 85 million bushels; the crop was 84.5 million.

Promoted to agricultural editor of the *Free Press* in 1906, Cora Hind continued to make her crop forecasts until 1933, and rarely was she more than a million bushels away from the actual count. She wrote on many other aspects of agriculture and became the best-known woman journalist of her time. Her energy seemed inexhaustible and in 1935, when she was already seventy-four, she set out on a two-year world trip to investigate agricultural developments in many countries. She died in 1942, having devoted the years of her retirement to compiling her best articles into books such as *Seeing for Myself* (1935) and *My Travels and Findings* (1939). She was a good journalist; she was also a living proof that in any field of practical knowledge—of which her crop estimates were an example—a keenly observing mind is as important as the most patient gathering of facts.

Princess and Poetess

Pauline Johnson, the poetess whose showmanship rivalled that of Grey Owl, was Indian by tradition and half-Indian by ancestry. She was born in 1862, on the Six Nations Reserve near Brantford, Canada West. The people of this reserve were Iroquois whose ancestors had remained faithful to their alliance with the British during the American War of Independence and had emigrated to Canada with other Loyalists when the war ended.

Pauline's father, George Henry Martin Johnson, was the Mohawk chief of the Six Nations: her mother, Emily Howells, was an Englishwoman from Bristol. While she was baptized Emily Pauline, the chief's daughter naturally received a Mohawk name as well; it was Tekahionwake. She was educated at the Brantford Modern School and at home her passion for reading was encouraged. What Pauline read consisted largely of the more sentimental and romantic kind of poems written in Victorian England and undoubtedly this poetry influenced her own work when she took to writing. This happened very early. She published her first poems in a New York magazine when she was twelve, and by her early twenties her lyrics were appearing widely in Canadian, British, and American magazines.

from year to year, she began to understand the factors that affected grain yields on the Prairies.

Prairie people in their turn were beginning to listen to Cora Hind when she talked about grain and livestock. She had developed a forceful personality, and she emphasized her intention to count in the man's world of the West by wearing what then seemed exclusively masculine clothes: breeches, high boots, buckskin jackets. Her reputation spread beyond Winnipeg to eastern Canada and one of the crucial days of her life came in 1898, when a Toronto firm of grain handlers invited her to estimate how that year's summer was likely to affect the wheat yields.

Cora Hind's estimate that year was remarkably accurate and this success at last gave her entry into the profession she had always wished to follow, for in 1901, when she was almost forty, she was hired by the *Winnipeg Free Press* as an agricultural reporter. The chance to prove how competent she could be in that role came in 1904 when black rust appeared in the prairie wheat fields. Little was known about the blight and the farmers turned to American experts for a forecast of the possible crop. The experts predicted a disastrously low harvest of 35 million bushels. Cora Hind decided to make her own prediction, and after returning from several

Pauline Johnson.

But the role of a poetic performer, which we associate with Pauline Johnson's name, did not materialize until she was thirty. In 1892 Pauline was invited to give a reading at an author's night at the Young Liberal Club in Toronto. The verses she recited gave a highly romanticized view of Indian traditions and so fascinated her audience that she was invited to give a second performance. For this occasion she wrote her most celebrated poem, "The Song My Paddle Sings"; the performance she gave was even more successful than the first and Frank Yeigh, the president of the Young Liberal Club, suggested that he would like to arrange a reading tour for her.

Pauline agreed and her sensational public career began. Dressed in a rather theatrical adaptation of Indian garb—or sometimes in heavily sequinned evening gowns—she performed under her Indian name of Tekahionwake. Her first tour through the towns and cities of Ontario was a success from beginning to end. In 1894 she set off on an equally well-received tour of England. Accustomed to the melodramatic theatrical style of the Victorian era, British audiences were deeply impressed by Pauline's striking appearance and by the passion with which she read.

Pauline's first book of verse, *The White Wampum*, appeared in London in 1895. The poems it contained extolled the virtues of the Indian peoples and blamed the white man for the destruction of the Indian way of life. But they were written according to the romantic conventions of the Victorian age and they have very little relation to the traditional oral literature of the Iroquois, or of any other Indian group. Yet, overwhelmed by Pauline's stage personality, those who went to listen and applaud rarely criticized the content of her poems.

From 1894 to 1907 Pauline Johnson travelled on a long series of Canadian tours, interrupted by a second visit to England in 1903. In all she crossed Canada, from Halifax to Victoria, a total of nineteen times. Most of the time, however, she was repeating herself, for during this whole period she only produced enough new poems to fill a second small volume, *Canadian Born*, which appeared in 1903. But her personality remained as intriguing as ever and the audiences always came.

In 1907 Pauline retired from touring and went to live in Vancouver. To earn a living she wrote stories for popular magazines. She also associated with the local Salish Indians, and worked with Chief Joe Capilano on a series of stories based on the tales of the Squamish tribe, whose main reservation was—and is—in North Vancouver. The stories were published in 1911 as *Legends of Vancouver* and the book still has a sale among visitors to the city. Later, in 1913, the year of her death, Pauline published two collections of greatly inferior and very sentimental stories, *The Moccasin-Maker* and *The Shagganappi*. She died in Vancouver and her monument in Stanley Park is a pilgrimage place for tourists.

Pauline Johnson was not a great or even a good poet, but her style of writing and her romantic stage presence undoubtedly appealed to the audiences of her time. She was really less important for what she created or for the way she interpreted Indian traditions than for what her great success as a stage personality tells us about the popular tastes of Canadians in the age of Wilfrid Laurier.

Imperial Traveller

Sara Jeannette Duncan was one of the first successful Canadian women journalists. She was also one of the few really good novelists to appear in Canada during the period before World War I.

Sara Jeannette was born in 1862 at Brantford, Canada West. Like most women of her time who aspired to something more ambitious that the kitchen and the nursery, she chose the principal profession then open to members of her sex, graduated from the Toronto Normal School, and took up teaching. But she had no intention of remaining a school mistress, and in her middle twenties she began to write for the Washington *Post* and later for the Toronto *Globe*. Women journalists were so rare at this period that she submitted her articles under the masculine nom de plume of "Garth Grafton" to make sure her work was accepted. When she had forced male editors to acknowledge her ability, she was able to come into the open and write under her own name; in 1888 she made Canadian newspaper history by becoming the first woman parliamentary correspondent.

The next year, in 1889, she turned into a kind of roving foreign correspondent, wandering around the world with a woman friend and sending back lighthearted and somewhat fictionalized columns. Upon her return she assembled the columns into her first book, *A Social Departure*, which was published in 1890 and subtitled, "How Orthodocia and I Went Round the World by Ourselves".

The subtitle set Sara Jeannette Duncan's tone as a witty young woman with a mind of her own, and the humour and the independent viewpoint were maintained when she took to novel writing. Her first novel, *An American Girl in London*, appeared in 1891; it was a well-polished but not very profound book which derived a great deal from Sara's own experiences as a young North American woman in Europe. In some ways, with its juxtaposition of New World innocence and Old World

Sara Jeannette Duncan.

experience, it reminds the reader of the novels of Henry James, whom Sara Jeannette Duncan greatly admired.

In 1891 Sara Jeannette Duncan married, but this did not mean she gave up her ambitions as a writer, though she did give up her profession as a journalist. Her husband, Everard Charles Cotes, a man of understanding and literary discrimination, was the curator of the Indian Museum in Calcutta.

Marriage to Everard Cotes took Sara Jeannette Duncan into a new and fascinating world, or rather, two worlds: that of the Indian people and that of their English rulers, the sahibs and memsahibs. Since the shock of the Indian Mutiny, the English rulers had isolated themselves from the country as a whole and formed a closed society in which social snobbery and personal eccentricity flourished like green plants in a hothouse.

Sara Jeannette Duncan spent over twenty years in India. Her husband's position as a museum director placed them somewhat outside both the official world of civil servants and army officers and the business world of the merchants, and this degree of distance helped her look with a delightfully ironic eye on the pretensions of the ruling class. Two of her Indian novels, *The Simple Adventures of a Memsahib* (1893) and *His Honour and a Lady* (1894) are certainly among the best and most

amusing novels written about the world of the Indian raj. Unfortunately Sara Jeannette Duncan did not have the same opportunity to observe the real India, the world of the many Indian peoples. So, while she was able to catch like a camera lens the futile life of the English rulers, she never succeeded in evoking the richness and vitality of native Indian life.

Even while she was in India, Sara Jeannette Duncan did not forget her Canadian roots. She kept well informed on Canadian affairs, and distance seemed to give her a more objective view of her own country, so that her one thematically Canadian novel, written in India, is remarkably perceptive in its exposure of the way Canadians in the Edwardian era thought and behaved. This novel is *The Imperialist*, published in 1904 and written about an election in a small Ontario town called Elgin, which is quite easily recognizable as a fictionalized version of Brantford. It is really a study of the interplay between political idealism and political realities. The hero is a supporter of the Imperial Federation movement, which really existed, and which advocated that the British Empire be turned into a great federation in which all the dominions would have equal rights with Great Britain. But such fine ideals seem very far removed from the local interests of Elgin's businessmen and Elgin's powerful church groups, and the defeat of the "Imperialist" is a foregone conclusion. It is a novel written with a sharp eye for character and a fine ear for language.

Sara Jeannette Duncan was more than a very lively pioneer woman journalist. She was also one of the first of the good Canadian novelists, and her best books, particularly *The Imperialist*, have stood the test of time so well that they are still extremely readable.

The Bird Man

Jack Miner was a school dropout who became a world-famous naturalist and a leading conservationist. He was born at Dover Centre, Ohio, in 1865, and left school the year before his family, which included twelve children, migrated north to take up an Ontario farm, at Kingsville near Windsor. He did not return to school, largely because he was needed to work on the farm and to hunt for game to supplement the family's food supply. In later years he established a small tile and brick works, but he still retained the family farm.

Jack Miner grew up an enthusiastic hunter, but gradually he realized that the once abundant wild animals and birds around Kingsville were fast diminishing in number, and that hunting could no longer be indiscriminate. Besides, as often happens to hunters, he found himself growing steadily more interested in the creatures he hunted and therefore less eager to kill them. Round about the turn of the century he helped found Ontario's first game protection association, devoted to educating people in the need to preserve the wildlife native to their forests and waterways. But he was not content with this modest effort and proposed to take his own practical steps by creating a bird sanctuary.

Miner, who rarely changed out of his baggy working dungarees and who looked far younger than his age, was already regarded by his neighbours as an eccentric. In 1904, when he dug ponds on his farm, released four clipped-wing Canada geese, and scattered grain in the hope of attracting wild Canada geese, they looked on with sceptical amusement. They continued to laugh when no geese landed beside Miner's ponds that year or for the next three years. But Jack accepted both disappointment and mockery, and in 1908 eleven geese finally dropped down from the sky into his little sanctuary. The next year thirty-two came, and the year after that nearly four

hundred. Every year the numbers grew until very soon more than fifty thousand ducks and geese were arriving annually.

Miner was not only concerned about giving wildfowl a safe haven on their migrations. He was also passionately interested in the mystery of migration itself and to solve this mystery he began an extensive program of banding in 1909. He had his first success when a mallard duck he banded in August 1909 was shot in the following January by a South Carolina doctor. Over the next six years Miner banded more than fifty thousand ducks. One of his problems was to induce hunters to return the bands, for this was his only way of charting the migration routes. He was a very religious man and it occurred to him that if he included Biblical texts on the bands this might bring a response. It was a better idea than he thought, for puzzled Inuit hunters in the far North took the bands to the local missionaries, who forwarded them to Miner. In this way he established the breeding grounds and showed that all the waterfowl nested in Canada and wintered in the United States or farther south. Later, in 1915, Jack Miner

Jack Miner releasing the first of his banded Canada geese in 1915.

94

began banding wild geese and again he was able to establish accurate patterns of migration routes. His findings eventually became the basis of the Migratory Birds Treaty between Canada and the United States.

By 1915 Miner found that the cost of feeding the ducks and geese that came to his sanctuary had risen to $6,000 a year, far more than he could afford, so he decided to earn some money as a lecturer. His lack of formal education proved no hindrance—for he had so many fascinating facts to reveal—and he became an extremely popular lecturer, using his tours to spread the idea of conservation as well as to earn money to sustain his sanctuary. But he was not only a pioneer conservationist; he was also aware, far ahead of his contemporaries, of the danger of pollution to human beings as well as to wildlife. As early as 1927 he made a public appeal to provincial and state authorities around the Great Lakes to halt the contamination of the waters by chemicals and sewage.

Though he still lived at Kingsville among the sounds of wild birds, Miner continued his lecture tours almost to the end of his life (the last one took place in 1940 when he was seventy-eight) and over the years he spoke in every major city in North America. But in these final years he was preaching conservation rather than asking for funds. In 1931 the Jack Miner Foundation was established to administer the Kingsville sanctuary and also to assist in founding two hundred sanctuaries in other parts of North America.

Jack Miner died in 1944. Three years later, in 1947, the Canadian Parliament passed unanimously the National Wildlife Act. One of its provisions was that National Wildlife Week should be celebrated each year so as to include April 10, the birthday of Jack Miner, the self-taught Canadian conservationist who solved the mysteries of bird migration.

The Lady Sourdough

Among the tens of thousands of people who were drawn to Dawson City in 1898, the great year of the Klondike gold rush, many were women. And by no means were all of them the kind of gold diggers—like the famous Diamond-tooth Gertie—who made their fortunes charming yellow dust out of the pokes of miners. Some of them went to find gold in the ground and did so. One of these women was a Chicago society lady named Martha Louise Purdy.

Martha Louise was the daughter of George Merrick Munger, a rich manufacturer in Chicago. She was born in Chicago in 1896 and had a sheltered upbringing and a convent-like education at St. Mary's College in Notre Dame, Indiana. When she was twenty-one, she married William Purdy and she seemed to settle contentedly into the gaslight and diamonds existence of a wealthy and fashionable young woman in the 1890s. But Martha Louise turned out to be far too spirited a young woman to remain content with the empty comforts her life offered. When the news of the bonanza discovered on the Klondike echoed through the United States in 1898, she was one of those who smelt the pine-scented air of liberation. She proposed an expedition to the Yukon; Purdy disagreed. So Martha Louise took off with her three children, found her way to Seattle, sailed to Skagway, and endured all the hardships of climbing the Chilcoot Pass with her youngsters and sailing down the Yukon River from Lake Bennett to Dawson City.

Martha Louise Purdy was even one of the fortunate minority who staked a claim that paid off, at least modestly. In 1899 she returned to the United States, but the Klondike fever was set in her bones, and in 1900 she came back to make the Yukon her permanent home.

In the hard competitive world of the North, Martha Louise turned into an able businesswoman and a capable organizer. She not only supervised the working of her own claim, but also managed a sawmill for several years. When her husband died in 1904, she married George Black, a Canadian who in 1912 was appointed commissioner of the Yukon.

Martha Black became a true Northerner, entering into every phase of Yukon life. During the summers she often wandered the countryside, collecting wild plants which she pressed and mounted by a process of her own that she called "artistic botany". She became eventually an authority on the flora of the Yukon, which earned her a Fellowship of the Royal Geographical Society in 1917, and in 1936 she published a standard work, *Yukon Wild Flowers*, which her husband George Black illustrated.

The Blacks moved to Vancouver for a short period from 1919 to 1921, but they returned to the North when George decided to run as parliamentary candidate for the Yukon. He was elected and represented the constituency until 1935 and during this period Martha Black gained a good deal of insight into the corruption with which her husband had to contend in the early days of Yukon political life.

By the 1930s, however, she herself had become something between a respected institution and a legend in the Yukon. When George Black was taken ill in 1935, she showed no hesitation—at the age of sixty-nine—in agreeing to contest his constituency that year. Her own popularity and George Black's reputation ensured her victory, and she became the second woman—the first was

Martha Louise Black.

Agnes Macphail—to sit in the House of Commons. She retained her seat in Parliament until 1940.

Nowadays Martha Louise Black is probably best known for the extremely lively autobiography which she dictated to Elizabeth Bailey Price and which appeared as *My Seventy Years* in 1938. It is a classic of the North, an extraordinary tale of a woman abandoning a rich and sheltered existence to risk the hardships of the Klondike. And it ends appropriately with her maiden speech in the House of Commons as the representative of the country whose rocks and plants and people she had come to love.

The Uneasy Nationalist

One of the most attractive Canadian political figures was Henri Bourassa. He was never a major leader, but he represented an idealistic strain in French Canadian nationalism that was compatible with a vision of an independent Canada in which people of different traditions could live together and strengthen each other's cultures. Often it is such men, rather than the dominant personalities of the political world, who express the deep longings that we, as a people, collectively share.

Henri Bourassa, born in 1868 in Montreal, was the son of Napoléon Bourassa, who was an architect as well as being one of the most talented nineteenth century Québec painters. On his mother's side Henri was the grandson of the Patriote leader, Louis-Joseph Papineau, and much of his childhood was spent on his grandfather's estate of Montebello. Papineau died when Henri Bourassa was three, but his tradition lingered, and there is no doubt that when Henri helped as a young man to manage Montebello and to colonize its unoccupied acres, he tended to identify himself with the old rebel of 1837.

Henri Bourassa's education was in the formal sense very irregular, but he grew up in an artistic and intellectual environment and developed an independent mind. This turn of mind ably fitted him for the roles he later assumed of an independent journalist and a politician committed to ideals rather than party platforms.

As a young man Bourassa attracted the attention of Wilfrid Laurier, the leader of the Liberal Party, and in the general election of 1896, when Laurier defeated the Conservatives, Bourassa was elected to the House of Commons. He was regarded as one of the best of the young Liberals and as likely cabinet material. There were some who thought he might eventually succeed Laurier as leader of the party.

But even this early on Bourassa had formed strong views on the need for Canada to liberate itself from the

Henri Bourassa on the porch of his summer retreat at Ste. Adele, 1912.

imperial domination of Great Britain. In 1899, when Laurier committed Canada to participating on Britain's side in the South African war, Bourassa regarded Canada's involvement as a surrender to imperialist domination. Rather than support it Bourassa publicly separated himself from the Liberals. From that time on he became an independent and a maverick, aloof from all the major Canadian parties.

Bourassa developed a nationalism of his own, but it was a bicultural nationalism. It was based on his idea that English Canadians should throw off their attachment to Britain and that they and the French Canadians should co-operate freely as two North American peoples who had shed the chains of their ancestral heritages. In 1903, with Oliver Asselin, he founded the Ligue Nationaliste. But his nationalism was very far removed from twentieth-century separatism, as he showed in a notable speech he made in 1904. In that speech he said:

> The fatherland, for us, is the whole of Canada, that is to say, a federation of distinct races and autonomous provinces. The nation that we wish to see developed is the Canadian nation, composed of French Canadians and English Canadians, that is to say, two elements separated by language and religion, and by the legal arrangements necessary for the conservation of their respective traditions, but united in an attachment of brotherhood, in a common attachment to a common fatherland.

He projected a vision very much like that idea of a loosely knit and regionally based confederation which some people of Québec, including Claude Ryan, are advocating in the 1980s.

Bourassa soon despaired of gaining anything by working in Ottawa and in 1907 he resigned from the House of Commons. Deciding to work on the provincial level, he successfully ran for election to the Québec Legislative Assembly. In 1910, to give his ideas a wider appeal, he founded *Le Devoir*, which ever since then has been the best French language newspaper in Canada, independent, anti-imperialist, loyal to French Canadian traditions, but never going as far as separatism.

Le Devoir opposed Laurier's creation of a Canadian navy in 1910 and contributed to the Liberal defeat in the elections of 1911. But the Conservative government of Robert Borden, which then succeeded to power, proved no better since it introduced conscription, opposed by the people of Québec, in World War I. Though Bourassa now had no party, his influence was very great and his newspaper provided a focal point for French Canadian resistance to the war.

Between the wars Bourassa returned to active politics, serving in the House of Commons from 1925 to 1935 and staying aloof from the more extreme nationalists; he felt they unnecessarily alienated the English Canadians, who in their own way were becoming nationalistic. But during World War II the re-emergence of the conscription issue made Bourassa draw close again to the nationalists. In 1943 he helped André Laurendeau found the Bloc Populaire as an expression of Québec opposition to Canada's automatic participation in England's wars. Shortly afterwards he retired from politics and lived in seclusion until his death in 1952. Bourassa never wished to see Canadians divided. He believed that their essential interests were the same. As André Laurendeau said of Bourassa, he "asserted in clear terms that we must be Canadians before being either Frenchmen or Englishmen".

Justice for Women

The Canadian Prairies have traditionally been the birthplace of movements that went against the political mainstream. The Progressive Party, the Co-operative Commonwealth Federation (CCF), and the Social Credit Party all emerged first in the region between Lake of the Woods and the Rockies. And it was also in the West that Canadian feminism won its first successes and found its best advocates.

One of these was Emily Murphy. Like many of the leaders of prairie society in the days before World War I,

she was born in Canada West (as Emily Gowan Ferguson). In fact she spent her first thirty-six years, from her birth in 1868 until her journey to Manitoba in 1904, in the town of Chatham on the Thames River.

Emily Ferguson came of a strict Tory family of Irish Protestant descent. Her grandfather, Ogle Gowan, was editor of the Brockville *Statesman* and later of the Toronto *Patriot*. He was a member of the Upper Canada Legislative Assembly and for twenty years he served as Grand Master of the Orange Association of British America. It was in keeping with her family traditions that Emily should be educated at Bishop Strachan School and at the age of nineteen should marry the Anglican rector of Chatham, Arthur Murphy.

Murphy was not the kind of parson who was content with a stuffy urban congregation. He spent a great deal of his time on missionary work in the rural areas, and in 1904 he and Emily, with their two daughters, moved to the recently settled Swan River district of Manitoba, where he engaged almost entirely in missionary activity. In 1907 they reached the end of their journeying in Edmonton and there Emily lived for the rest of her life.

Emily Murphy was never satisfied with the ordinary duties of a clergyman's wife, and by 1907 she had already begun a career as a writer. She had inherited her grandfather's gift for writing and observed the life around her with a sharp eye: she had started to keep a diary while she was still in Chatham and after taking a trip to Europe, Emily decided that her journals were worth printing. So in 1901 she published an account of England and Germany under the title of *Janey Canuck Abroad*. The spirit of reform which later inspired her activities was already there in her criticism of the English class system and in her vivid descriptions of the London slums. In these descriptions she stressed how women became the victims of the double curses of poverty and drink.

Janey Canuck in the West (1910) shifted attention to Emily Murphy's life at Swan River, and later books, such as *Open Trails* (1912) and *Seeds of Pine* (1914), dealt with life in the western Prairies around Edmonton. These books were all published under the nom de plume of Janey Canuck, but as Emily Murphy became a social activist in the 1910s, she published magazine articles on issues of the day under her maiden name, Emily Ferguson. Her most important later book was *The Black Candle* (1922), which concerned the crusade she was carrying on, as early as the 1920s, against illegal drug trafficking.

But Emily Murphy's principal concern in the ye just before World War I, and for some time after it, with the movement for equal rights for women. She campaigned for the property rights of married women, as

Emily Gowan Murphy.

Stephen Leacock.

well as for a women's court in which cases involving women could be heard in a sympathetic atmosphere, so that women could testify without embarrassment.

Wartime Alberta was responsive to reformist causes. In 1916 women were allowed to vote in provincial elections and in the same year the province accepted Emily's arguments and set up a women's court in Edmonton. Appropriately, Emily Murphy presided over it and she made history by becoming the first woman magistrate in the British Empire.

A similar court was set up in Calgary, presided over by Alice Jamieson. Anti-feminist lawyers, who found Murphy and Jamieson competent and uncompromising judges, attempted to unseat them by arguing before the higher courts that women had no legal status in matters of rights and privileges. The Supreme Court of Alberta rejected these arguments and thus confirmed the right of women to hold judicial office.

Emily Murphy and her feminist associates followed up this landmark decision by fighting the famous Persons Case* for the admission of women to the Senate. When the Privy Council overruled the Supreme Court of Canada in 1929 and declared that a "person" eligible for appointment to the Senate could be a woman, an even more important step had been taken towards equality of rights.

The first woman senator was appointed in 1930, and when Emily Murphy resigned her post as magistrate in 1931 it was thought she would become the second. But in 1933 her life and her courageous campaigns for the rights of women were brought to a sudden end by a fatal heart attack.

Quiet Laughter in Mariposa

By profession, Stephen Leacock was a political scientist. By vocation he was a writer, and he was celebrated not for his knowledge of political science but for his humour, for the comic stories and essays that were the products of his gently acid pen. Yet for decades Leacock combined without any apparent difficulty the serious and the light-hearted halves of his life. And he established himself securely as a political scientist before he began to reveal the humorous side of his personality.

Leacock—Stephen Butler Leacock—was born in Hampshire, England, in 1869, and came to Canada with his parents when he was six. He was educated in Ontario at Upper Canada College and the University of Toronto and then went on to the University of Chicago, where he

*The Persons Case is described in the profile of Nellie McClung.

took his Ph.D. in 1903. In the same year he became lecturer in economics and political science at McGill University. Promotion was quick for brilliant scholars in the universities of those early days, and by 1908, when he was thirty-nine, Leacock was already a professor and head of his department. He remained in that position until his retirement twenty-eight years later in 1936.

The academic side of Leacock's career was surprisingly dull for a man with such a reputation for humour. He wrote a boring basic handbook in his speciality, *Elements of Political Science*, which was published in 1906, and after that he left the subject well alone, though he did take up history and wrote six books in the field, all of them very tedious reading. One of them, however, involved the kind of incongruous situation Leacock loved to exploit when he turned to humorous writing. The book was called *Canada—the Foundations of Its Future*, and it was published in 1941, not by a firm of publishers, but by a firm of distillers—Seagrams—which made its money exporting gin to the United States during the Prohibition period.

To this day critics disagree over the real nature of Leacock's wit—the power of amusing that has survived even translation into languages as remote from his native English as Japanese and Gujarati. Some regard him as a satirist who set out to expose the faults and follies of mankind. Others treat him as a humorist who merely intended to amuse. In fact, he seems to have combined both these roles.

Leacock's first book of humour, *Literary Lapses* (1910), was distinguished by a kind of self-deprecating fun. The reader felt that Leacock was laughing at his own expectations as well as at the people who failed to meet them, and the same rather gentle spoofing characterized his next book, *Nonsense Novels* (1911). But by 1912, when he published *Sunshine Sketches of a Little Town*, which is probably his best book, Leacock was writing a different type of humour. He was beginning to attack with a sharp edge the pretensions he saw in Canadian society—the difference between what people and institutions liked to appear as and what they really were. *Sunshine Sketches* tells of the deceptions and self-deceptions that keep society moving in the sleepy little town of Mariposa, modelled on the real town of Orillia, where Leacock had his summer home. The real point of Leacock's satire in this case seems to be that without these pretenses, society would disintegrate; we need illusions about ourselves to maintain our self-respect. And Leacock shows us that the acceptance of each other's illusions is what makes it possible for us to live together.

Leacock once defined humour as "the kindly contemplation of the incongruities of life", and *Sunshine Sketches* is certainly kind in its laughter. But there are darker tones to some of Leacock's other books, such as *Arcadian Adventures of the Idle Rich*, which he published in 1914 and which is probably his best-known work after *Sunshine Sketches*. Here Leacock is satirizing the life of the wealthy plutocrats of Montreal, which was then the financial centre of Canada. And there is no doubt that his "kindly contemplation" at times gives way to anger and contempt when he exposes the selfishness that isolates the rich from the rest of humanity. At this point in his literary career, Leacock seems to be using satire as a corrective, trying to change men's behaviour by exposing them to ridicule.

Altogether Leacock published more than thirty books that hover between humour and satire. Sometimes he is quite obviously doing nothing more than trying to be funny and sometimes his efforts fail like damp fireworks. But in almost every book there are barbed attacks on institutions, prejudices, and illusions, which are masked under the self-deprecating irony that Leacock chose as his personal tone. But Leacock remains one of the most popular Canadian writers—many of his books are still in print nearly forty years after his death in 1944—because of his laughter rather than his anger. And this is because the institutions and prejudices which satirists attack tend to change or vanish with time, whereas the human foibles which humorists mock are always there within all of us. These foibles are part of our nature as men and women, and to laugh at our own faults helps us to live with them.

The Laughing One

Nowadays Emily Carr's painting seems as important to our mental picture of Canada as the work of the Group of Seven. Like most great landscape artists, she taught us to see in our environment things we had never imagined, and in this way she changed our perceptions of the world. Yet few artists have waited so long to be recognized. We now remember Emily Carr as a great painter and a fine writer. Yet the first major exhibition of her paintings was not held until she was fifty-six, and her first book was not published until she was seventy, four years before her death.

Until receiving this late recognition, Emily Carr had been regarded by people in her native city of Victoria as an eccentric ageing woman who kept a ramshackle boarding house, bred sheep dogs for sale, made pottery decorated with Coast Indian designs for the tourists, and did her shopping with a perambulator whose passengers were monkeys, cats, and dogs.

Emily Carr's own view of that life in Victoria was recorded in the autobiographical volumes she wrote in her later years, such as *The Book of Small* (1942), *The House of All Sorts* (1944), and *Growing Pains* (1946). That life began in 1871, when she was born the daughter of a Victoria merchant. Her mother died when she was twelve and her father when she was fourteen. She grew up under the control of a strait-laced and detested elder sister until she broke free to study art in San Francisco.

Emily did not get a great deal from the academic training she found in San Francisco. It was not until she returned to Victoria in 1895 and made a visit to the Indian villages on the west coast of Vancouver Island that she discovered the landscape and the way of life that would provide the content for a life of painting. In these villages she did her first sketches of the Coast Indians and their vanishing totemic art, and tried to capture on whatever surface was available—paper, cardboard, or canvas—the feeling of the dense primeval rain forests of the Pacific Coast.

Later Emily Carr went to England, where she saw Queen Victoria's funeral, studied at the Westminster School of Art, and painted in Cornwall. She returned to Canada in 1904, but, though she was now in her middle thirties, she still felt she had not learnt enough to paint what she wanted. So in 1910 she went to Paris and studied at the famous Académie Colarossi. But apart from a little technique, European art did not have a great deal to teach her. What she saw in the landscape of British Columbia was a very personal vision, and she had to invent her own way to express it.

By the age of forty, it was quite evident to Emily Carr that she could not make a living by painting, and when she returned to Victoria in 1911 she was forced to turn her home into a boarding house and find other ways to eke out a living. For fifteen years the only opportunities she had to paint as she wished were during the summer vacations she took to work among the Indians of the Queen Charlotte Islands and the Skeena and Nass rivers. In the deserted native villages, with their decaying carvings, she found herself as a painter, developed her special range of colour, and learnt to convey the strange alternations of shadow and light which characterize the coastal world.

Though they never knew it, the Indians opened for her a way to recognition. When the ethnologist Marius Barbeau was working in northern British Columbia, they told him of the strange white woman who came to paint in their villages. On his way home, Barbeau made a side trip to Victoria to call on Emily. He was impressed by her paintings and on his return to Ottawa he talked of them to Eric Brown, then director of the National Gallery. Brown

Emily Carr, round about 1916.

travelled west, was as impressed as Barbeau, and that year arranged an exhibition in Ottawa. It was Emily's first major show, and a highly successful one, praised by the Group of Seven, who welcomed Emily Carr like a sister. The stimulus enabled her to return to painting with renewed vigour, and during the decade that followed she painted the great interpretations of the coastal forest which are now regarded as her finest work.

In 1937 Emily Carr found that she was suffering from heart disease and would have to conserve her energies. Up to that time she had continued to make her arduous summer trips to the Indian villages; now she had to give them up. But her creative urge would give her no rest, and when she could not express herself fully in painting, she turned to writing. First she related, in *Klee Wyck*, her memories of encounters with Indians; published in 1941, *Klee Wyck* was immediately recognized as a highly original work and was awarded the Governor General's Gold Medal. In her later books, Emily Carr wrote evocatively of her childhood and young womanhood in Victoria. Two of them, *The Book of Small* and *The House of All Sorts*, were published while she was still alive; the last,

Growing Pains, appeared a year after her death in 1945. There are not many artists who are as successful with words as they are with visual images; Emily Carr, like William Blake, was one of them.

The Holy Terror

The most striking personality among the pioneers of the movement for women's rights in Canada was undoubtedly Nellie McClung. She was born as Nellie Letitia Mooney, the daughter of a farmer in Chatsworth, Ontario. When Nellie was seven, her father was attracted by the promise of free land in the Prairies, which were just opening up to settlement, and in 1880 the family began farming in the Souris Valley about thirty miles from Brandon.

From this time on Nellie Mooney never lived anywhere but in the West, though her public activities were to take her all over Canada as well as to other countries. She began this career of public service by taking up the one

Nellie McClung.

profession open to women at that time; after attending the Winnipeg Normal School, she began to teach in a one-room school near Manitou. In 1898 she gave up teaching when she married Robert Wesley McClung, a young Manitou druggist who later became an insurance agent.

For almost a decade Nellie McClung was content with the life of a housewife in a small prairie town. But in 1907 she became inspired by the great crusade against drinking that was sweeping the Prairies, and she joined the Women's Christian Temperance movement. For the rest of her life she remained a fervent advocate of Prohibition, which she believed was the only cure for the heavy drinking that caused so many of the social ills of the Prairies and that particularly brought unhappiness to the wives and children of drunkards.

She soon realized that the fight for temperance and the fight for women's rights were closely linked. When her husband was transferred to Winnipeg, she joined the Political Equality League there, and when he was moved to Edmonton in 1914 she continued to work for her two causes. She developed into an aggressive and flamboyant orator, and became very popular on the public speaking circuit which took her over the entire Canadian West. Her motto was: "Never retract, never explain, never apologize", and she became known as the "Holy Terror". She reinforced her success as a public speaker by writing a great variety of books to spread her gospel to a wider public.

In many practical ways the activities of Nellie McClung and her associates were highly successful. In Alberta, her home province, women were allowed to vote in 1916, and in 1921 Nellie herself was elected as a Liberal to the provincial legislature. In 1927 she became involved, with Emily Murphy (the first woman magistrate in the British Empire) and three other women, in the precedent-setting "Persons Case". The case arose over the definition of the word "persons" in the clause of the British North America Act relating to appointments to the Senate. Canadian governments up to that time had interpreted "persons" as meaning exclusively "men". Nellie and her associates petitioned the Supreme Court for an interpretation that would include women. The court decided against the petitioners, who carried the case to the Privy Council in London, which was then the court of final appeal in disputes over constitutional questions. This time the appeal succeeded and in 1929 the Senate was finally opened to women.

Nellie McClung never entered the Senate, but she was given other appointments that broke precedent in favour of women. In 1921 she was selected as the first woman delegate to a Methodist world congress, which was held in London. In 1936 she was appointed to the first Board of

Governors of the newly founded Canadian Broadcasting Corporation. In 1938 she was a member of the Canadian delegation to the League of Nations and she served on the League's committee for social legislation.

As a writer Nellie McClung was very popular in her day. Her first novel, *Sowing Seeds in Danny*, went into seventeen editions and sold a hundred thousand copies. Her great fund of energy enabled her to write seventeen books, including novels, short stories, and essays. Although she wrote in a lively manner, nowadays her books seem sentimental, sanctimonious, and rather shallow. The most interesting to a modern reader are two volumes about her own life, *Clearing in the West* (1935) and *The Stream Runs Fast* (1945). Apart from telling of the causes for which she worked so hard and so successfully, these books depict with a good deal of vividness the prairie society of the pioneer years.

When she was seventy, in 1943, Nellie McClung decided that she had struggled enough and so retired to Victoria, where she died in 1951. Her fate has been that of many reformers, whose books no longer interest us because many of the causes for which they speak have been won. But in her time she was a fearless fighter and a powerful influence.

Conscience of the West

In an amazing number of instances Canadians have found their way into left-wing politics through an apprenticeship in the pulpit, largely as a result of the wave of social concern that swept the Canadian churches at the beginning of the twentieth century. It produced minister-writers like Salem Bland and the novelist Ralph Connor (in real life the Reverend Charles William Gordon) who suggested that the responsibility of Christians for their fellow men must lead to basic reforms in a society that was divided into two nations: the rich and the poor. It also produced the first socialist premier in Canada in T. C. Douglas, the former Baptist minister who headed the Co-operative Commonwealth Federation (CCF) government in Saskatchewan, and the first national leader of the socialist CCF in J. S. Woodsworth, a former Methodist minister.

James Shaver Woodsworth was born in 1874 in Islington, Ontario, of a lineage of clergymen; his father and grandfather were both Methodist pastors. When James was a child, his father joined the great trek westward that followed the laying of the CPR tracks and he became a missionary at Portage la Prairie in Manitoba. James attended Wesley College in Winnipeg and finished his education at Victoria College in Toronto, the mecca of Canadian Methodist scholarship. He followed the example of his forebears and was ordained a minister in 1896.

Woodsworth first served as pastor in Winnipeg and then in Revelstoke, British Columbia. But he served with growing uneasiness for he felt the Church was not adapting its message to the needs of the modern age, with its great divergences of poverty and wealth. He felt it was the Church's duty to set right such injustices and in 1907 he proposed to resign his ministry.

He was persuaded to stay on and take charge of the All People's Mission in Winnipeg. This work brought him into contact with the most destitute people in the city, many of whom were unskilled immigrants unable to earn a living in their new country. The need to do something more than preach to such people haunted Woodsworth and in 1908 he published a scholarly but also compassionate study of their condition, *The Strangers within Our Gates*. Two years later, in *My Neighbour*, he stressed more strongly the social obligations implied in Christian teachings.

Woodsworth was rapidly moving out of the orbit of formal Christianity. In 1912 he resigned from the All People's Mission to become field secretary of the Canadian Welfare League. In 1916 the three Prairie Provinces set up a joint Bureau of Social Research to investigate the persistence of poverty and Woodsworth was appointed director, only to be sacked in 1917 because he opposed Canadian participation in World War I and spoke out against conscription. He found a post in a mission at Gibson's Landing, British Columbia, but was again sacked, this time for helping to organize a co-operative. He resigned finally from the Methodist ministry and found work as a longshoreman in Vancouver.

Yet he kept his links with the Prairies and in 1918 he helped to organize a radical farmer's group, the Non-Partisan League, in Alberta. He was present during the General Strike in Winnipeg in 1919, and was arrested for the speeches he made, but was released when the case against another of the strike leaders was thrown out of court. From this point on he dedicated his life to the labour movement.

In 1921 Woodsworth entered the House of Commons as a labour member for Winnipeg North; he retained the seat until his death in 1942. They were important years for the Canadian political left. In the early days Woodsworth often had to fight virtually alone in the House for necessary reforms, but his eloquence and obvious honesty gave him a great moral influence. So he was successful in winning better conditions for industrial and farm workers and in shaming Mackenzie King's government into passing the first federal old age pension legislation. He formed alliances with other labour members and with the farmer radicals of the Ginger Group, and from these alliances emerged in 1932 the CCF, the first Canadian social-democratic party. Woodsworth was president and leader of the party when it won seven seats in the 1935 election.

Woodsworth was a convinced pacifist, and in 1939 his was the only vote cast in the House of Commons against Canadian entry into World War II. His fellow members of the CCF disagreed with him but respected his convictions, so he remained president of the party, and his constituents, who supported the war but loved Woodsworth, returned him in the next election. He did not live to see the peace. In 1940 he suffered a severe stroke and retired from active politics; in 1942 he died. Of all Canadian political leaders Woodsworth was the most respected, for his intelligence and his integrity. Other party leaders listened always when he spoke, and his influence on Canadian life extended far beyond the tiny party he led. He showed that even in politics, which we usually consider an amoral kind of activity, moral power can still be made to count.

James Shaver Woodsworth at the time of his wedding.

An Island Idyll

The best children's books are those that can still be read and enjoyed after one grows up. They deal with the process of awakening to the meaning of life, which interests people of all ages. Books of this kind are very rare and *Anne of Green Gables*, an idyllic portrayal of youth in Prince Edward Island long ago, is one of them.

L. M. Montgomery, whose name appears on the title page of *Anne of Green Gables*, was Lucy Maud Montgomery. She wrote many other books, but none of them struck the imagination of children and adults in the same way as *Anne of Green Gables*, which reflected a great deal of the setting and atmosphere of Lucy Maud's own childhood.

Lucy Maud was born in 1874 at Clifton on Prince Edward Island. Her mother died when she was very young and she grew up on her grandparents' farm at Cavendish. The country around Cavendish is typical of the red-earth agricultural land of the island; the beaches and the rocky northern shore were not far away, and as a child Lucy Maud absorbed the feeling of country life in the days before machines had taken control of rural existence.

Early on in her life, Lucy Maud showed a passion for reading; she began to write verse in her teens and eventually published a poem in the local newspaper. Then, when she was training as a teacher at Prince of Wales College in Charlottetown, she sold her first piece of writing, a short story, for which she was paid five dollars. By this time she had decided that writing must be her career, and after a spell at Dalhousie University, she joined in 1901 the staff of the *Daily Echo*, a Halifax newspaper. But this work as a journalist came to an end when her grandmother became ill and she had to return to Cavendish to look after her. So Lucy Maud put her college training to use and taught in the local school.

All this time, while working as a journalist and while teaching, she continued the work that really interested her, writing stories and poems, and she published many of them, mainly in American magazines. There was nothing very original about her work at this time. She followed the formulae that made stories acceptable to popular magazines, mixing romance and sentiment as her main ingredients.

And then she hit on the idea for *Anne of Green Gables*. In 1904 she was invited to write a serial for a juvenile newspaper. While she was thinking of a plot, she came across a newspaper clipping that she had put aside because the heading intrigued her. It ran: "Elderly couple apply to orphan asylum for a boy; by mistake a girl is sent to them." She herself had been an orphan, and this was

Lucy Maud Montgomery.

why the situation had appealed to her as a good plot for a story. After thinking it over, she decided that instead of wasting the idea on a serial, she would use it for her first book.

The result was *Anne of Green Gables*, a book whose appeal has lasted for three quarters of a century and has survived adaptation for the stage and for television. It is one of those clear and joyful visions of childhood, set in an unspoilt world, that haunt the imagination, particularly in an age when the world has become crowded and hurried and noisy with machines. Today *Anne of Green Gables* has become part of the mythology through which Canadians see their past.

The timeless quality of *Anne of Green Gables* comes, at least in part, from the faithfulness with which the book portrays not only the life but also the mood of the time to which it belongs. It has the feeling of a lost paradise because it was written in and about a rural countryside where traditional values were still accepted and did not seem to be threatened. It is hard to imagine a book such as this being written after 1914, when World War I changed our view not only of the human future, but also of human nature itself.

Because it enshrined so much of Lucy Maud Montgomery's own childhood, *Anne of Green Gables* was the kind of success that could not be repeated. But Lucy Maud went on writing nevertheless. Anne's adventures were taken up in a series of books which ran to seven further volumes, and a variety of other novels for girls were undertaken. All these books were popular in their time and sold widely. But none of them had quite the same freshness of appeal that strikes one even today on reading *Anne of Green Gables*.

While all these books were being written, there were considerable changes in their author's life. Lucy Maud was able to give up teaching, and in 1911 she married a Presbyterian minister, Ewan MacDonald, and with him she moved away from Prince Edward Island to live in Ontario. But marriage and motherhood—she had two children—did not stop her from writing. She published book after book; *Anne of Ingleside*, the last of the series, appeared in 1939, thirty-one years after *Anne of Green Gables*. Her books were published all over the world, but they always concerned life in Prince Edward Island. After Lucy Maud Montgomery died in 1942, the house where she had lived with her grandparents in Cavendish was preserved as a national monument.

Finding the Colours of Canada

It was when the Group of Seven looked at the Canadian countryside with a fresh eye and applied to the landscape the new techniques of light and colour developed by European painters, that modern art began in Canada. A true Canadian school of painting appeared then and changed our way of looking at our own land. But the man we most often associate with that movement was never actually a member of the group. He is Tom Thomson, whose great paintings, *The West Wind* and *The Jack Pine*, seem in their brilliance of colour and concept to project all that was vital in the group's approach to Canadian landscape. By the time that the Seven emerged as a group and exhibited together, Thomson had been dead for three years. Yet he was so close to the Seven, and influenced them so much, that it would have been a Group of Eight if he had not drowned in the summer of 1917.

Tom (Thomas John) Thomson was an Ontario farmer's son. He was born in 1877 at Claremont, but shortly afterwards his father moved to a farm at Leith, near Owen Sound. Tom's childhood was spent on Georgian Bay, and there, among other things, he learnt to become a first-rate boatman. He had very little formal education, and as he did not want to become a farmer like his father, he started his working life as apprentice to a machinist at Owen Sound. He found the work tedious and left to study at a business college in Chatham, but he quickly realized that he was no more suited for the office desk than for the work bench. The Thomsons were a restless family, for two of Tom's brothers had wandered off and worked their way westward until they finally settled in Seattle. There Tom joined them in 1901.

In his youth Tom's one enduring interest had been painting and drawing, which he had taught himself. So when he found a job as draftsman in a firm of Seattle photo-engravers, he realized that he had at last established a direction for his life. In 1905 he returned to Toronto, still interested in draftsmanship, and in 1911 he made perhaps the most important decision in his life when he joined the famous commercial art firm, Grip Limited.

Grip employed many artists and some of them had ambitions that went far beyond the commercial studio. Two were men who became great names in Canadian art and founding members of the Group of Seven: Arthur Lismer and J. E. H. MacDonald. They encouraged Tom to share their aim of presenting a new image of the Canadian landscape and under their influence he took up oil painting. Almost equally influential was an artist who is now remembered only for his connection with more famous men: it was Tom McLean who told Tom Thomson about the dramatically beautiful country of the Canadian Shield, which centred on Algonquin Park in northern Ontario.

In the summer of 1912 Thomson went for the first time to Algonquin Park. He was fascinated by the geological formations there and the vivid colouring of the vegetation. From sketches made on that tour he prepared the painting, *A Northern Lake*, that brought him his first recognition. The Government of Ontario bought it, and the painting earned him the friendship of Dr. James MacCallum, who encouraged him and helped him financially.

By May 1913, Thomson gave up his job and became a professional artist, living by the money he made from his paintings. In winter he worked in Toronto, first in a small shack behind the Studio Building, and later in the Studio Building itself, where he shared a room with another young painter, A. Y. Jackson. In the summers Thomson

Tom Thomson.

went to paint at Canoe Lake in Algonquin Park, where he sometimes eked out his funds by working as a forest ranger.

Thomson had three years of remarkable productivity left to him. All his important canvases—which we now regard as among the great treasures of Canadian painting—were painted between the spring of 1914 and the summer of 1917. In July of that year he disappeared on Canoe Lake. His craft was found, empty, and later on his body floated to the surface of the lake. A mystery still overshadows his death. Thomson was both an expert canoeist and a good swimmer, and it seemed unthinkable that he should have died accidentally. Murder has always been regarded as a possibility, but no clues have been found that satisfactorily explain how Thomson died or identify a possible murderer. All we can say for certain is that Tom Thomson's death in 1917, at the height of his powers, cut short the most promising career in the whole history of Canadian art.

Bible Bill

Social Credit has a strange history. It originated in the mind of a British engineer, Major C. H. Douglas, who evolved a theory that the social injustices he saw in the world were not due to factories and railways and other sources of wealth being in private hands, as the socialists argued. These injustices, according to Major Douglas, were due instead to the fact that most of the people did not have enough purchasing power. He argued that it would be possible to calculate the productivity of a nation, and then to print vouchers to the equivalent amount and distribute them as a national dividend equally shared among the population.

Major Douglas's ideas appealed to many British and American poets and writers, including T. S. Eliot and Ezra Pound. But it was only in New Zealand and Canada that political parties emerged which carried the name of Social Credit. And only in the Canadian provinces of Alberta and British Columbia have such parties held power for long periods of time. In both provinces the original doctrine of Major Douglas has been greatly diluted; Social Credit in political practice has resulted in safe and conservative economic and social policies.

The first Social Credit government in the world came into power in Alberta in 1935. The man who led the Social Crediters to their landslide victory in that year's election was William Aberhart, who was already well known in Calgary as "Bible Bill".

"Bible Bill" was born in Hibbard, Ontario, in 1878; he went to Queen's University and after graduation in 1906 he taught school in Ontario until 1910, when he moved to the greener pastures of Alberta. There he rose quickly to the position of principal of Crestwood Heights High School in Calgary. But Aberhart had other things on his mind than education. He was a religious zealot, a fundamentalist who believed that every word of the Bible must be taken as literal truth, and in 1918 he established a combination of church and school called the Calgary Prophetic Bible Institute. There he gave classes in the interpretation of the Bible.

Aberhart recognized early on the importance of the new information media emerging after World War I, and during the 1920s he set out to broaden his religious following by instituting a "Back to the Bible Hour" for a local radio station. From this time on, Aberhart's influence was no longer restricted to Calgary. He gained a regular audience of people on remote farms in every corner of Alberta. It was a following that gathered round him when he turned to politics, which meant Social Credit.

Aberhart did not actually introduce Social Credit to Alberta when he began in 1932 to insert a simplified version of the political doctrine in his radio talks. Major Douglas had come to Canada in 1923 to address the House of Commons Standing Committee on Banking and Commerce and he had made a great impression on some of the M.P.'s who belonged to the United Farmers of Alberta. When they returned to their constituencies they began to distribute Social Credit literature. Thus the ground was prepared when Aberhart entered upon the scene. By 1932 the Depression-ridden farmers were ready to accept any new gospel that seemed to offer a solution to the world financial disaster in which they had become entrapped.

At this time the provincial government was in the hands of the United Farmers of Alberta. Aberhart tried to persuade the government to endorse a modified version of Social Credit, but the party leaders refused to commit themselves and Aberhart hurriedly organized a Social Credit Party of his own. To the astonishment of everyone but "Bible Bill", who believed in the intervention of Divine Providence, the new party won a landslide victory in the provincial elections of 1935, taking fifty-six seats out of sixty-three.

Aberhart had stood outside the fray; he did not contest a seat. But a Social Credit government without "Bible Bill" was unthinkable; one of the successful candidates resigned, Aberhart won the by-election, and he became premier.

It was hardly a victory for Social Credit, which most of the electors understood even less than Aberhart; it was a

William Aberhart inspiring the faithful.

cry of despair at the failure of the other parties to solve the problems of the Depression years. Aberhart tried to institute monetary reform in various ways, promising a $25 a month "dividend" to every Albertan and proposing a local currency called "prosperity certificates". But the federal courts disallowed all these proposals. Aberhart was forced to rely on conventional measures of economizing in government spending until the Depression ended and oil discoveries brought a prosperity for which Aberhart and his successors took the (Social) credit. Aberhart was still unchallenged premier of Alberta when he died suddenly in Vancouver in 1943. His party was so strongly entrenched that it kept power for another twenty-eight years.

All Golden Lads and Lasses Must...

Émile Nelligan was the most romantically tragic of all the Canadian poets. He was also one of the best Canadian poets. Like those golden boys of European poetry, Thomas Chatterton and Arthur Rimbaud, he had a genius that blossomed and faded early. By the age of twenty his career as a poet was already at an end. If Louis-Honoré Fréchette represented the peak of the classical tradition in French Canadian poetry, Nelligan represented the beginning of the modern tradition in Canadian poetry as a whole.

A mon ami Albert Lozeau, ce
portrait du grand Nelligan.
   Tous trois, nous avons adoré
la Poésie; nous l'avons
adoré, puisqu'elle
est divine. Est-ce
pour cela que
nos trois nous
se rencontrent
ici, ou bien
est-ce
parce que le
malheur
nous a
frappés
tous trois?
   Charles Gill

Émile Nelligan.

Nelligan was the son of an Irish doctor who had settled in Montreal and a Québecois mother. He was brought up in an almost completely French Canadian setting and educated in Montreal at the Collège Sainte-Marie, where he was a reluctant student in every subject except literature. This was mainly because he had become passionately devoted to poetry and impatient of any other studies. By the age of fourteen he had discovered the great French Symbolist poets, Charles Baudelaire and Paul Verlaine. In comparison with anything being written in Canada at the time, their work was highly innovatory, and under their influence Nelligan began to develop in directions quite different from those taken by the poets then accepted in Québec.

He started to produce poetry seriously at the age of fifteen and for the next five years he wrote with enthusiasm and intensity. At first he saw himself as a solitary poet—the only one in his corner of time and place who understood what the great poets of Europe were writing. But he later encountered two kindred spirits, Jean Charbonneau and Paul de Martigny. They were law students who had also discovered the modernist poetry being written in Paris, and they and Nelligan decided to imitate the French example by founding a "school" of poets, a group dedicated to developing a particular kind of writing.

They called their group the École Littéraire de Montreal; it was comprised of young critics as well as poets who met regularly at the historic Château de Ramézay in the old quarter of Montreal. As well as Nelligan, the group included many poets who are now recognized as the pioneers of modern writing in Québec: Charles Gill, Albert Lozeau, Louis Dantin, and Gonsalve Desaulniers. A kind of mutual excitement inspired them and together they produced a kind of poetry quite unlike anything previously written in Québec. It was cosmopolitan in the sense of being highly conscious of what was being done in Europe at the time, but it was genuinely experimental in form and theme.

The other poets recognized Nelligan's extraordinary brilliance, and the portrait reproduced here was given by Charles Gill to Albert Lozeau as a memento of their friendship with him. Nelligan's reading of his great poem, "La Romance du Vin", at the Château de Ramézay stimulated such enthusiasm that the event has been regarded as one of the key stages in the development of modern Québecois literature.

Another poem by Nelligan that has enjoyed a great reputation is "Le Vaisseau d'Or"—"The Golden Ship"—a poem filled with great sadness and foreboding. The last lines seem to anticipate Nelligan's own tragic fate:

Qu'est devenu mon coeur, navire déserté?
Hélas, il a sombré dans l'abîme du Rêve!

"What has become of my heart, abandoned ship?/Alas, it has foundered in the abyss of dreams!"

And Nelligan's mind, if not his heart, did founder. Many of his poems revealed a mind in torment and as it turned out this was no mere pose of romantic agony. From childhood, Nelligan had shown strong depressive tendencies and in 1899, before he had even reached his twentieth birthday, his mind broke down completely. He wrote no more. But he lived on, in a series of mental institutions, into his early sixties. He died in 1941. During those four decades of silence the light never seemed to shine in his mind. When his first book of poems was published in 1903, with an introduction by his friend and fellow poet Louis Dantin, he understood neither what he was being shown nor what he was being told. He had indeed foundered in the abyss of dreams!

Yet if Nelligan forgot that he had ever been a poet, the world did not. The poems which this youth of genius produced during the brief but intense years of his writing life have become classics, not only of Québecois literature but also of French literature. His memory is as greatly honoured in Paris as it is in Montreal—and of few Canadians can that be said.

Icelander in the Land of Ice

No man learnt or applied John Rae's innovatory methods of Arctic travel more thoroughly than Vilhjalmur Stefansson, perhaps the greatest of all the Canadian explorers. Not only did Stefansson travel by living off the land, as Rae had done; he also shared the lives of the Eskimo themselves over long periods and learnt from experience how superbly their hunting culture was adapted to its special environment.

Stefansson was of the same breed as the Viking explorers who discovered Canada round about A.D. 1000. He was of Icelandic origin and was born in 1879 at Gimli, the Norse settlement on Lake Winnipeg. Two years later his family moved to North Dakota and as a young man Vilhjalmur went to the University of North Dakota and then on to Harvard. After graduation he travelled to his ancestral country, Iceland, to study anthropology. His first opportunity for real field work came in 1906, when he was appointed anthropologist to the Anglo-American Arctic Expedition led by Leffingwell and Mikkelsen.

His involvement in the expedition was a story of

Vilhjalmur Stefansson at the sailing of the Karluk *from Esquimalt harbour.*

hunters; he never starved and he became an expert hunter of seal, polar bear, and barren land caribou.

While he was on this expedition Stefansson discovered the famous Copper Eskimo of Victoria Island. They were a tall and fair-skinned people, often with reddish hair, and Stefansson was convinced that they were descended from the Norsemen of Greenland. As a result of this expedition he was able to describe the daily life of the Eskimo with an intimacy that had been unknown in accounts of the Canadian North. Books such as *My Life with the Eskimo* (1913) and *Hunters of the Great North* (1922) were splendid travel narratives that introduced Stefansson to a large and fascinated readership.

In 1913 Stefansson returned to the Arctic on an expedition organized by the Canadian government to locate hitherto undiscovered islands in the Arctic archipelago, and this time he was five years in the North. The expedition began unluckily when the leading ship, the *Karluk*, drifted away and was crushed by ice in the Siberian sea. Several of the members of the expedition died of exposure. If it had not been for Stefansson's experience of Arctic living, the whole expedition might have failed at this point. Stefansson divided the party into two groups. Rudolph Anderson was left with a group of scientists from the Geological Survey to survey the Arctic coast between Coronation Gulf and the Alaskan border. Stefansson himself set off with two companions, travelling across the ice to Banks Island, and then exploring the seas northeast of Prince Patrick Island. He discovered Borden, Brock, Meighen, and Lougheed islands and thereby completed the map of the Canadian Arctic, for these were the last uncharted territories left. The expedition finally came to an end in 1918, when Stefansson was stricken with typhoid fever on Herschel Island.

Stefansson described these travels in *The Friendly Arctic* (1921), but this was not the only account. During the expedition he and Anderson had quarrelled, and Anderson had become Stefansson's bitter enemy. Upon their return Anderson started a campaign of denigration in which he blamed Stefansson for the loss of the *Karluk* (a somewhat unjust charge since Stefansson was not there when it drifted away) and accused him of unscientific procedures. Government scientists, even ministers, became involved in the dispute and Stefansson was so discouraged that he left Canada for good and never went on another Arctic expedition.

He remained interested in the far North, wrote books about other Arctic explorers as well as writing an autobiography, *Discovery*, which was published after his death in 1964. Stefansson was a great explorer and a great Canadian, driven away from us by the jealousy of smaller men.

misfortune turned to good use. When he reached the rendezvous of Herschel Island in the Beaufort Sea, Stefansson found that the expedition had been trapped in the ice about two hundred miles away, off the coast of Alaska. He transformed disappointment into opportunity by travelling and living with the local Eskimo over the winter. When he did manage to join the expedition it was about to return south to the United States so Stefansson decided to stay on the rest of the year among the Eskimo. He then made his way south to Fort Yukon. His long sojourn among the native people of the Arctic had convinced him that Europeans could survive there for long periods if only they would adopt the Inuit way of life.

Next year, in 1908, he set off with the Canadian zoologist, Rudolph W. Anderson, on a journey to Coronation Gulf and the surrounding islands, where he hoped to put his recently acquired knowledge to the test. He spent four years there, all the time living among the nomad

Summer in Jalna

Perhaps there have been other novelists who, in terms of their income from writing and the number of their books that have been sold, deserve even more than Mazo de la Roche to be regarded as the great Canadian bestseller. But Mazo de la Roche's success came early, in the 1920s, when few people expected a great deal from Canadian writing. And her reputation was remarkably widely spread. She was as popular in Britain and the United States as she ever was in Canada and for decades she was better known in France than any writer from French Canada. Her books sold in France in the millions, even after they had ceased to be popular in the English-speaking countries.

Yet Mazo de la Roche is not one of the writers whose work is usually taught in courses in Canadian writing. She was a popular writer and in some ways a shallow one. But her appeal was immense and there is no doubt that in her best-known novels, the series of sixteen books about the Whiteoaks family and their Ontario estate of Jalna, she appealed on a deep level to the dreams of many readers.

We can only suggest the reasons for the popularity of her novels by considering her life and its relation to her work. Mazo de la Roche was born in Newmarket, Ontario, in 1879. From childhood she had a special attachment to her father, William Roche (the "de la" in Mazo's name was her own romantic addition), and to her cousin, Caroline Clement, who remained her constant companion throughout her life. As children she and Caroline created an imaginary world which they called "the Play", or sometimes "the Game"; they populated this world with characters and developed episodes, and it was out of this kind of dream-play that Mazo's decision to become a writer emerged.

She was—as one critic has remarked—"a full-time writer from childhood"; the problem she faced in the beginning was not finding what to write about, but the much more practical matter of persuading editors and publishers that what she wrote was worth publishing. She was educated at schools in Galt and in Toronto; she then went on to the Parkdale Collegiate Institute in Toronto and to the University of Toronto, where she studied art. But all this time she was busily writing and in 1902 her first story appeared in *Munsey's Magazine*. It was not until 1915, when another story appeared in the *Atlantic Monthly*, that her fiction was printed in an internationally recognized journal. During the 1920s she published a volume of short stories and two novels, *Possession* and *Delight*, but they were not widely read and she made very little money from them. She depended on her small private means for survival until she finally struck the vein of popular success in 1927.

In that year her novel *Jalna*, the first of the famous series, won the first $10,000 *Atlantic Monthly* fiction award. Within three months of winning the award, it had sold one hundred thousand copies in the United States alone, and Mazo de la Roche's career was assured. Eventually, including translations, *Jalna* sold nine million copies in hardcover.

Jalna was the product of Mazo's long experience of the rural landscape in Ontario and the romantic fantasies she had cultivated in those childhood games with Caroline Clement. She had lived for some time on a fruit farm in southern Ontario; it was a district where there were many large estates whose owners actually earned their living, not from the soil, but from businesses in Toronto. Later she gained a more intimate view of this kind of life when she stayed in a cottage on one such estate near Clarkson, Ontario. She felt very strongly that the house and the land had been divorced from their original purpose of farming and she felt that the people who inhabited the house were in their turn cut off from the basic realities of existence. She tried out this theme in *Possession*, which appeared in 1923 and which concerns a city man who inherits a fruit farm and fails. Mazo's evocation of the countryside and even of the house in *Possession* was quite successful, but the characters were not convincing.

Mazo de la Roche.

It was in *Jalna*, when she created not only a house, but a whole dynasty of landowners that degenerates when it loosens its links with the soil, that she succeeded in writing a dramatically romantic novel which appealed to the millions. She wrote more than thirty other novels in a long career that lasted almost to her death; *Morning at Jalna*, her last novel, appeared in 1960 and she died in 1961 at the age of eighty-two. Apart from the four years she spent in England after the success of *Jalna*, Mazo de la Roche had lived all her life in the Ontario that gave her the inspiration and the material for her books.

Beaverbrook

Not many years ago we heard a great deal about the "brain drain" that was taking brilliant Canadians to the United States because they could not make careers for themselves in Canada. But within Canada there was another brain drain that had been in existence since Confederation. This one had brought many hundreds of capable young Nova Scotians and New Brunswickers, Prince Edward Islanders and Newfoundlanders, to find careers for themselves in Montreal, in Ontario, and in western Canada. Such Maritimers were frequently encountered in financial institutions and universities, but those who went into politics often found Canada too small a pool for their ambitions and they went on to success in Great Britain. Among this group were Andrew Bonar Law, who eventually became prime minister of Britain, and his fellow New Brunswicker, William Maxwell Aitken, who ended up as Baron Beaverbrook and who was the only man other than Winston Churchill to serve in the British cabinet during two world wars.

Max Aitken was actually born in Maple, Ontario, in 1879, but he was brought up in Newcastle, New Brunswick, and he always regarded himself as a Maritimer. He briefly attended the University of New Brunswick, but never took his degree, since he very soon revealed a talent for financial manipulation. He moved to Montreal, became a stockbroker, and by the age of thirty-one he had made his first fortune by engineering the merger of thirteen cement companies into Canadian Cement and by assisting in important bank and steel industry mergers. At the age of thirty-one he was able to retire from business and sail to England where he proposed to build a new career in politics.

Bonar Law was already there. Max Aitken became his private secretary, and when Arthur Balfour resigned the leadership of the British Conservative Party, it was Aitken who masterminded the intrigue that made Bonar Law his successor. Aitken himself had no difficulty getting elected to the House of Commons in 1910 and he so dazzled the British that honours came quickly to him. He was knighted in 1911, was made a baronet in 1916, and was raised to the peerage in 1917, all before his thirty-eighth birthday. For his title he chose the name of the little Acadian village of Beaver Brook, near his home town of Newcastle.

The First World War provided Beaverbrook with further opportunities for personal advancement. He was deeply involved in the 1916 plot to remove Herbert Asquith as prime minister and to put Lloyd George in his place. And later, in 1922, he helped to dissolve Lloyd George's coalition government and establish his friend Bonar Law in the position of prime minister. He himself became British minister of information in 1918. At the same time he was in charge of Canadian War Records and was responsible for commissioning the many remarkable paintings which Canadian artists executed during the war.

But already Beaverbrook had decided that real power lay in other directions than politics. He understood the influence that could be wielded through the popular press and in 1916 he acquired the *Daily Express*, around which he built up a whole constellation of papers, including the *Sunday Express*, the *Evening Standard*, and the *Scottish Daily Express*.

Beaverbrook used his papers as political instruments. He was a devoted imperialist, believing that the British Empire should be transformed into a confederation of equal states. He thought that if the empire were made into a great free trade area and raised high tariff walls against the rest of the world, then all Britain's economic problems could be solved. Even though he held no government post between the two world wars and was distrusted by the Conservative leaders in Britain, he had a great following among the ordinary people. His ideas seemed to offer a simple solution to their problems. When war broke out again he could not be ignored, particularly as Churchill, who also had been out of favour with the Conservative hierarchy, recognized in him a fellow maverick.

Throughout Churchill's wartime administration, Beaverbrook served in his cabinet. He was minister of aircraft production from 1940 to 1941, at a time when a vigorous organizer was needed to create a British air force out of almost nothing; he was minister of supply from 1941 to 1942 and lord privy seal from 1943 to 1945, when he left active politics. He was also for a while the administrator of the British lease-lend program in the United States.

When the great effort of the war ended, Beaverbrook retreated to his personal newspaper empire, but he was

William Maxwell Aitken, the young Beaverbrook.

increasingly disillusioned with the progressive break up of the other empire—the British Empire. Realizing that his power to influence affairs had dwindled in the post-war years, he retired to the English countryside. At the same time he renewed his interest in Canada, and particularly in his own province, where he built and endowed the Beaverbrook Art Gallery of Fredericton in 1957. He died in 1964 in the Surrey countryside, but it was to Canada that he left his fortune, administered by the Beaverbrook Canadian Foundation.

Operating with equal fervour through finance, politics, and the press, Beaverbrook understood more than most men in his time how power was acquired and sustained in a modern democratic society, and how the will of the people could be manipulated or ignored.

Painting the Look of the Land

Few people ever called A. Y. Jackson by his given names. To his many admirers, he was always "A.Y." Under these initials his work was known until he died in 1974 at the age of ninety-two, the dean of Canadian painters, the stubborn survivor from the great days of the Group of Seven.

Jackson was born in Montreal in 1882. As a boy he showed a talent for drawing and at the age of twelve he left school to become apprenticed to a lithographer. This work brought him into contact with artists and he soon decided to become a painter. But there was little artistic training to be had in Montreal at that time and he had to

A. Y. Jackson sketching in the Arctic.

be content with evening classes until he went on to Chicago, where he could attend a regular art school. During this period many American art students went to France to finish their training and Jackson followed their example, studying at the Paris art academies which were open to all comers who could pay a small fee. He wandered through the galleries of Europe, absorbing not only classical but also modern art. It was the period when Gauguin was most influential and the Art Nouveau movement was encouraging the use of vivid primary colours and dark sinuous outlines. Jackson's later painting showed that he absorbed such influences.

Jackson returned to Montreal excited by what he had seen in Europe. He felt that if the Impressionists had found ways to portray the French countryside with a new truthfulness and vibrancy, some artist should be able to do the same for the Canadian landscape, in a manner that was true to the land and its traditions.

Montreal was not receptive to ideas of this kind. The few artists it did produce preferred to go to Europe, often to stay and be absorbed into its artistic world. Discouraged by the attitude of his fellow townsmen, Jackson moved in 1913 to Toronto, where he had already made contact with J. E. H. MacDonald and other painters. In 1914 he shared Tom Thomson's studio. Thomson introduced him to the lakes and rocky hills of the Canadian Shield and under his influence—which lasted until Thomson's death in 1917—Jackson painted the earliest of the works by which he is now known, such as *Red Maple* (1914).

Though Jackson was already in contact with the men who were to join him in forming the Group of Seven, the group did not take formal shape until 1920. This was the year of the first joint exhibition of seven friends who shared the conviction that Canadian painting must seek out the true character of the Canadian landscape without being merely representational, as the earlier landscapists had been. A Canadian style was needed; these seven young men believed they had discovered it. The original Group of Seven—who took part in the historic 1920 show—consisted of A. Y. Jackson, Arthur Lismer, F. H. Varley, Lawren Harris, J. E. H. MacDonald, Frank H. Johnston, and Franklin Carmichael; missing was Tom Thomson who in his tragically brief career had inspired them all.

The first reaction of many Canadians to the Group of Seven was similar to that of most people faced with a new kind of art which they do not understand. They saw the paintings in terms of crude colour and tortured outline. But very soon art lovers began to recognize that by these means the painters of the Group of Seven were drawing attention to the real nature of the Canadian land, to its vastness of form and its extremities of colour as well as climate.

Not that the opinion of other people mattered very much to A. Y. Jackson, who was a remarkably single-minded painter, intent on following his art regardless of how it might be received. He continued, for years that span into decades, to wander over the Canadian terrain—to Québec, to British Columbia, to the Arctic. He painted vivid sketches everywhere and later turned them into canvases as vibrant as those he had done in northern Ontario, a region that he always returned to as the source of his inspiration.

In the late 1930s the work of the Group of Seven was finally accepted by Canadians. Their vision fitted in with the growing tendency towards artistic as well as political nationalism. By this time, however, Jackson had ceased to be a great original painter. He had become frozen in the formulae he created at the beginning of his career and his later paintings were little more than imitations of his earlier work. But he kept on painting. He worked in his old Toronto studio until 1955 and then he moved into the country at Manotick near Ottawa. There he took to the pen to write a fine autobiography. *A Painter's Country* (1958). During his last years he lived on the premises of the McMichael Collection at Kleinburg, Ontario, an artistic revolutionary who had outlived his own revolution.

Epics of Canada

One of Canada's finest poets, E. J. Pratt, was born a Newfoundlander, and long before the island colony entered Confederation in 1949, he was writing fine poems on Canadian themes, though a touch of the craggy islander remained with him to the end.

E. J. (Edwin John) Pratt was born at Western Bay in 1882. His father was a Methodist minister who travelled among the small fishing communities of Newfoundland, and Pratt's childhood was spent in a succession of outports where he learnt very early on the hardships and the compensating vitality of the fisherman's life. In his youth he thought of following his father's example and he was trained for the ministry at the Methodist College in St. John's. For a few years after graduation he worked in coastal villages such as Portugal Cove and Moreton's Harbour, Clarke's Beach and Bell Island, preaching and teaching to the Newfoundland fishermen among whom he had grown up.

In 1907 Pratt left Newfoundland to carry on his studies at Victoria College in Toronto, and he never returned to live on the island or take up again the task of the preacher. He graduated in philosophy in 1911 and gained his doctorate in theology in 1917. But E. J. Pratt was a versatile man and when he decided to become an academic rather than a clergyman, the first subject he taught was psychology, at University College. In 1920 he joined the department of English at Victoria College and there he remained until he retired in 1953.

The switch in academic disciplines was undoubtedly linked to Pratt's discovery that his real passion was not for religion or philosophy, but for poetry. It was only in poetry that he was able to express the Newfoundlander's sense of the sea as a symbol of destiny, and give words to his experience of the rugged life of the coast and outports of his native island. In 1917 he published his first book, a cycle of poems entitled *Rachel*, about a mother waiting for news of her son, who has actually been drowned at sea. *Newfoundland Lyrics*, which in 1923 established Pratt's name as a poet, ranged more widely over the griefs and joys of life in a land where men faced nature in a direct and cruel way.

Out of these early poems emerges Pratt's immense admiration for the kind of courage that makes a man put his life on the line even if the odds against him seem impossibly heavy. His admiration for the hero was even greater than his compassion for the sufferer and this was why, after his first collection of short lyric poems, he turned to the longer epic form that would allow him to work out grand stories of human audacity. But there was another side to Pratt. He also realized that the grand could easily degenerate into the grandiose. So along with his serious epics that paid tribute to heroism and endurance, he also wrote comic epics that mocked at man's pretensions to greatness.

Among these comic epics were poems such as *The Witches' Brew*, which satirized Prohibition and showed how a seemingly good idea could produce evil results if it failed to take into account such negative factors as human greed. There were other brilliant satires of this kind, in which Pratt showed an enormous power over words. But his best poems were still those which showed men fighting against great natural—or sometimes human— odds.

The Roosevelt and the Antinoe told the story of a spectacular rescue at sea. *The Titanic* was a poem about the conflict between human arrogance and the great impersonal forces of nature. These forces are symbolized

E. J. Pratt.

Conrad Kain after the first ascent of Mount Robson, 1913.

in the poem by the iceberg that destroyed the "unsink-able" ship on its first journey. Once the iceberg strikes and the liner begins to sink, attention turns to the spectacle of men face to face with death, the powerful often showing weakness and those who seemed weak showing strength and courage. In *Brebeuf and His Brethren* Pratt turns to the conflict between man and man, and tells the story of the Jesuit martyrs of Huronia and the courage with which they faced almost unendurable torment at the hands of the Iroquois. And *Towards the Last Spike* is perhaps the greatest poem written about the creation of Canada. While the poem is concerned ostensibly with the building of the CPR, it is really the story of how a nation became unified by human will imposing itself on vast distances and apparently insurmountable natural obstacles like the Rockies.

No one now writes heroic poems like those of E. J. Pratt, who died in 1962. Partly that is because we no longer take heroism as seriously as people did a genera-tion ago. But it is also partly because in his finest poems Pratt set an example of powerful writing about action which few later poets have tried to equal.

The Man from the Alps

He climbed, as another would read,
because his mind was incurably curious, . . .
and he was bred to the game.

Earle Birney, a man in love with mountains, wrote these lines in his fine poem celebrating the feats of Conrad Kain, who was probably the greatest of all Canadian mountain-eers.

Conrad Kain was born in 1883 in the village of Nasswald, eighty miles southwest of Vienna, where the land lifts upward from the plains of Lower Austria towards the mountains of Styria. His father was a miner and one of the rare Austrian Protestants; his mother was an Italian woman from Florence. When Conrad was nine his father died in a mine accident. When he was fourteen he left school, having learnt almost nothing in a class where one teacher taught a hundred children, and went to work as a goatherd in the local mountains. Later he took up work as a quarryman, an occupation he sometimes varied with poaching.

A two-thousand-metre mountain near Nasswald, called the Raxalpe, proved to be Conrad Kain's salvation from a life of labouring. Like all the young men of his village, he had been climbing mountains since boyhood, and in 1903 he began to guide Viennese climbers for payment. The next year he had to take military training, but when he returned to Nasswald he spent so much time on the mountain that the quarry owner sacked him, and he was forced to take up guiding for a living. He travelled over the whole Alpine region, climbing peaks in Austria, Italy, France, Switzerland, and even Corsica, until in 1906 he received his *führerbuch*, the official guide's passport.

Conrad carried on with this work for another two or three years. He perfected his climbing techniques, but found it hard to make more than a bare living through his skills and in 1909, thanks to a Viennese doctor named Erich Pistor, he received a promise of employment from the Alpine Club of Canada (ACC). He arrived at Banff in time to help complete the construction of the ACC clubhouse on Sulphur Mountain and then was commis-sioned as the club's first official guide. He had already shown his abilities by climbing Mount Odaray with two companions and climbing Mount Victoria alone.

During this year Kain developed a pattern of employ-ment that he was to follow in later years: he guided and surveyed in the summer, and in winter he did farm and railroad work. Once again, as in Austria, he could not live entirely by guiding. In 1911 he took part in the Yellow-head Pass expedition and was a member of the groups that made the first ascents of Pyramid Mountain and Mount Resplendent. In 1912 he joined a scientific expedi-tion sent to collect rodents in the Altai Mountains of Siberia. He then went home to Austria for the last time and sailed to Australia and New Zealand. There he found little employment, so when a call came from the ACC to take part in an attempt on Mount Robson, he responded enthusiastically. On July 31, 1913, he and two compan-ions completed the first ascent of that formidable peak; it was a task of endurance as well as skill, for in the process Kain cut no less than six hundred steps.

He returned to New Zealand, hoping to make a career there as a guide in the Southern Alps, and carried out one of the most spectacular early climbs of Mount Cook. But the New Zealanders mistrusted him—it was already wartime—because of his Austrian origin, even though he was by then a Canadian citizen. He returned to Canada in 1916, added a few more peaks to his list of achievements and then retired for a long winter of introspection and Bible reading in a cabin in the bush. He began to feel he had wasted his life on mountaineering and resolved to give up guiding.

He did not keep his resolution. When he returned to civilization in the early summer of 1917 he married a Guyanese woman named Henriquita Ferreira and shortly afterwards bought a small holding, overlooking the Co-lumbia Valley. He resumed a yearly cycle of employment: trapping in the winter, gardening and guiding in the

Davidson Black (centre) at Chou-k'ou-tien, September 10, 1927.

summer, and hunting in the fall. During the summers of 1923 and 1924 he took part in a series of spectacular climbs, including several "firsts" around the Columbia Icefield and the Athabasca Pass. These were his greatest seasons, when he was described as "the best guide that has ever been in the country".

Conrad Kain continued climbing into the summer of 1933, though by this time he had to admit occasional defeats. His wife had died early in that year and Kain began to suffer long periods of depression, complicated by loneliness. Yet it was not solitude that killed him, but encephalitis lethargica, the dreaded sleeping sickness. He died in Cranbrook hospital on February 2, 1934, mourned by the mountain men of Canada as the best of their kind.

Tale of a Tooth

The ancestry of the human race—where it came from, how it evolved—has been a subject haunting scientists ever since Charles Darwin published in 1878 his epoch-making book, *The Descent of Man*. In this book Darwin boldly asserted that man was biologically a mammal and not a special kind of being entirely outside the animal world. If man shared his physical nature with the animals, Darwin suggested, then he too must have his place in the great chain of evolution. Somehow, and at some time in history, the human species must have stemmed from one branch of the animal kingdom.

Once Darwin had made this suggestion the search

began for what was often called the "Missing Link". This was the succession of species that might link man to some ancestor that he shared with creatures such as the gorilla and the chimpanzee, which in terms of intelligence stood at the apex of the non-human animal world. It was obvious that between the brightest of chimps and the most stupid of men there was still a considerable gap. How could it be filled? Only by discovering species which in terms of intelligence and manual skills lay between the higher apes and our own species (known as *Homo sapiens)* and which may have appeared on the earthly scene about a quarter of a million years ago. But no such intermediary species exist today; they must be sought in the record of past life which the world's rocks preserve in the form of fossil remains.

A series of crucial archaeological discoveries have led to the view that there were at least two and possibly more manlike beings who differed from other animals in their ability to use their hands, make tools, and communicate by some form of speech. The farthest from man in this chain of species is *Homo habilis*, the tool-using hominid from three million years ago whose remains the Leakeys discovered in East Africa. The nearest in the chain is *Homo erectus*, who was certainly wandering the earth until three hundred thousand years ago. And in the discovery of *Homo erectus* the Canadian scientist Davidson Black played one of the key roles.

Davidson Black was born in Toronto in 1884, the son of a leading Ontario lawyer. He took up medicine as his vocation, but his avocation was always the study of man's past, and he sought to utilize his anatomical knowledge in that cause. From 1909 to 1916 he taught at Western Reserve University in Cleveland, Ohio, but he was only waiting for an opportunity to study the early history of mankind, and he eagerly accepted in 1918 the post of professor of neurology at the Peking Medical Union College. He believed that eastern Asia, which had so rich and ancient a record of human cultures, might offer some clue to the origins of man. After he was appointed professor of anatomy in 1921, he began to organize exploratory digs in the northern Chinese province of Jehol as well as in Thailand. Then, in 1927, Davidson started to excavate the site of Chou-k'ou-tien near Peking, where a series of caves were rich in relics. He found, to begin with, a single lower molar tooth that obviously belonged to some creature akin to man, yet it was highly unusual in form. On the basis of this single tooth, Black inferred, by an astonishing feat of anatomical reconstruction, the existence of an intermediate species, living about half a million years ago. He called this species *Sinanthropus pekinensis*, or Peking Man.

Excavations continued in the Chou-k'ou-tien caves,

and by 1930 Black's inferences had been dramatically confirmed by the discovery of fourteen skulls, several jawbones, some arm and leg bones, and many teeth. These enabled scientists to reconstruct a being with a large brain who walked upright and used his hands. Even more dramatic, the uses to which *Sinanthropus*—as he was still called—put his brain and hands were revealed by the stone tools, charred bones, and stone hearths that were discovered alongside his bones. It was even shown that he extracted the brains from human skulls in a way which suggested the existence of some kind of magical or religious ritual.

For many years *Sinanthropus* was regarded as a separate species. But this classification was to change to take into account another discovery made in the late nineteenth century. In the 1890s a Dutch doctor had discovered in Java a few hominid bones that were thought to establish a species called *Pithecanthropus erectus*—the Upright Ape-Man. It was Davidson Black who pointed out in 1932 the close resemblance between *Pithecanthropus* and *Sinanthropus*. Black, who died in Peking in 1934, did not live long enough to witness the merging, in scientific opinion, of the two species into one, *Homo erectus*, which seems to have originated in Africa and spread east into Asia. It was probably the direct ancestor of our own species, so curiously named *Homo sapiens*—Wise Man! Peking Man's place in the ladder of evolution is still unchallenged, whatever name he bears. And so is the achievement of Davidson Black, who inferred his existence from a single tooth!.

His Excellency . . .

The name of Vincent Massey is closely linked with Canada's coming of age as a nation during the years after World War I. He was the first native-born Governor General of the country. And as chairman of the Royal Commission on National Development in the Arts, Letters, and Sciences (which most people remember as the Massey Commission), he helped to change the very nature of Canada's cultural life.

In 1887 Vincent Massey was born into the two-family industrial dynasty which controlled the famous farm implement firm of Massey-Harris; his younger brother was Raymond Massey, who became an internationally famous actor.

Attending the University of Toronto and Balliol College in Oxford, Vincent Massey first seemed inclined to follow an academic career. For two years, from 1913 to 1915, he was lecturer in modern history at the University

Vincent Massey.

of Toronto, and while there he supervised the construction of Hart House, the cultural centre built in memory of his father, Hart Massey. This brief academic service gave Massey an understanding of the problems of scholars, particularly in the humanities, and in later years he put this to effective use. But World War I drew him away from the university community to act as a staff officer, and when the war ended he went into the family business; from 1921 to 1925 he was president of the Massey-Harris Company.

Except in financial terms, he found it unrewarding work, for his interests lay in culture and in Liberal politics, and in 1925 Mackenzie King took him into his cabinet as minister without portfolio. Massey failed to win election to the House of Commons, however, and had to give up his ministerial position. But his attendance at an imperial conference in 1926 gave him an interest in international affairs and he entered the newly formed Canadian external service at the top level, becoming in 1926 Canada's first minister to Washington. He returned to Canada in 1930 to immerse himself in party politics and he served as president of the National Liberal Federation from 1932 to 1935. As a reward for this work he received what was then regarded as the plum in the Canadian diplomatic service, the High Commission in London, which he held from 1935 until 1946.

During this time he sustained an interest in the life of the arts and scholarship in Canada; he was a trustee of the National Gallery and encouraged the arts through the Massey Foundation, which he created. When Prime Minister St. Laurent reluctantly agreed in 1949 to set up a commission to inquire into the state of cultural affairs in Canada, Massey—a hallmarked Liberal and an internationally known representative of Canada—seemed the obvious person to direct it. He and his associates on the commission recognized the importance of the arts and of scholarship in developing and defending a national consciousness among Canadians and they went about their task with great thoroughness. Their hearings, which lasted for two years before the historic report was issued in 1951, revealed a great hunger among Canadians for a better system of education and a fuller artistic life. At the same time, the hearings showed how little financial support had been received by the arts and the humanities in Canada. The main recommendations of the commission were that the universities should be generously assisted from federal funds and that a Canada Council should be set up (which was done in 1957) to encourage "the Arts, Humanities, and Social Sciences". Coming at a time when Canadians were prepared psychologically for the great cultural upsurge of the 1950s, these developments helped to change the very nature of artistic and scholarly life, which hitherto had been officially neglected and financially impoverished.

Lord Alexander was the last of the Governors General to be sent out from Britain. When his term of office came to an end in 1952, it was recognized in Westminster as well as in Ottawa that Canada's role as an independent nation demanded a Canadian representative of the Queen. Massey's diplomatic record and the prominence he had gained through his masterly conduct of the recent commission made him the obvious candidate for the role—as one writer put it—of making "the Crown Canadian".

Massey served for seven years as Governor General, and he was tireless in the task, travelling more than two hundred thousand miles through the provinces as well as through the territories of the North to familiarize himself with the country and the problems of its people. He maintained an interest in cultural affairs, and after he retired as Governor General in 1959 he devoted himself to supervising the creation of Massey College, which was built between 1960 and 1963. Providing a residence for scholars, it was designed to reproduce the kind of college atmosphere Massey remembered from his days at Oxford. He was a man to whom the forms and ceremonies of the past were as important as visions of the future. And in that sense he was an appropriate man to serve as the symbolic head of the Canadian state during the crucial years of transition from dominion to nation.

The Beleaguered General

Canadians are not a warlike people, but occasionally warfare has been thrust upon them, either by invasion, as in 1812, or because they felt unable to stand aside from world conflicts, as in 1914 and 1939. In situations where physical courage was needed, Canadians have often done more than was expected of them, and the battle honours of Canadian divisions, corps, and armies compare favourably with those of other countries. At the same time, the military tradition has always seemed alien to the Canadian nature. When Canadians have had to be soldiers, they have usually preferred to be part-time ones, amateur warriors, willing to turn professional for a period. And the few examples of Canadians who have devoted themselves to soldiering as a vocation are often unhappy ones, as the strange, distinguished, yet frustrated career of Andrew McNaughton clearly shows.

McNaughton was born in 1887 in the almost too typical prairie town of Moosomin, Saskatchewan. He attended Moosomin's elementary school and then went

General A. G. L. McNaughton.

on to Bishop's College at Lennoxville in Quebec's Eastern Townships. From Bishop's he continued to McGill University, specializing in electrical engineering; he graduated in 1910 and was granted his M.Sc. in 1912.

While he was at McGill, McNaughton entered a course that trained students for commissions in the Canadian militia and in 1909 he became a provisional lieutenant; in 1910 he was given the rank of full lieutenant and in 1913 the rank of major. This meant that immediately war broke out in 1914 he was commissioned as an officer in the Canadian Field Artillery. In 1915 he was wounded in the second battle of Ypres and in 1918 at Soissons. Wounds and promotions alternated; he became lieutenant colonel in 1916 and in 1918 he was given the Distinguished Service Order and made brigadier general in command of the Heavy Artillery attached to the Canadian Corps.

Returning to Canada, McNaughton decided to make soldiering his profession. He remained with the Permanent Active Militia, then Canada's equivalent of a regular army, and took his courses at the Camberley Staff College and the Imperial Defence College in England. In 1919 he was promoted to major general and appointed chief of the Canadian General Staff, a post he held until 1935. During the Depression he devised his own contribution to solving the unemployment question; it consisted of using unemployed men to construct airfields. He argued that such construction would encourage the development of civil aviation; in fact the airfields were most useful as centres for the Commonwealth Air Training Plan in World War II, and McNaughton may have had this possibility secretly in mind when he made his recommendation.

Involved as he was in military matters, McNaughton did not forget that his original vocation had been electrical engineering. In 1926 he helped to invent the cathode ray direction finder and he willingly left the army in 1935 to become chairman of the National Research Council. For the next four years he worked hard to strengthen the council by recruiting Canadian and foreign scientists. But when war broke out in 1939 he returned to the army and was immediately appointed to the command of the First Canadian Infantry Division, which was immediately sent to England. In 1940 he was promoted to the rank of lieutenant general commanding the Seventh Corps; he commanded the Canadian Corps in 1941 and the First Canadian Army when it was formed in April 1942.

Like the Canadian generals in World War I, McNaughton fought on two fronts; against the acknowledged enemy and against the British generals—notably Bernard Montgomery—who wanted to submerge the identity of the Canadian forces in those of Britain. Finally, McNaughton resigned in despair in November 1944, with the rank of general, and entered the field of politics, which

in his case turned out to be even more perilous than the field of battle.

At this time Mackenzie King, the prime minister of Canada, was entangled in the difficult problem of how to recruit enough soldiers for overseas service without imposing conscription, which would antagonize Liberal supporters in Québec. James R. Ralston, minister of national defence, was an ardent conscriptionist; McNaughton agreed with King that conscription would damage the unity of Canada which was vital in wartime. King engineered Ralston's resignation and appointed McNaughton in his place. It turned into a fiasco so far as McNaughton was concerned, for he lost two successive by-elections and in 1945 resigned as minister.

Yet McNaughton's career was far from tailing off into oblivion. He served as chairman of the Canadian section of the Permanent Joint Board on Defence from 1945 to 1959; he was for several years president of the Atomic Energy Control Board; and from 1948 to 1949 he was Canada's representative on the Security Council of the United Nations. In 1950 he became chairman of the Canadian section of the International Joint Commission, which regulated matters of common interest between Canada and the United States. But once again his involvement in politics resulted in his downfall. McNaughton objected to the Columbia River Treaty, which he rightly believed highly favoured the United States, and in 1962 he was removed by Prime Minister Diefenbaker in an attempt, as McNaughton put it, to throttle his "objections to a very damaging arrangement". McNaughton stepped out of public life in a way greatly to his credit as a Canadian patriot. Time—which has seen the spread of American economic power in Canada—has proved him right. When all the controversy occurred, McNaughton was already seventy-five. He died four years later, in 1966.

The Great Pretender

Archibald Stansfeld Belaney was a highly inventive man. He not only created a good number of very successful books; he also invented a fictional personality to write them. This was the "half-Indian" Grey Owl, or Wa-sha-quon-asin, who travelled on arduous lecture tours in North America and Britain, always dressed in Indian buckskin garb, and who span a romantic tale about himself from which even now the fragments of truth have not been entirely disentangled. A number of writers have tried to reveal the real man behind the mask known as Grey Owl. Lovat Dickson, in his fascinating book, *Wilder-*

Grey Owl.

ness Man: The Strange Story of Grey Owl (1973), perhaps came nearest to the truth. But there still remain many cloudy areas of doubt, many points in Grey Owl's career that could be interpreted in more than one way.

Among the facts we do know with certainty is that Archibald Stansfeld Belaney was born in England in 1888. Archibald's father, George Belaney, was something of a wanderer; it was in Florida that he married Katherine Cox, who was Archibald's mother. Many years later her son asserted that she had Indian blood and on this supposition was based the claim he sometimes made of being part Apache. But there seems to be no reason to believe that Katherine Cox was anything but English. She left England with George Belaney and her sister Elizabeth, who was George's common-law wife, and after Elizabeth's death she married him. The couple returned to England a short time before Archibald was born but did not remain together, and when they parted their son was brought up by two aunts in Hastings on the south coast of England.

Archie grew up a lonely boy. He was deeply interested in natural history and in taming wild animals. He was captivated by dreams of the Wild West and of Indians, and he never outgrew them. His later life was in fact a sustained effort to fulfil his childhood dreams.

He was only seventeen when he took the first steps towards realizing his fantasies by sailing to Canada. To earn some money he worked in Toronto for a few months and the next year he headed for northern Ontario where he became a guide and trapper and spent a great deal of time with the Ojibwa Indians. In 1910 a girl from one of the local bands became his common-law wife, but it is not at all certain that her relatives accepted him, and the marriage seems to have been an intermittent one, since Belaney was often away.

When World War I broke out, Belaney volunteered for service abroad and went to France where he was wounded in the foot. While convalescing in an English hospital, he married a childhood friend from Hastings, Constance Holmes. But Constance seems to have had no enthusiasm for a life in the Canadian bush, and she refused to accompany Archie when he went back to northern Ontario. He found the region changed greatly by indiscriminate logging and trapping, and from this time on the preservation of the wilderness and its natural inhabitants became one of his chief concerns.

Soon after his return Archie adopted the name of Grey Owl and began to claim that he was a Métis; he wore Indian dress and followed the Indian way of life as far as he could. He went to live with a beautiful Ojibwa girl, Anahareo, in Temiscouta County, Québec, and there they started to breed beaver to restock the depleted waterways of the wilderness. But such practical conservation mea-

sures did not seem sufficient and in 1929 Grey Owl began to lecture and write articles on the need to preserve the wilderness.

Very soon Grey Owl's activities attracted the attention of the department of the interior, which was developing its program of national parks. In 1931 he was employed as a ranger, first in Riding Mountain National Park in Manitoba and then in Prince Albert National Park in Saskatchewan, where he built a cabin and lived, when he was not travelling, the rest of his life.

There was not much of it left, and the work Grey Owl crammed into those few last years was hardly that of a wilderness hermit. The public legend of Grey Owl began to take shape with the publication of his first book, *The Men of the Last Frontier* (1931). In it he posed as an Indian working to save the ways of the wild and this appealed to the nostalgia of North Americans and Europeans alike. Almost immediately Archie Belaney, alias Grey Owl, was an international celebrity. His descriptions of the Canadian woodland, his success in taming beavers, and his moving appeals for conservation made bestsellers of his later books, such as *Pilgrims of the Wild* (1934) and *Tales of an Empty Cabin* (1936). While he was writing these books, Grey Owl also travelled on exhausting lecture tours to advertise himself and his ideas, and at the end of one of these tours he died, only fifty years old, in 1938.

Archibald Stansfeld Belaney was a poseur and in some ways a fraud. But that is too simple a view of a very complex man who remained in the fantasy world of his boyhood, when he played Indians with such zest. He kept on playing Indians, but his concern for conservation was entirely sincere and he ranks as one of the true pioneers of modern environmentalism. And if he acted a role—the role of the fictional Grey Owl—he acted it so well that thousands of people were convinced.

Pioneer in Parliament

While women such as Emily Murphy and Nellie McClung campaigned mainly for the rights of women, Agnes Macphail went a step further. She demonstrated in her own life the ability of a woman to fight equally with men for the rights of all people, regardless of sex or race or any of the other categories that are constantly used to divide human beings from one another. She campaigned— among other issues—against war and for producers' co-operatives; against the existing Canadian political system and for a better deal for the farmers. She walked into political life as if sexual differences did not exist and perhaps that is one of the most effective ways of establish-

Agnes Macphail in 1921.

ing the political relevance of women.

Agnes Macphail was born in 1890 in Grey County, rural Ontario, and embarked on a teaching career by attending the Stratford Normal School. After graduating, she taught in a succession of small rural schools—never in towns—and this gave her a sharp insight into the problems which Ontario farmers faced. She became increasingly concerned by the fact that the main political parties represented the interests of those who exploited the cultivators of the soil—the manufacturers, the bankers, the railway magnates.

In 1919 Agnes became an active member of the United Farmers of Ontario (UFO). The UFO was a political movement based on the idea of "occupational" representation. This form of representation would allow farmers and other rural people to elect representatives committed to speaking in their interest. The farmers' representatives could become associated with representatives of the urban workers in alliances that would make it unnecessary to accept the leadership of the existing parties, which the UFO regarded as entirely corrupt.

Speaking at public meetings on rural grievances, Agnes Macphail impressed the Ontario farmers with her integrity, her intelligence, and above all her energy. In 1921 the UFO members in the federal constituency of Southeast Grey chose her as their candidate over several male rivals, and she was successful in that year's election. In this way she became the first woman to sit in the Canadian House of Commons.

Agnes Macphail entered the House as an independent, but she immediately joined the Progressive Party led by T. A. Crerar, which in the 1921 election had come second with sixty-five seats, fifteen more than the Conservatives. But when Crerar led the Progressives to support Mackenzie King's Liberal government in return for a few small concessions, Agnes Macphail and five Alberta M.P.'s formed themselves into a critical opposition to the party line. The press called them the Ginger Group, a title Macphail and her associates gladly accepted.

When the Progressive Party disintegrated, the Ginger Group remained intact, working in alliance with the handful of labour representatives headed by J. S. Woodsworth. Eventually it joined other similar organizations in 1932–33 to form the Co-operative Commonwealth Federation (CCF), which was the forerunner of the present day New Democratic Party. Agnes Macphail herself remained rather aloof from this development. She usually voted in Parliament with the CCF, but she held her Ontario federal seat as an independent until she was finally defeated in 1940.

It was then that she joined the CCF, and in 1943 she was elected on the party's ticket to the Ontario Legislative Assembly. She continued to represent the CCF there until 1951, when she retired from political life.

Her parliamentary activities were only one side of Agnes Macphail's extremely active public life. She was one of the leading members of the Ontario Co-operative Union, and spent much time organizing co-operative stores and marketing agencies in the rural areas of the province. She was also a convinced pacifist, who opposed any kind of participation in war. As a member of the Canadian delegation to the League of Nations, she became the first woman to be elected to the League's disarmament committee. She was a passionate advocate of penal reform and her criticism of the way criminals were treated in Canadian jails was largely responsible for the establishment in 1938 of a royal commission to investigate prisons. The commission's sensational report revealed abuses of which the general public had hitherto been quite unaware.

Agnes Macphail had no desire to be a political leader; she realized that a leader is always the prisoner of his party. She proved by her own life and by the many ways in which she helped to better the lot of neglected sectors of the populace, such as country people and prisoners, how much a single dedicated person can do to change the world.

The Discovery of Insulin

The career of Frederick Grant Banting, the discoverer of insulin, demonstrated that extensive scholarship and a wide background in research are not needed to conceive a brilliant idea that may be of great scientific and practical value. Banting thought of insulin—which has saved the lives of many thousands of diabetics—before he became a research professor; after becoming a research professor he made no other great discovery.

Banting was an Ontario farmer's son, born at Alliston in 1891. When he was a schoolboy he saw a scaffolding collapse and watched the doctor giving first aid to two badly injured masons. He was so impressed by the idea of giving immediate help to human suffering that he decided on the spot to become a doctor, and when he went to the University of Toronto he entered the medical school and graduated in 1917.

It was the middle of World War I, and Banting enrolled in the Medical Corps. In the battle of Cambrai, he was tending casualties under fire when he himself was badly wounded; for that day's action he won the Military Cross. On returning to Canada after the war he started a practice in London, Ontario. It was not a very busy one and he had time to think about medical problems, particularly the problem of diabetes. He had the idea that if a pancreatic hormone in a pure form could be injected into the blood stream, this might enable the body to use up the blood sugar, and so the notorious "wasting" effects of the disease could be controlled. How to do it was the problem. On the night of October 30, 1920, he woke up with the basic idea in his mind and wrote in his notebook: "Tie off pancreas ducts of dogs. Wait six or eight weeks. Remove and extract."

Banting immediately went with his idea to Professor J. R. R. Macleod, head of the department of physiology at the University of Toronto, and Macleod was sufficiently interested to give him laboratory facilities and the assistance of a graduate student, Charles H. Best. In the summer of 1921 Banting and Best isolated insulin and purified it with the assistance of J. B. Collip, so that it could

Frederick Grant Banting.

be experimentally tested on human patients. It proved an immediate and dramatic success and in 1923 the Nobel Prize was awarded jointly to Banting and Macleod, who in fact had nothing directly to do with the research though he was nominally in charge of the project because of his professorial status. Banting was at first inclined to refuse the award because Best was not honoured. But in the end he shared his half of the $40,000 award with Best, while Macleod shared his with Collip, for whom Banting had conceived a rooted dislike during their period of working together.

On the strength of his achievement and his celebrity, Banting was appointed the University of Toronto's first professor of medical research in 1923. He was knighted and elected to the Royal Society of Canada and to the much more prestigious Royal Society in London. But though he later suggested some interesting directions of research which other men followed up, Banting remained essentially a man of one great insight—the midnight hunch that led him, even before he had the means of research, in the direction of discovering insulin. He made no other discovery of major medical or scientific importance.

When World War II began in 1939, Banting enlisted again in the Canadian Army Medical Corps, with the rank of captain. In February 1941, he was sent on a scientific mission to Britain, but the plane crashed while attempting a forced landing on a frozen lake in eastern Newfoundland. Banting's lung was pierced by the wreckage and he died long before help could reach him.

A Musical Life

In terms of performance, music has been a highly successful art in Canada. The thanks for this goes largely to a public broadcasting system, the CBC, which made sure in its better days that orchestras survived and that musicians had enough employment to prevent their giving up in despair. But the actual creation of music is another matter, and Canadian composers have found it difficult to win an audience. We know our conductors and our pianists—such as Glenn Gould—better than we know our composers, and the fact that Sir Ernest MacMillan is probably the best known of all Canadian musicians is an illustration of this fact. For Ernest MacMillan was a very minor composer compared with Barbara Pentland, who has received little attention from the general public. Where Sir Ernest shone was as a performer and as a conductor: he was a teacher and a great propagandist in the cause of bringing music to the Canadian people.

Ernest MacMillan first attracted public attention as a child prodigy. Born in Mimico, Ontario, in 1893, he was the son of Dr. Alexander MacMillan—church organist, composer of hymns, and editor of such collections as the Presbyterian Book of Praise and the United Church Hymnary. Trained as an organist from the age of eight, young Ernest showed an extraordinary power of improvising, and at ten he gave his first recital before an audience of four thousand people in Massey Hall. He then went to study in Edinburgh and by the age of thirteen he was an associate of the Royal College of Organists in London. When he returned to Canada he was appointed organist at Knox Church in Toronto. Later he studied at Oxford and graduated at the age of seventeen as Bachelor of Music. But he still wished for a broad liberal education so he also attended the University of Toronto, where he took his B.A. in modern history.

This meteoric career was brought to a halt in 1914, when Ernest MacMillan went to the annual Wagner Festival in Bayreuth; he stayed a little too long and was caught in Germany at the outbreak of war early in August. He was interned in the famous Ruhleben Prison Camp, and there he filled his time by arranging operatic and musical events for his fellow prisoners, studying Russian, and preparing the setting of Swinburne's *Ode to England* for choir and orchestra. When he completed this piece of music he sent it to England, and while he was still interned, it won him his Doctorate of Music at the University of Oxford.

Returning to Canada in 1919, MacMillan found himself a nine-days'-wonder; he was feted everywhere and invited to lecture on his experiences. But he was not diverted from the serious business of music. He accepted an appointment as organist to the Timothy Eaton Memorial Church and joined the staff of the Canadian Academy of Music. Shortly after this the academy became the Toronto Conservatory and MacMillan took over as principal in 1926. In 1927 he added to his growing list of responsibilities the position of dean of the faculty of music at the University of Toronto. At the same time he began to develop his talents as a conductor, directing the Toronto Mendelssohn Choir, and in 1931 becoming conductor of the Toronto Symphony Orchestra. He remained with the Toronto Symphony for a quarter of a century, until his retirement in 1956.

An untiring worker who was accustomed to fifteen-hour days; a man of dour and patient disposition; a conductor given to virile rather than subtle performances: MacMillan suited the needs of Canadian music in its stage of development between the two great wars. He also developed a considerable international reputation. Not content with triumphant conducting progresses in Britain

Ernest MacMillan.

and North America, he went on tours in Australia and Brazil; he even judged Welsh choirs at the National Eisteddfod. At the same time he became an indefatigable propagandist for music in Canada, eating the rubbery chicken of a thousand luncheons where he was guest speaker and encouraging the foundation of Ernest Mac-Millan Fine Art Clubs all over Canada.

MacMillan never really gave up. By 1956 he had retired from the conservatory, from the University of Toronto, even from the Toronto Symphony Orchestra. But there were still CBC festivals and choral performances and all those temptations to repeat "last appearances" which performing artists enjoy. Like all such artists, MacMillan was too enamoured of music ever to retire completely, and until he died in 1973 he was part of the Canadian musical world. Even if he composed nothing that has survived him, by the time he died in 1973 he had made millions of Canadians aware of the importance of music to a full and satisfying life.

The Chief

John Diefenbaker was the first representative of Canada's "Third Solitude" to become prime minister of our country. All his predecessors had been either of British or of French descent, but Diefenbaker's ancestry was German. He was also elected, at his great moment of triumph in 1958, with the largest majority any Canadian prime minister has ever enjoyed. Yet his fall from the pinnacle of power was so rapid that nine years later, in 1967, he was expelled from the leadership of his own party.

Political success, dramatic when it finally arrived, was slow in coming to John Diefenbaker. He was born of a farming family in Grey County, Ontario, in 1895. It was the period of the great migration to the Prairies, and when John was eight years old the Diefenbakers moved out to Saskatchewan. There John was brought up in the neighbourhood of Prince Albert and as a young man he studied law at the University of Saskatchewan. After serving in World War I, he went into legal practice and was made a King's Counsel in 1929. He gained a high reputation as a successful criminal lawyer, whose eloquent speeches for the defence could wring acquittals from the hearts of the toughest prairie juries.

Diefenbaker's concern over the problems of the Depression years in the Prairies, as well as his experiences as a lawyer defending criminal cases, led him into politics. He started on the provincial level and from 1936 to 1940 he was the leader of the Saskatchewan Conservative Party. Then, in 1940, he won election to the House of

Commons, of which he remained a member until his death in 1979.

From the beginning, Diefenbaker was a Conservative of a peculiarly western kind. This branch of Conservatism was influenced by the populist doctrines that had long been current in the Canadian West, and was strong on moral issues, such as the abolition of the death penalty, which Diefenbaker advocated without any regard to the possible political disadvantages. This meant that he was unpopular with right-wing Tories, who controlled the Progressive Conservative Party in eastern Canada, and when he competed for the party leadership in 1948 he was unsuccessful.

But Diefenbaker had a strong sense of mission and was willing to wait. After successive eastern leaders had failed to dislodge the Liberals from power, his opportunity came, and in 1956—at the age of sixty-one—he was chosen as party leader. He immediately went on a crusade against Liberal arrogance, as displayed in the famous Pipeline issue of 1956, when—at the insistence of C. D. Howe—the Liberals arbitrarily imposed closure during a debate in Parliament on a government loan to an American-owned pipeline company. (Closure is a procedure by which a government with a parliamentary majority can end debate on a question by moving an immediate vote.)

In the election of 1957, with their slogan of "Follow John!", the Conservatives were able to defeat the Liberals and form a minority government. Diefenbaker became the first Conservative prime minister in twenty-two years. In 1958 he called another election. An unprecedented—and unrepeated—swing in Québec, where many Tories were elected, gave Diefenbaker his historic majority: 208 Conservatives were elected in a house of 265.

It was a great opportunity for "the Chief" (as Diefenbaker now was in more than name) to show that the Progressive Conservative Party was really progressive, but Diefenbaker turned out to be concerned with symbolic issues rather than real ones. He was largely responsible for South Africa being forced out of the Commonwealth because of its racist policies, and he showed his respect for minorities by insisting that a reservation Indian be appointed to the Canadian Senate. But the Bill of Rights he set out to enshrine in the Canadian judicial process was ineffectually conceived and changed little in practice. Like many brilliant opposition leaders, he was inept and indecisive in the practical affairs of government, and intolerant of criticism and often misled by his own vanity.

Diefenbaker's position weakened dramatically in the election of 1962, after which he again led a minority government, and in 1963 the Conservatives were de-

John Diefenbaker points an accusing finger in the House of Commons, 1948.

feated by Lester Pearson's Liberals, who also set up a minority government. The Conservatives did not forgive Diefenbaker for destroying their dream of a long period in power, and in 1967 he was voted out of the leadership of the party and Robert Stanfield took his place.

But Diefenbaker did not decline into anonymity, even though he had lost the prime ministership and had been ousted from the party leadership. As the respected member for Prince Albert, he remained a powerful spokesman for political decency and he continued to be active and eloquent to the end. He died in 1979, a little before his eighty-fourth birthday, in Ottawa. During his last years he dictated his memoirs, which appeared in three volumes under the general title of *One Canada*. His devotion to the Commonwealth and the link with Britain, his compassion for the underdog and his sense of being a man of the people, are as clearly evident in these books as they were in his life. But the memoirs also show that he regarded himself in his final years as a man badly betrayed by his associates. He could not accept the fact that a fine and generous crusader, which he was, could be splendid in opposition but ineffective as a leader of government.

Bush Pilot

Among the legendary figures of the Canadian North are the bush pilots who appeared there in the 1920s—before modern methods of direction finding had been perfected—and flew in small planes over the bush and the barren lands. In the process these pilots revolutionized the life of a region that had been accustomed to transport by dog teams and by the annual boats which sailed to the remote outposts in the years when the ice allowed such travel. Before the bush pilots arrived, the people in the North were months away, especially in winter, from the southern world which they called "Outside". The bush pilots reduced that interval to days and they brought the possibility of rescue or cure in situations where death would have been certain in the past.

The legend has it that the bush pilots went into action immediately after World War I. This is not really true, though many of them learned their flying skills as air aces in that war. G. W. Gorman and E. G. Fullerton piloted two planes to Fort Simpson on the Mackenzie River in 1921, but this was an isolated feat. The era of the pilot who was

"Punch" Dickins in winter garb.

willing to fly—at calculated risk—anywhere in the North did not really begin until the late 1920s. Two pace-setting flights occurred in 1928, both connected with mining exploration. "Doc" Oaks flew a party of prospectors in to the Nahanni River that year, but failed to find them when he returned to pick them up; they made their way out on foot in the traditional way. And "Punch" Dickins arrived at Fort Smith to complete a much more successful and spectacular trip, the first of the great northern flights.

By this time "Punch" Dickins was already a seasoned flyer. He was a prairie boy—Clennell H. Dickins was his real name though he seldom used it—who was born at Portage la Prairie in 1899. He grew up during World War I and in 1917 at the age of eighteen he joined the Royal Flying Corps which later became the Royal Air Force. Though he was never so famous an ace as Billy Bishop or Wop May, he won the Distinguished Flying Cross for his exploits and then returned as a veteran to study at the University of Alberta. When the Royal Canadian Air Force (RCAF) was re-established in 1924, Dickins joined it. For almost a decade the RCAF was involved mainly in developing civil flying operations, and by the time Dickins left the force in 1927 he had a good deal of experience flying in Canada south of the 60th parallel.

In the autumn of 1928 he was hired by two American mining men to undertake the great flight that carried him into the true North. It extended for three thousand miles, from Winnipeg north to Hudson's Bay and Chesterfield Inlet, then west to the Thelon River and southwestward to Fort Smith; it took Dickins just twenty-seven hours to do a journey that, with conventional Arctic transport, would normally have taken a year. He arrived at Fort Smith on September 6, and received the McKee trophy for pioneering in the air.

The next year he became the Mackenzie district superintendent for Canadian Airways, which was involved in a bitter competition with a rival group of bush pilots, Mackenzie Air Lines. This did not mean that Dickins sat in his office and let others fly. In fact, during his years as superintendent he completed eight hundred thousand miles of flying. Much of it was in unmapped country and was undertaken in winter with temperatures reaching down to minus fifty degrees Fahrenheit, and it was done without radio contacts with outer civilization. Among his pioneer flights Dickins crossed the Arctic Circle in March 1929. He landed at Aklavik in July, and he later flew from Aklavik to Edmonton—fifteen hundred miles—in seventeen hours. He survived these arduous flights with few accidents, and this was at least partly due to his passion for always being well turned out, which extended from his immaculate flying garb to the plane that he insisted on keeping clean and tuned to perfection.

Like most of the bush pilots who survived, "Punch" Dickins found himself in the end drawn into managerial work in the quickly expanding Canadian air transport industry. He became general superintendent of Canadian Airways in Winnipeg in 1935 and during the war he organized the Air Ferry Service to Britain. Then he served for a couple of years as general manager of Canadian Pacific Airlines before he went on to the de Havilland Aircraft Company of Canada, in which he eventually became executive vice-president before retiring to become an aviation consultant in 1966.

The world of great corporations may seem a far cry from the small operations and the lonely daring of bush pilots in the 1920s. Yet it was these men who led Canada into the air age; they reaped the rewards and also the regrets for an exciting way of life that lasted a short time and in which, in the words of Stephen Spender, they "left the vivid air signed with their honour".

Through the North-West Passage

In Vancouver, above the beach at English Bay, stands the Maritime Museum, and beside it, in an A-shaped shed of wood and glass, a sturdy schooner-rigged ship faces out to the sea. It is so small and snub-nosed a boat that at first its history strikes you as incredible. For this is the *St. Roch*, the second ship to sail the legendary North-West Passage, the first to sail it in a single season.

The first conquest of the North-West Passage, after centuries of efforts going back to the 1500s, was by the Norwegian, Roald Amundsen. It took him three years, from 1903 to 1906, to nose his ship, the *Gjoa*, through the series of frozen straits, gulfs, and channels between Hudson Strait and the Beaufort Sea. After Amundsen, the passage went unconquered for another thirty years; then the *St. Roch* travelled through it, under the command of Henry Asbjorn Larsen, who was a fellow countryman of Amundsen, at least by birth.

Larsen was born in 1899 in a village near the mouth of the Oslo Fjord. He grew up in sight of the sea and heard much talk of ships during his boyhood, for his family was a seafaring one. It was not merely the sea, but the northern sea that fascinated him as a boy, and he read avidly the narratives of the great polar explorers, especially the Norwegians, Amundsen and Nansen, and the great Icelandic Canadian, Stefansson. When he was fifteen, Larsen began his sea-going career on a timber ship captained by one of his uncles, and throughout World

Henry Asbjorn Larsen.

War I he worked on sailing ships. In 1919 he signed on his first steamship, the *Vinstra*, as boatswain. After graduating from navigation school and spending two years of compulsory service in the Norwegian navy, he sailed as mate on a series of freighters.

It was not until 1924 that Larsen finally reached the Arctic, on a two-masted schooner, *The Maid of Orleans*, which was later renamed *The Old Maid*. He spent two years in northern waters, making his first contact with the Eskimo and also with the RCMP, who in that period were establishing posts around the Arctic sea. His experience confirmed him in his intention to become an Arctic explorer, and he had the shrewd and original idea that the best way to do it might be to become a water-borne Mountie.

Accordingly, he stayed in Canada and in 1927 took out citizenship. This enabled him to join the RCMP and he

did so in 1928. The force needed an experienced navigator for its new Arctic patrol ship, the *St. Roch*, which had just been built in the shipyards of North Vancouver. So, as soon as it was launched, the *St. Roch* sailed north with Henry Larsen as master; owing to the strange conventions of RCMP promotion, he ranked as a mere constable.

The first years of Larsen's service on the *St. Roch* were comparatively uneventful and no opportunity presented itself for the exploration he longed to carry out. For eleven years he and the other crew members sailed the Arctic waters, patrolling in the western islands, supplying the police outposts, and acting as a floating detachment available in case of emergency. It was only with the outbreak of World War II, when Canada again became concerned about asserting its sovereignty over the Arctic archipelago, that Larsen's opportunity arrived.

The most dramatic way of showing the flag, it was

decided, would be to send a Canadian ship through the North-West Passage, and in 1940 Larsen—who had been promoted to sergeant—was instructed to leave Vancouver with supplies for a year and a half. He was to visit the northern outposts as if he were going on a customary trip, and then he was to attempt sailing the *St. Roch* through the passage from west to east—the opposite direction to Amundsen's—with Halifax as his destination.

The *St. Roch* set sail on the first of its great voyages on June 21, 1940. Weather conditions were bad and the ship had to spend two winters in the ice before it reached Halifax in the autumn of 1942. Larsen's experience on that first voyage showed that a more powerful engine was needed for dealing with the ice floes. But the wartime commitments of the shipyards in Halifax prevented this work from being done in time for a return voyage in 1943, and it was July 1944, before the *St. Roch* was in fact ready to sail.

This time Larsen took a more northerly route than Amundsen's, guiding the *St. Roch* through Lancaster Sound and Barrow Strait. The ice conditions were unusually favourable and the *St. Roch* reached Vancouver in an amazing eighty-six days, the first ship to enter the North-West Passage and pass through it without being trapped over at least two winters.

The two great voyages of the *St. Roch* satisfied Larsen's desire for exploration. He remained with the RCMP, reaching the rank of superintendent in 1953 and retiring in 1961. He died in 1964, the last of the great Arctic travellers.

Outsider in Power

In 1952 William Andrew Cecil Bennett, known to his friends as "Cece" and to his opponents as "Wacky", came out of the back country of British Columbia at the head of a new party. He won the provincial election that year and ended for ever the influence of the old parties, the Liberals and the Conservatives, in West Coast politics. Since 1952 politics in British Columbia has been polarized between two rival populist parties: the right-wing populists of the Social Credit Party and the left-wing populists of the New Democratic Party (NDP). Populism is the doctrine of rule by the people and for the people; populist politicians give the illusion that this actually happens when they are in power.

Populist movements arise out of discontent, when large numbers of people think they have no control over their lives. When Bennett came to power in British Columbia, and stayed in power for twenty years, the voters who supported him were those who believed that the old parties ruled in the interests of a minority of rich people in the cities and that the country districts were being sacrificed to Vancouver. Bennett was the charismatic outsider, the political loner, who appeared at the right time to focus this popular discontent and turn it into power.

Bennett was a Maritimer who had found New Brunswick—where he was born in 1900—too limited for his ambition, and had moved as a young man to Edmonton. In 1930 he crossed over the mountains into the Okanagan Valley and bought a hardware business in Kelowna. It was the height of the Depression yet "Wacky" Bennett not only survived but prospered, becoming a notable local figure and easily gaining election as a member of the provincial legislature in 1941.

Bennett started out as a Conservative, and perhaps the one element that remained constant in his political career was his fear of a political takeover by the CCF and later by the NDP, the socialist movement that had always been strong on the Pacific Coast. Bennett wished to build a party strong enough to keep the socialists from power for ever. At first he thought the Conservatives might serve as that party, but throughout World War II the provincial Tories ruled the province in a coalition with the Liberals, and Bennett believed that this prevented the party from being fully effective.

If only he were in control, Bennett believed, the Tories might be revitalized. Twice, in 1946 and 1950, he tried to win the leadership of the party. He was defeated on both occasions. More than that, he was passed over when there were cabinet vacancies, though he was an able man with a strong rural following. Finally, in 1951, he resigned from the Conservative Party and denounced the coalition with the Liberals. Declaring himself an independent, he began to gather followers not only in the rural constituencies but also among discontented urban office workers and small businessmen.

Bennett had the will and the friends and the purpose; he lacked a party machine, but he soon found it in the small Social Credit movement which had polled a mere one and a half per cent of the vote in 1949. Between them, Bennett's personal followers and the Social Credit members set afoot an extraordinary propaganda campaign, and the 1952 elections showed a massive uprising of the small men and the political outsiders against the old party establishment. Social Credit won nineteen seats and the NDP eighteen; they shared sixty-four per cent of the vote between them. The following year Bennett called another election and won a massive majority of twenty-eight seats, with forty-five and a half per cent of the vote. The old parties between them received twenty-four per cent of the

W.A.C. Bennett (centre) inaugurating a railway extension in northern British Columbia.

vote. A new dispensation had come to British Columbia.

Loud and aggressive, emotional and always sure he was right, Bennett fitted the expanding economy of the period. He ruled by making spectacular gifts. The road system of British Columbia was transformed into the most splendid in Canada, the government-owned British Columbia Railway was pushed north to the Yukon border, the powerful British Columbia Electric Company was expropriated and turned into a crown corporation. Government ferries were established linking Vancouver Island with the mainland, hospital treatment was made free, and house taxes were reduced. Rural electrification went ahead, two new universities were founded, and a Bank of British Columbia was created.

For two decades Bennett fascinated the people with his strident personality and pleased them with his gifts, but many important issues were neglected and discontent grew up among such groups as teachers, unionized workers, and the poor. In 1972 what had been regarded as impossible happened: after twenty years in power Bennett's Social Credit Party was defeated by the NDP, led by Dave Barrett. Unwilling to serve as opposition leader, "Wacky" Bennett resigned and left the field clear for his son William to lead the Social Credit Party. In 1975, after three years of the NDP's greatly watered-down socialism, the people of British Columbia returned Social Credit to power. W. A. C. Bennett died in 1979, conscious that he had changed the whole nature of British Columbian politics by destroying the power of the old parties that had ruled the province since Confederation.

The All-round Man

Lionel Conacher was Canada's most versatile sportsman. His nickname, the "Big Train", suggested the number of sports in which he participated and, very often, excelled. There was, indeed, hardly a single athletic activity in which Conacher did not at some time or another participate, but he was among the best in no less than six sports—boxing and wrestling, baseball and lacrosse, football and hockey.

Born in Toronto in 1900, Conacher came from a working-class family whose main way of escape from the dreariness of their daily lives was through sports. All his brothers were ardent sportsmen; one of them, Charles Conacher, became a famous hockey player. But none of them succeeded in so many fields as Lionel Conacher.

At the age of sixteen, he was the Ontario 125-pound wrestling champion. Four years later he became the Canadian light heavyweight boxing champion. He even fought an exhibition match in 1922 with Jack Dempsey, the world's heavyweight boxing champion, and came off well.

In every North American team sport Conacher excelled. He played with the Toronto Hillcrests team in 1922 when they won the Ontario baseball championship; on the same day he also played with the Toronto Maitlands team which won the Ontario lacrosse championship.

The two games to which he gave most attention though were hockey and football. Hockey he played because it gave him the money to ensure the financial security of his children, a security which he himself had not enjoyed when he was young. He joined the New York Americans in 1926 and later played seasons with the Montreal Maroons and the Chicago Black Hawks.

Football he played because it was his favourite game, and here again he took part in some notable triumphs. In the historic game in 1921, when the Toronto Argonauts won the Grey Cup, defeating the Edmonton Eskimos 23 to 0, Conacher scored 15 of the Argonauts' points. It took thirty-five years before another player scored more points in a Grey Cup game.

In his late twenties Conacher took to coaching for Rutgers University and for other university teams. In his late thirties he gave up professional sports entirely and devoted himself to public service on various levels. He became chairman of the Ontario Athletic Commission and in 1937 he ran successfully for a seat in the Ontario Legislative Assembly. He served in provincial politics for twelve years, concerning himself with the needs he knew best: providing community parks and athletic opportunities for the poor districts of Toronto. Lionel Conacher never forgot the place he came from or the people among whom he grew up.

Finally, in 1949, Conacher was persuaded to seek election to the House of Commons. His opponent was the Communist Party leader, Tim Buck, and Conacher was chosen to run against him because of his popularity in working class constituencies. He won the election, and held his seat until 1954, when he died, as it were, on parliamentary business. During a baseball match between members of the House of Commons and members of the press gallery, he collapsed at third base and expired twenty minutes afterwards. It was an appropriate passing, the death in action that he had doubtless wished.

Lionel Conacher in a rare moment of inaction.

Joey Smallwood in his element before the microphones.

Living Father of Confederation

Joey Smallwood has based his claim to recognition on the fact that he is "the only living Father of Confederation". This claim is true to the extent that he was the man who led Newfoundland, which had avoided entering Confederation ever since the idea was first broached in 1867, into the clutches of the "Canadian wolf", as Newfoundland patriots used to call us, in 1949.

It was—given the craggy independence of Newfoundlanders—a genuine feat. The man who brought it off was born in St. John's in 1900; he grew up small and energetic, a notable jester and a great braggart. But underneath the bravado there developed in Joey Smallwood a sense of solidarity with the ordinary people of Newfoundland, who were then near the lowest end of the scale of North American poverty.

Joey was educated in St. John's and then in New York, where he did not study in any of the universities, but at the Labour Temple and the Rand School of Social Science. He returned to Newfoundland to take up journalism as his profession and he served on the staffs of papers in Newfoundland and Nova Scotia, in Boston and New York. He moved on to edit various Newfoundland newspapers and eventually to become a radio commentator of great popularity and influence.

But he never forgot the condition of his people. He was a great admirer of William Ford Coaker, who had founded the Fishermen's Protective Union in 1909, and Smallwood's first publication, in 1927, was actually a pamphlet entitled *Coaker of Newfoundland: The Man Who Led the Deep-sea Fishermen to Political Power*. He supported and imitated Coaker by helping to set up labour unions and fishermen's co-operatives in an attempt to break the power of the big merchants in St. John's. In this way he began to build, as early as the 1930s, his basis of popularity and power. He moved into politics, first as a Liberal campaign worker and then, in 1932, as an unsuccessful Liberal candidate.

Smallwood's great political opportunity came at the end of World War II when Newfoundland, which had gone bankrupt and had been ruled since 1932 by a British colonial office commission, was forced to give consideration to its future. In 1946 a national convention was called to discuss three possible courses for Newfoundland to follow: it could return to its original autonomous status as a poverty-stricken miniature dominion; it could remain under the receivership of a British-appointed commission; or it could join Canada as the tenth province. Smallwood was convinced, though many New-foundlanders disagreed, that Newfoundland, on its own, could never build up the kind of economic base that would ensure a significant improvement in its people's standard of living. Within the convention he became the leading advocate of integration into Canada and in 1947 he was appointed secretary of the delegation that went to Ottawa to explore the terms on which Newfoundland might enter Confederation. When he returned he began to advocate union with Canada by all the means at his disposal, especially through his radio programs and through the press. His efforts were responsible for the fact that Newfoundlanders voted by a narrow margin to give up their threadbare independence and let their rugged island become a part of Canada. On March 31, 1949, Newfoundland ceased to exist as a sovereign political unit. On April 1 it became a province of Canada with Joey Smallwood as its first premier.

The benefits he promised did to a large extent materialize. Newfoundlanders became more prosperous and gained greater social benefits than they had ever enjoyed in the past. In six consecutive elections Joey Smallwood and his Liberal Party were returned to power. But in the end Newfoundlanders grew tired of his autocratic ways, and in 1972 he was defeated. None of his later attempts to return to power were successful, and he spent his unwelcome leisure time writing one of the most lively of political biographies, *I Chose Canada* (1973).

Whatever his failures and failings, Joey Smallwood has never lacked wit and audacity, though his compassion for human suffering was somewhat negated by an urge to force on people measures that he considered good for them, whether they liked it or not. The most striking example of this trait was his attempt to make many thousands of Newfoundlanders leave the traditional neighbourliness of their little outport villages for larger settlements that were more accessible and seemed more convenient. But life in these communities was too impersonal for the taste of most Newfoundlanders.

The Greatness of History

Donald Creighton treated history as an art. He believed that facts were its necessary basis, but he also believed that they had to be presented in dramatic ways for the real outlines of a country's history to show up. And he believed that history, as much as fiction or poetry, deserved to be well written. He put these precepts into practice, and for this reason he was the most widely read, the most influential, and perhaps the best historian to present the strange and splendid record which is the story

Donald Creighton, in touch with tradition.

of Canada as a land and as a group of peoples uniting into a nation.

Creighton was born in 1902 in Toronto, in the midst of the great system of lakes and waterways that he always regarded as the heartland of Canadian history. Except for a period of time at Oxford, he was never away for long from his home city. He was a lifelong teacher, joining the department of history at the University of Toronto when he was twenty-five, and staying there until he retired in 1970 at the age of sixty-eight. He was head of his department from 1954 to 1959, was active in the Royal Society of Canada, and served his time as president of the Canadian Historical Association. He was heavily garlanded with honorary doctorates and medals. But none of these honours turned him into a routine, dry-as-dust academic historian. His books were always daring in thought and fluent in writing, and for this reason he was read far beyond the universities.

In his early years at the University of Toronto, Creighton was under the influence of the economist Harold Innis, who actually contributed a great deal to our understanding of Canadian history. Innis showed that the various phases in Canadian history were linked to certain staples, natural products that became the basis of trade, such as cod in the early days and furs afterwards. In Creighton's first book, *The Commercial Empire of the St. Lawrence: 1760–1850,* he developed Innis's insights to show how the fur-trading system of the St. Lawrence and the Great Lakes provided a direction of political and economic development that extended over the Prairies. This direction of development was at right angles to the rival geographical pattern of the mountain ranges that ran from north to south and that tended to draw Canada into the American orbit. He regarded the creation of Canada as a nation as one of the results of the natural transcontinental drive that built up its impetus in the fur trade along the St. Lawrence.

Creighton was really suggesting that Canada, no less than the United States, had a manifest destiny, which was to become the great nation of the north and he expressed this in the title of his second major book, *Dominion of the North: A History of Canada* (1944). In *Dominion of the North* Creighton's Canadian nationalism is clearly shown. He suggests that a union with the United States would constitute treason to the real goals of Canadian history, which are determined by the natural trade routes, later supplemented by the railroads and highways that led from Montreal to the Pacific Ocean.

In *The Road to Confederation: The Emergence of Canada, 1863–1867* (1964), Creighton showed how Confederation emerged out of a recognition by people throughout British North America, from Nova Scotia to Upper Canada, of the economic interests they shared and the political dangers—of American takeover principally—that made their union necessary. For Creighton the personification of the drive to create an independent nation north of the United States was Sir John A. Macdonald, the first prime minister of the Dominion of Canada. It is therefore appropriate that what is perhaps Creighton's best book was the first good biography that was written about Macdonald; it was divided into two volumes, *The Young Politician* (1952) and *The Old Chieftain* (1955).

During his later years Creighton became deeply concerned over the threats to Canada's independent existence. He recognized that the north-south pull was stronger than he had first believed, and that Canada's natural east-west ties were threatened by economic and cultural invasion from the United States. His last important book, *Canada's First Century, 1867–1967* (1970), was more pessimistic than any other of his works. Creighton believed that the rise of Québec nationalism and the trend towards provincial autonomy were weakening the political structure of Canada and making it an easy prey to American pressures.

Creighton, who died in 1979, was not always popular with other historians. Many of them believed that in his concept of a natural east-west Canadian bond he was creating myths which he never properly supported with facts. But for many Canadian novelists and poets Creighton provided a historical pattern with which they could develop their intuitions about the nature of Canadian life. Hugh MacLennan and Margaret Laurence, Al Purdy and Margaret Atwood—in all of these writers, with their deep sense of history conditioned by Canada's unique geography, the influence of Donald Creighton is obvious. There are probably very few Canadian writers who have really escaped it. Perhaps one of the reasons is that even if many Canadian historians have rejected Creighton, Canadian writers have always regarded him as one of their own.

The First Socialist Premier

Tommy Douglas became Canada's first socialist premier when the Co-operative Commonwealth Federation (CCF) gained power in Saskatchewan in 1944. He held that position for seventeen years until 1961. Then he became the first national leader of the New Democratic Party (NDP), which emerged in 1961 after the reconstruction of the CCF; he held that position until 1971, when he withdrew to become an ordinary Member of Parliament. In that setting he has won as much respect from the Canadian public for his good sense and integrity as he ever did when he held positions of authority and prestige.

Douglas was born in 1904 at Falkirk in Scotland, the son of an iron moulder. In 1910 the family emigrated to Canada and settled in Winnipeg, but in 1914, when war broke out, the elder Thomas Douglas returned to serve in the army and his family went back with him. At the age of thirteen, Tommy Douglas began working in a Glasgow factory. When the family returned to Winnipeg in 1919 he became an apprentice printer and eventually worked as a fully trained typographer.

Brought up in a pious Baptist household, Tommy Douglas decided to enter the ministry of his church. He attended Brandon College, from which he graduated with a B.A. in 1930, and then he went on to obtain an extramural M.A. from McMaster University in 1933. After that he took up his first pastorate in Weyburn, Saskatchewan.

The hardships which the Depression caused in the Prairies soon had their effect on Douglas's view of his duties as a clergyman. He felt that he could not stand aside from social issues, and his involvement in social issues

soon led to his participation in politics. By 1934 he was already involved in active prairie radicalism; that year he ran unsuccessfully as Farm-Labour candidate in a provincial election. The next year he joined the newly founded CCF and was successful in the federal elections of 1935, being elected to the House of Commons as member for Weyburn South.

The Saskatchewan farmers continued to support him and he sat among the small group of CCF members in Parliament until 1944, when he resigned from the House of Commons to lead the Saskatchewan CCF in the provincial election of 1944. The party was successful, and as premier of Saskatchewan, Douglas became leader of the first socialist government ever elected in North America.

He remained in power in Saskatchewan for seventeen years, until he resigned to lead the national NDP in 1961. His style of government was low-key, unaggressive, almost well-mannered, though there is some truth in Douglas Fisher's remark that, "You don't stay in office as long as he has without a streak of Machiavelli."

Douglas in fact had a very real sense of the political possibilities in the Canada of his day. While he led the government of Saskatchewan he enacted no measures of

Tommy Douglas.

extreme socialism, preferring to regulate businesses rather than expropriate them. But he did experiment broadly in the area of social service, so that by the time he left the office of premier, Saskatchewan was ahead of other Canadian provinces in terms of health and welfare.

On the national scene Douglas was less effective than he was locally, largely because he could not command such intense and personal loyalties away from his home ground of Saskatchewan. Under his leadership the NDP had no great electoral successes. The party was most effective during the period of Liberal minority government from 1963 to 1968, when the NDP pressured Pearson's administration into passing social welfare measures that might otherwise have waited long before being entered in the statute book.

Throughout his life Tommy Douglas has been a reformer rather than a revolutionary, dedicated to gradual process rather than abrupt and spectacular change. Like most Canadians he seeks his place in the middle way that has always made us a nation which develops public and private service in a unique equilibrium.

The Black Canvas

Paul-Emile Borduas, one of the most important Canadian painters in the modern idiom, was trained as an artist in a way that had not changed since the days of the painting masters of Renaissance Italy.

From the days of New France until the early twentieth century, painting in Québec was done mostly in the service of religion, and many of the best Québecois artists spent part of their careers painting altarpieces or murals on church walls. One of the last and finest of the great church decorators of Québec was Ozias Leduc, who lived like a recluse in the little community of St. Hilaire. Leduc has a special place in the history of Canadian art, for as well as painting church decorations he also painted beautiful still lifes of humble subjects, such as apples, glowing with marvellous light, and in this way he was one of the forerunners of the modern movement in painting.

Paul-Emile Borduas was born in 1905 in Leduc's village of St. Hilaire. The church he attended as a boy was decorated with Leduc's murals, and in his teens Borduas became an apprentice to the older man, patiently learning all the techniques of ecclesiastical painting, in exactly the same way as a young painter in fourteenth century Italy learnt from his master in a painting workshop.

But Ozias Leduc quickly realized that Paul-Emile was much more than a promising church decorator. He saw in the boy something resembling his own urge to find a personal form of expression that was outside the conventions of sacred art, and he encouraged Borduas to leave St. Hilaire and study in the École des Beaux Arts in Montreal. From Montreal Borduas went on to Paris, where he attended the École d'Art Sacré, the most important centre of religious art in France.

Yet it was not what Borduas learnt of religious painting under the great teacher Maurice Denis that most affected him in Paris. His future career was really determined by his encounter with the work of the great French modern masters, from Renoir to Matisse. For a short time after returning from Paris, he continued to work as a church decorator, but he found that this work conflicted with his painting, which was steadily growing more simplified and modernistic. So in 1935 Borduas started to teach art in secondary schools during the day and to paint in his studio long into the night.

In 1937, when Paul-Emile Lemieux resigned his position in the École du Meuble in Montreal, Borduas took his place. The École du Meuble was something more than its name of School of Furniture suggests. It was a provincially funded school of craftsmanship that was run on progressive lines, and many of the students whom Borduas encountered there, such as Riopelle, were already more advanced in their understanding of modernist art than Borduas himself. But Borduas was always open to inspiration, no matter what direction it came from, and during his years at the École du Meuble he and his students explored together the problems of painting. As a result, master and students developed along parallel lines, and it is often hard to determine who learnt most from the association, Borduas or the younger men like Riopelle.

All of them were extremely sensitive to contemporary art movements in France. Borduas became interested in movements like Cubism and Fauvism, which had attracted the earlier Montreal painter James Wilson Morrice, whom he admired. In 1938 Borduas met the English Canadian painter John Lyman, who persuaded him to declare his modernist sympathies by becoming vice-president of the Contemporary Art Society when it was founded in 1939. Through Lyman, Borduas also became aware of the Surrealists, who emphasized free association as a means of creation. From this time on his painting moved away from figurative representation—based on forms taken from life—and in the direction of abstraction—the creation of forms independent of the natural world. In the early 1940s, under the influence of Surrealism and Abstractionism, Borduas began his great creative period. He and some other painters formed a group they called Les Autonomistes, meaning artists who worked freely as their moods and the nature of their materials directed.

Paul-Emile Borduas in Paris, 1956.

Hugh MacLennan.

Borduas saw such a development as a liberation from all the restraints that artists had hitherto endured. In 1948 he and his associates issued a famous manifesto, *Refus Global* (Global Rejection) in which he denounced all forms of authority, including the Church. It created a scandal in Québec of the 1940s and Borduas was dismissed from the École du Meuble.

His immediate response was to turn back in on himself. He returned to St. Hilaire and worked there for several years. Then, from 1953 to 1955, he worked in New York, and finally he went to Paris, where he spent the rest of his life. His health began to fail in 1949, and in Paris he was poor, sick, and unhappy. His mood was reflected in the increasing simplification of his art, until in the end he was painting only in black and white. His final paintings, before he died of a heart attack in 1960, were entirely black. Borduas had followed the rejection of natural forms to its logical end. Nothing could be more abstract than a black canvas.

Novelist as Historian

Hugh MacLennan has never been a prolific writer. The first six novels he wrote slowly and with much revision were spaced in terms of publication over twenty-six years, from *Barometer Rising* in 1941 to *Return of the Sphinx* in 1967. But at no time in his career has MacLennan been silent as a novelist for so long as he was during the period between 1967 and 1980, when his seventh novel appeared. There is a clue here to understanding his special position in Canadian literature.

MacLennan dominated Canadian fiction in the 1950s. There was no other novelist then writing who seemed better to express the difficult process by which Canadians were becoming aware that they belonged to a nation which at last was creating its independent destiny. No other novelist then writing was so intensely aware of the two great problems that have haunted Canadians: the failure of the "two solitudes" of English Canada and French Canada to come to a genuine and lasting understanding, and the threat to both solitudes posed by the confident and more ruthless culture of the United States. MacLennan may not have been a great novelist; he was too busy passing on messages ever to master the creation of entirely believable characters. But his vision of the choices before us, and his anxiety that we should not choose wrongly and thereby destroy the noble confederal experiment of Canada, made him a great Canadian.

MacLennan was born in 1907 in the Cape Breton mining community of Glace Bay; in his childhood, Gaelic came more easily to most of its inhabitants than English. But MacLennan drifted away from the land of his childhood, though he never forgot the blackness of its Calvinist sense of guilt or the music of its speech. He studied classics at Dalhousie University, went as a Rhodes scholar to Oxford, and in 1935 took his Ph.D. at Princeton University. But it was the height of the Depression, and though MacLennan had written a splendid thesis on a Roman Empire town in Egypt called Oxyrynchus, there were no positions to be had in the universities of North America. He had to accept a job at Lower Canada College, Montreal, teaching Latin and history to the sons of Westmount bankers and brokers.

MacLennan taught at Lower Canada College from 1935 to 1945. During that period he wrote his first two novels, *Barometer Rising* (1941), which is about events connected with the great explosion that ravaged Halifax in 1917, and *Two Solitudes* (1945), which is about the tensions between Francophones and Anglophones in Québec. They were powerful novels, even though MacLennan could not always keep his dialogue from sounding like a lecture on the destiny of Canada. And they were powerful because of the passion with which MacLennan felt his themes: the awakening sense of nationality among Canadians in *Barometer Rising*, and in *Two Solitudes* the danger confronting that emergent nationality of a rift between the two great Canadian cultures.

MacLennan's first two novels were successful enough for him to try the experiment of living from his writing, and from 1945 to 1951 he worked as a free-lancer. He wrote two more novels: *The Precipice* (1948), a very shallow work emphasizing the perils of American domination, and *Each Man's Son* (1951), an almost flawless novel in which MacLennan examines guilt and violence in Nova Scotia.

MacLennan found that he could not live by merely writing novels. Much of his time was consumed by journalism. And it was as a journalist that he wrote the fine essays which appeared in *Cross Country* (1949), *Thirty and Three* (1954), and *Scotchman's Return* (1960). There are many readers who think that MacLennan is at his best as an essayist and that his novels are really essays in disguise, using fiction to state points of view. There is a great deal of truth in this argument. But, good though his essays were, MacLennan could not endure the strain of making his living by writing for magazines, and in 1951 he accepted a part-time post in the English department at McGill University; he became a full-time professor in 1964.

MacLennan's entry into the academic world coincided with a decline in his creative energy. After *Each*

Man's Son, eight years elapsed before he published in 1959 his largest and most complex novel, a study of the psychological heritage of the rebellious 1930s entitled *The Watch That Ends the Night*. And another eight years passed before *Return of the Sphinx* appeared in 1967. It was his most pessimistic work, in which he seemed to express a view that the battle to keep Canada together was almost lost through the fanaticism of Québec separatists and the stupidity of their opponents.

Since *Return of the Sphinx*, MacLennan published no novel until 1980, when his futurist fiction *Voices in Time* appeared. Perhaps this slowness in completing his books is linked to the seriousness with which he takes his fiction as a didactic art, an art that is meant to teach lessons. But whether this is the case or not, by writing major novels on major Canadian themes, MacLennan has done more than any other writer to make Canadians realize that fiction should have a more serious and important purpose than merely entertainment.

The Fisherman's Life

Roderick Haig-Brown was a man of many guises and many causes. With the possible exception of Hugh MacLennan, he was the best of all Canadian essayists. But there were some people to whom he was best known as an expert on fishing and others to whom he was most important as a pioneer conservationist. There were yet others who remembered standing in the dock of his magistrate's court on northern Vancouver Island and being treated gently if they were harmless drunkards and sternly if they offended against the laws protecting wildlife. His friends remember him as a gentle and laconic man, wise but too humorous to take his own wisdom very seriously.

Roderick Langmere Haig-Brown, to give him his full name, was born in rural Sussex, England, in 1908. He received his formal education at Charterhouse School in Surrey, but he probably learnt more that was important to him in later life while fishing as a boy in English brooks and rivers and learning natural history by watching the wild animals and birds which survived in the long-cultivated English countryside. This interest, as much as anything else, led him to leave England as soon as he possibly could for a country where wilderness areas still existed, and at the age of seventeen he migrated to the Pacific Coast, first journeying to the state of Washington and working in a logging camp.

A year afterwards, in 1926, Haig-Brown went north into British Columbia. There he moved from occupation to occupation—working as logger, trapper, guide, fisherman, and farmhand—while he gathered the experience that he would use when he turned to writing, which he did on returning for a time to England in 1930.

It was in England that he wrote his first book, *Silver: The Life of an Atlantic Salmon* (1931), a fictionalized account of the salmon's life cycle. It was in England too that he began his second book, *Pool and Rapid: The Story of a River* (1932), which dealt with the Tahsis River on northern Vancouver Island and reflected Haig-Brown's growing concern for what happens to a natural landscape when man moves in and changes the country by logging, farming, and mining.

Returning from England, Haig-Brown took up a farm on the shores of the Campbell River on Vancouver Island and, to supplement what was at first a very unsure income from writing, he accepted the post of magistrate in the local community, also called Campbell River. And there, except for an interlude as a personnel officer for the Canadian army during World War II, he remained for the rest of his life, until in 1976 he died suddenly in his garden beside the river he loved, the river that was the great presence in so many of his books, such as *Return to the River* (1941) and *A River Never Sleeps* (1946).

Haig-Brown was as versatile in his writing as he was in the other aspects of life. Books such as *The Western Angler* (1937) are authoritative accounts of Canadian game fish, useful to the angler and the naturalist alike. Novels such as *Timber* (1942) and *On the Highest Hill* (1949) show a fine awareness of life on the shores and in the forests of British Columbia. And Haig-Brown also wrote excellent novels for juveniles, such as *Starbuck Valley Winter* (1943), *Saltwater Summer* (1948), and *The Whale People* (1962). But perhaps the best of all Haig-Brown's books are those in which he reflects on man and his relationship to the natural world, books that are closely related to his own life, such as the essay collections, *Measure of the Year* (1950) and *Fisherman's Spring* (1951).

In addition to his writing and his work as a magistrate, Haig-Brown was an ardent conservationist long before the environmental movement became fashionable in the 1960s. He led energetic campaigns against the promoters of hydro projects and industrial installations that ruined areas of the wilderness and endangered wildlife. Later he became chancellor of the University of Victoria and served on a variety of government commissions.

In his later years, after *Fisherman's Fall* appeared in 1964, Haig-Brown wrote far less than in the earlier decades. Perhaps this was due to the pressure of the community work he undertook so unselfishly. But per-

Roderick Haig-Brown fishing in his beloved Campbell River.

Gratien Gélinas in the title role of Bousille et les Justes, *1960.*

haps the reason was that he felt the books he had already written said all he needed to say. For Roderick Haig-Brown was much too modest a man ever to write merely for the sake of fame, and much too honest a man ever to write merely for the sake of money.

The Comedy of Pathos

Gratien Gélinas is more than merely a good actor or a fine dramatist. He has been both of these, but he is also, as John Robert Colombo once said, "Canada's leading man-of-the-theatre". He has combined his talents in playwriting and acting with an extraordinary sense of the role of drama in the modern world: this has also made him a remarkable impresario—producer, director, and in the end film executive. In spite of the challenge offered by many younger Québec playwrights and actors, Gélinas remains one of the major figures in Québec theatre, and he holds that position because of a talent for representing and also for arousing the feelings of ordinary people. Gélinas has been a true populist of the stage.

Gélinas was born in 1909 in the small Laurentian community of Saint-Tite de Champlain, but he was brought up in Montreal, where he attended the Collège de Montreal, the École des Hautes Etudes Commerciales, and the Université de Montreal. In accordance with his business training, he started out as an accountant in an insurance company, but he then began to write, and a little later to perform in, radio dramas.

Out of this activity Gélinas developed the idea of a revue centred around a simple Chaplinesque clown figure named Fridolin. Gélinas scripted the revue and also played the central, and indeed the only, role. As *Fridolinades*, the revue first appeared on the Montreal stage in 1938, and was immediately successful. Each year thereafter Gélinas produced an entirely new revue centred around Fridolin; in all there were nine of them, the last appearing in 1946.

During the later 1940s Gélinas turned to writing plays which were largely vehicles for his own bittersweet kind of comic acting. The first of them, *Tit-coq*, which appeared in 1948, represented the search for acceptance on the part of a young soldier, a bastard by birth with no real family ties, acted—of course—by Gélinas himself. The play was highly successful, running for fifty performances in Montreal, and marking the real beginning of the modern theatre in Québec. *Bousille et les Justes*, about another naive man, this time caught up and victimized in a family intrigue, was first produced in 1959 and once again Gélinas appeared in the title role. Finally, in 1966, Gélinas's third and most recent play appeared. It was *Hier les Enfants Dansaient*, which concerned a family that was divided over the question of separatism.

It is significant of Gélinas's personal viewpoint and perhaps also of his generation that the interest of *Hier les Enfants Dansaient* was centred less on the political issues involved in separatism than on the interplay of relationships when an outside influence disturbs a family equilibrium. And Gélinas has indeed been accused, by a younger generation in the theatre, of misrepresenting Québec and its state of mind. These criticisms have been aimed largely at his inclination to create and to act characters who are ineffectual victims and therefore far removed from the self-image of the modern separatist Québecois. Yet it was Gélinas who pioneered the exploration of ordinary Québecois life as a source of drama and led the way for the later group of the playwrights of defiance.

After the success of *Tit-coq*, Gélinas turned to the problem of an indigenous Québec theatre. In 1957 he organized his own company, La Comédie Canadienne, which began performing from its own theatre in 1958 and continued to do so until 1966. The same theatre is now used by the Théâtre du Nouveau Monde.

But Gélinas's dramatic interests have not been confined to the stage. He was interested from an early period in the potentialities of the cinema, and particularly so after *Tit-coq* was successfully adapted into a film. In 1969 he became an influential figure in Canadian film-making when he was appointed chairman of the Canadian Film Development Corporation, a position from which he has only recently resigned.

Gélinas was not a prolific playwright, though at least two of his plays, *Tit-coq* and *Bousille et les Justes*, are likely to remain classics of the Québec theatre. But his influence as an all-round man of the theatre has been very great, largely through his constant emphasis on the interdependence of the functions of dramatist, actor, and director.

Tin Flutes and Water Hens

Gabrielle Roy is undoubtedly the best-known Québec writer in English-speaking Canada. As long ago as 1947 her novel about poor people in Québec, *Bonheur d'Occasion* (1945), was translated into English as *The Tin Flute*, and it was immediately recognized as a major Canadian novel.

Since that time Gabrielle Roy has been more successful than any other Québec writer in appealing to people in all parts of Canada. To an extent this is because both her background and her experience have been different from those of most other Québec writers.

Gabrielle Roy was actually born—in 1909—in St. Boniface, Manitoba. Her family had come west from Québec under an abortive scheme to establish French-speaking settlers in the Red River district. She herself went to the Winnipeg Normal School, and then taught for several years in small schools in the rural areas of Manitoba. Not until she was almost thirty did Gabrielle Roy settle in Montreal, after spending two years in France and England studying drama, an interest she had developed while living in Winnipeg.

In Montreal Gabrielle Roy began to write seriously, first stories and articles, and then her novel *Bonheur d'Occasion*, for which she had patiently gathered material and impressions while living close to the people of Québec. For as a Manitoban, Gabrielle Roy regarded Québec at least partly as a strange land.

Always in Gabrielle Roy's writing there is the feeling that she looks at what she describes with a kind of detachment; it is a quality that other Québec writers do not possess for they are describing the world in which they were born and bred. This quality gives her books a greater accessibility for readers not familiar with Québec and its way of life; like them she is an observer, even if a

Gabrielle Roy.

154

deeply involved one. Indeed books such as *The Tin Flute* and her later novel *The Cashier* (originally published as *Alexandre Chenevert*, 1955) have done a great deal to help English-speaking Canadians understand French Canadian society and the attitudes of Québec people.

But Gabrielle Roy's broad appeal is also related to the fact that she has written more on other parts of Canada than most Québec writers. In fact, most of her books are set either in the Manitoba of her childhood or in the Arctic, which has always fascinated her.

Her Manitoba books are not so much novels as groups of interlinked short stories. *La Petite Poule d'Eau* (translated as *Where Nests the Water Hen*, 1950) tells of life in a remote settlement of northern Manitoba. *Rue Deschambault* (translated as *Street of Riches*, 1957) concerns the experiences of a girl growing up among the people of many origins who lived in St. Boniface during the pioneer era. Even if the book is not strictly autobiographical, it obviously embodies many of the experiences and observations of Gabrielle Roy's own childhood, as does its sequel, *La Route d'Altamont* (translated as *The Road Past Altamont*, 1966).

In writing of Manitoba Gabrielle Roy was dealing with the familiar terrain of her childhood and her young womanhood as a rural school teacher. In writing of Québec she was dealing with a province whose culture and language she shared and to which she belonged by ancestry. But the Arctic was an unfamiliar world, to which she was not linked either by experience or by ancestry. So she used the Arctic as the setting for novels and stories that had broader themes than the Manitoba fiction (which was so largely dominated by personal memories) and the Québec fiction (in which the frustrations of poor and narrow lives were seen in the context of Depression-ridden French Canada).

For example, *La Montagne Secrète* (*The Hidden Mountain*, 1962) tells of a young artist's discovery, loss, and rediscovery of a mountain in the far North, and here Gabrielle Roy is really telling of the struggle which all artists undergo to find an authentic way of expressing their subjects once they have decided what they want to paint or write about. And *La Rivière sans Repos* (of which part has been translated as *The Windflower*, 1970) is a group of stories which tells of a society—that of the Eskimo—which is in transition and whose people are being forced by circumstances to accept the gifts of the white man's world. These gifts inevitably destroy their traditional cultures which are based on very specialized hunting techniques. It is a profound and passionate study of the difficulty in the modern world of remaining true to one's self and one's past. And that is a sentiment close to the heart of every French Canadian.

The Drowned Poet

Like Émile Nelligan, Hector de Saint-Denys Garneau was one of the tragic figures of Québec literature. He was born in 1912 at Sainte-Catherine-de-Fossambault, Québec, where the Garneau family had its summer home; he died there at the age of thirty-one in 1943.

Saint-Denys Garneau came of one of the leading literary lineages of French Canada. One of his grandfathers, Alfred Garneau, was a notable romantic poet in late Victorian Québec; his other grandfather was the historian, François-Xavier Garneau.

Saint-Denys Garneau spent the early years of his childhood at Sainte-Catherine. There his closest playmate was his cousin, the little girl who was four years younger than Garneau and who eventually became the poet Anne Hébert; her family also owned a summer home at Sainte-Catherine. In 1923 the Garneaus returned to Montreal, and Hector was sent to the Collège Sainte-Marie, run by the Jesuits. In his early teens he had showed a talent for painting, and in 1924 his family sent him to the École des Beaux Arts in Montreal. The year after that he returned to the Collège Sainte-Marie. In 1928 he suffered from a severe attack of rheumatic fever, and in 1933 the effects of this illness showed themselves in a cardiac lesion, which left him for the rest of his life with a weak heart that made any major physical exertion impossible.

At this point Saint-Denys Garneau abandoned his academic ambitions. Realizing that he would never be able to follow a professional career of any kind, he divided his time between the family house in Montreal and the summer home at Sainte-Catherine, where Anne Hébert was often his companion. He continued to paint; he began to keep a journal of intimate thoughts that would be published only after his death; and he wrote poems and essays.

At first Hector de Saint-Denys Garneau attempted to maintain his contact with the world of arts; he did not immediately allow his illness to cut him off from the world. In 1934 he held an exhibition of his paintings at the Montreal Art Gallery. And about the same time he helped to found an art magazine called *La Relève*; translated as "The Reawakening", its title reflects the inclination of the magazine, which was to use art in support of the Christian revival movement then going on in France and spreading to Québec. For several years Saint-Denys Garneau continued writing regular art criticism for *La Relève*.

But already he was beginning to cut himself off more and more from all except a few human beings, and to live like a hermit. Poor health undoubtedly played a part in turning him into a recluse; he was physically incapable of

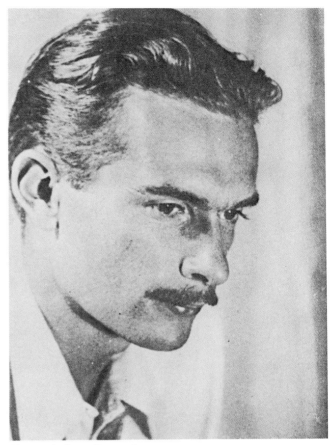
Hector de Saint-Denys Garneau.

making the effort to live an active social life. But there was also something in his mental make-up that welcomed these disabilities. It now seems that the combination of physical and mental renunciations that Saint-Denys Garneau made at this time was linked with the fact that at the same period—between 1935 and 1939—he wrote his best poetry. Many critics have suggested that art is often the product of a psychic wound; in the case of Hector de Saint-Denys Garneau this was undoubtedly true.

There was still a side of his personality that regretted the loss of the world outside his personal circle of vision, and in 1937 it impelled him to make a journey to Paris. But this was the last of his excursions into the world outside Québec, and he did not stay long. After he returned to Canada he began to withdraw for long periods from any kind of human companionship, and in 1941 he went back to Sainte-Catherine, the place of his birth, and never left it.

At Sainte-Catherine, Saint-Denys Garneau lived in the same house as his parents, but apart from them and Anne Hébert he saw few people, and it is obvious that during these years he was living through a major inner crisis. His retreat from the world may have been a renunciation, but the diary he wrote at the time suggests that every day he was struggling to establish his spiritual identity, his relationship to the universe or, as he would have had it, to God. In 1937 he published the only book that appeared during his lifetime: *Regardes et Jeux dans l'Espace*. Its title, which can be translated as "Games and Glances in Space", shows how Garneau, like so many modern men, was trying to locate himself in a world where the traditional signposts were gone.

The games and glances came to an end in 1943; on October 24 of that year Hector's body was found in a stream near Sainte-Catherine. Whether he drowned himself or drowned by accident or fell into the water during a heart attack has never been established.

After he died, the journals of Saint-Denys Garneau and his last poems were discovered. John Glassco has translated them into English. The *Journal* was published in 1962 and the *Complete Poems* in 1975. The two books show why, since his early and tragic death, Hector de Saint-Denys Garneau has been such a growing influence on the young people of Québec. His personal sense of spiritual isolation seemed to express their own collective sense of alienation in a Canada which they felt did not respect or give equal status to their culture and their traditions.

The Caribou Hunter

It is at the same time difficult and gratifying to write about a man like the Inuit artist Tiktak, because the ordinary standards we apply in writing the biography of a *kabloona* do not really fit in with the Inuit attitude to life. As *kabloonas* (the Inuit expression for white men which literally means "eyebrows"!) we attach great importance to concepts such as *time* and *art*. The Inuit do not, and so we come to the first question about Tiktak; we expect an answer to it but he may very well prefer it to remain a question. It is the date of his birth. The people who exhibit art in Canada or anywhere else in the world are accustomed to having exact biographical data, and so whenever Tiktak's works are exhibited, the date of his birth is given with due precision as 1916. When I met Tiktak for the first time in 1968 he told me with a great gap-toothed laugh that he had no idea when he was born!

Still, we can form a rough idea. As a middle-aged man Tiktak arrived in what white men call civilization, which means the bleak little settlements on the western shore of Hudson's Bay. It was to Rankin Inlet that Tiktak came in the middle 1950s. In the early 1960s he began to make the stone carvings—strange round human heads with gashed eyes and mouths—that have made him famous.

Until he arrived on the shore of Hudson's Bay, Tiktak was an Inuit of the barren lands, that vast area north of the tree line between Hudson's Bay and the Mackenzie River which in summer is studded with thousands of lakes and laced by hundreds of rivers; at the height of the season the name is belied by the abundance of minute flowering plants. Over the barren lands roamed the great herds of caribou, and the Inuit of that region were as dependent on these migrant ruminants as the Inuit of the coast were dependent on sea mammals like seal and beluga, like walrus and narwhal.

Tiktak was born sixty or more years ago—give or take a few years—in a tiny encampment on the barren lands, probably in a tent of caribou skin. He was reared to the hunter's life which he carried on into his forties. The herds of caribou provided almost everything for his people, as the herds of bison had done for the Plains Indians. The skin of the caribou was used for clothing and for tents; the sinew was used for thread and the bones and antlers for various implements and tools; the meat was eaten with festive prodigality when a hunt had been successful, but some was dried and some was frozen and cached for the winter. Sometimes the supplies ran out, or the caribou did not appear on their usual route, and then there would be starvation. When I met Tiktak at Rankin Inlet, I also met two other Inuit hunters of the barren lands; Erkuti sang to me a song called "Caching the Meat", but Okoktuk sang one called "The Hungry Camp"!

During the late 1940s and the early 1950s the Hungry Camps occurred more often. The introduction of the rifle, used by the Inuit and also by alien hunters, had not only reduced the herds, but also changed their routes. Many Inuit starved and died because the caribou did not come. Eventually the Canadian government decided to bring the people in from the nomad camps of the barren lands and resettle them in coastal places such as Rankin Inlet, to which Tiktak came.

It was hard for old hunters to live in these tacky new settlements, and for a long time Tiktak would go out each year with his dog team to the barren lands and kill what meat he could. He preferred this meat since, as he told me, he found store food distasteful and "too sweet". But he had an accident, was partly crippled, and could no longer travel far from the settlement. It was then that he started carving, and immediately began to create his highly original sculptures, so that, though few of his works date from before 1963, he was the first Inuit sculptor to have an exhibition devoted entirely to his work, in 1970.

Like most Inuit sculptors, Tiktak has no great pretensions as an artist. When we talked about his work he told me he did not start with an idea of what he would carve; he took the stone and let the shape within it emerge. But

Tiktak with Robert Williamson in Ottawa, 1973.

the shape was usually figurative, a man's head, a beast, however stylized the execution might be. When someone else asked him a similar question, Tiktak said: "My thought comes out while I work. My work expresses my thought." Tiktak also summed up the character of his work and its strange relation to sculptor and material when he said: "I like to carve faces. Round ones when the stone is soft and flat ones when the stone is hard."

He also said to me, "I am a bad carver!" But that was for the ear of any envious spirit that might be listening, and he was pleased when I said, as I believe, that he was a great artist.

The Muse of Manawaka

Margaret Laurence may well be the best living Canadian novelist—perhaps even the best novelist who has ever written in Canada. Certainly she has created in the imaginary town of Manawaka, where so much of her fiction is set, a little universe that embodies with faith and intensity the reality of being born in the Prairies. It is a universe that embodies, in a wider sense, the reality of setting our roots in Canada no matter where the seed from which we or our forefathers came as immigrants may have originated.

Yet Margaret Laurence came to write of her native small-town Manitoba by a remarkably circuitous route. It went by way of Somalia and Ghana before her attention finally homed in on Manawaka. She was born—Jean Margaret Wemyss—in a small Manitoba community named Neepawa, which is north and west of Winnipeg. She was educated at the University of Manitoba, and then after marrying in 1948, she went to England with her husband Jack Laurence. Jack is an engineer, and in 1949 he was given a contract by the Crown Agents for the Colonies to build earth dams in the deserts of Somaliland, then part of the British Empire. There he and Margaret lived for two years, moving among the nomad peoples of the desert and witnessing, if not sharing, the sufferings of droughts and the joys of other seasons.

Margaret Laurence found those years to be a discovery of herself, as she shed her Canadian middle-class prejudices, as well as a discovery of a strange land. Not surprisingly it took her a decade after leaving Somaliland before she could write an account of her experiences in

Margaret Laurence.

The Prophet's Camel-Bell. It is a searching fragment of autobiography as well as one of the best and most moving travel books ever written by a Canadian.

After two years in Somaliland, Margaret Laurence and her husband moved on to another assignment in the Gold Coast, which was shortly to become independent as Ghana. It was here that she first began to write stories and she based this fiction on her experiences of Ghanaian life. But not until she finally left Africa in 1957, and settled down to living in Vancouver, did she determine to make writing her career. Her first novel, *This Side of Jordan* (1960), and her first book of short stories, *The Tomorrow-Tamer* (1963), were both set in Ghana. Only after she had worked the African experience out of her system was she able to start on her more mature work, the series of Canadian novels that began with *The Stone Angel* (1964) and came to a halt with *The Diviners* (1974).

For most of her career as a writer, Margaret Laurence has preferred to work at a distance from the settings for her novels, and if she wrote of Africa in Vancouver, she moved to England (where she lived for several years in an old house in a Buckinghamshire village) to write most of her Manawaka books.

These are the four novels, *The Stone Angel, A Jest of God* (1966), *The Fire-Dwellers* (1969), *The Diviners*, and a collection of short stories, *A Bird in the House* (1970). Margaret Laurence has described *A Bird in the House*, whose stories reveal various stages in the maturation of Vanessa MacLeod, as "fictionalized autobiography". The book therefore gives us some idea not only of the world in which the young Jean Margaret Wemyss grew up, but also of the kind of experiences she eventually turned into the four novels, which she very resolutely maintains are invented works whose action is not parallelled in real life.

The characters populating the four novels all originate in Manawaka, though in most cases life takes them away from the little prairie town. Many of them cross each other's paths from novel to novel, even though the novels are not a formal sequence.

In spite of the lack of strong structural links, there are obvious patterns uniting Margaret Laurence's four Canadian novels. In all of them the central character is a woman. The youngest, Rachel Cameron in *A Jest of God*, strives to escape from her closed off existence as a spinster school teacher who has never lived away from Manawaka. Rachel's elder sister, Stacey MacAindra in *The Fire-Dwellers*, is trapped by her marriage and her children, and even when escape is offered she cannot take it. Ninety-year-old Hagar Shipley, in *The Stone Angel*, has spent a life raging against life, and on the eve of her death she is still trying to run away from the care of her son, who is elderly himself and who wants to put her in a rest home. In a way, all this feminine rage and frustration is reconciled in Laurence's last and largest novel, *The Diviners*, which she returned to Canada to write. It tells of the novelist Morag Gunn, who had been brought up in poverty in Manawaka and who finally reaches peace with herself and her past, largely by recognizing that the centre of her life lies in the land that bred her.

Margaret Laurence has said that *The Diviners* will be her last novel; the only fiction she has published since has been written for children. It is true that *The Diviners* is written in such a way that the train of thought and experience set out in the Manawaka novels is brought to an effective close. One cannot imagine the series resuming after such a summing up of the whole relationship between Canadians, their land, and their past.

But Margaret Laurence's readers find it hard to accept that there will be no more novels from a vigorous writer who was only fifty-three when the 1980s began. We can only hope she is waiting for the well of inspiration to fill once more, before she starts on a new area of the imagination, as different from Manawaka as Manawaka was from Ghana.

Picture Credits

Archives nationales du Québec, collection Initiale, 12.
Archives of Ontario, 22, 26, 47, 115, 128.
Archives of Saskatchewan, 63.
Archives of the Canadian Rockies, Banff, 120.
Banting and Best Institute, University of Toronto, 131.
Mme. Gabrielle Borduas, 147.
Canada's Sports Hall of Fame, 141.
Canadian Eskimo Arts Council, 157.
City of Edmonton Archives, 99.
Irma Coucill. Drawing taken from *Founders & Guardians* and reprinted by permission of John Wiley & Sons Canada Limited, 124.
Glenbow-Alberta Institute, 53, 64, 73, 104.
Historical Society of Montana, 68.
Jack Miner Foundation, 94.
La Comedie Canadienne, 152.
Dr. Stuart Macdonald, 107.
Maclean's Magazine, 93.
Manitoba Archives, 90.
McMichael Canadian Collection, Kleinburg, 118.
Metropolitan Toronto Library Board, 24, 25, 32, 33, 48, 54, 71, 77, 86, 140, 155.
National Film Board of Canada, 130, 151.
National Gallery of Canada, 17, 46.
National Geographic Society, 84.
Notman Photographic Archives, 58, 100.
Peter Paterson of Toronto. Photo taken from *The Other Side of Hugh MacLennan* and reprinted by permission of The Macmillan Company of Canada, 148.
Provincial Archives of British Columbia, 16, 55, 66, 91, 103.

Public Archives Canada, 9, C7298; 11, C6643; 13, C34199; 15, C4765; 18, C167; 20, C1348; 23, C7760; 28, C5462; 30, C23580; 31, C7044; 35, C1993; 36, C6087; 38, C34218; 39, C7043; 40, C1862; 41, PA61930; 43, C44304; 44, C6721; 52, C9078; 57, C23565; 61, PA25397; 65, C59290; 67, C9480; 70, PA25944; 75, C3844; 80, C1879; 85, PA26689; 88, PA28125; 96, C81812; 97, C27483; 106, C55449; 111, C9452; 112, C88566; 114, C9439; 117, PA6467; 126, C33103; 135, C80883; 136, PA88763; 138, C70771; 142, PA113253; 145, C36220.
RCMP Archives, 78.
John Reeves, 154.
Eldie Steiner, 158.
St. Joseph's Oratory, Montreal, 82.
Tom Thomson Memorial Gallery of Fine Arts, Owen Sound, 109.
Toronto Symphony Orchestra Archives, 133.
University of Toronto Archives, Dora Hood Papers, 122.
University of Toronto Library, Department of Information Services, 144.
Victoria University Library, Toronto, 119.